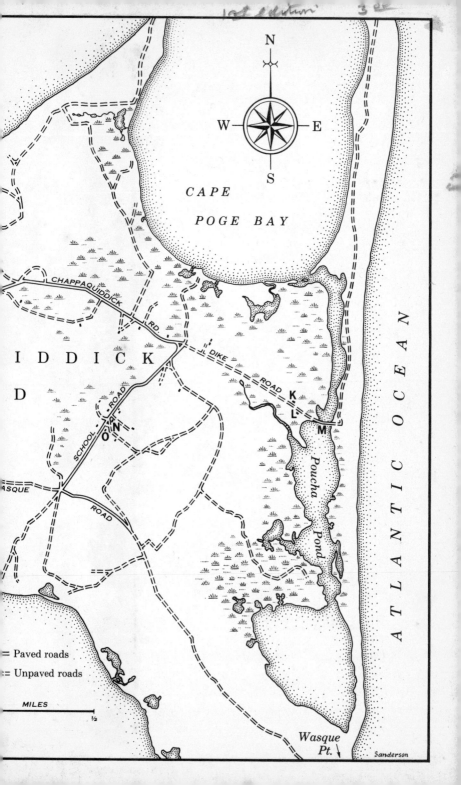

N

W   E

S

CAPE

POGE BAY

CHAPPAQUIDDICK RD.

I D D I C K

D

DIKE ROAD

K

L

M

SCHOOL

ROAD

O **N**

ASQUE

ROAD

Poucha

Pond

ATLANTIC OCEAN

= Paved roads

= Unpaved roads

MILES

½

Wasque
Pt.

Sanderson

The Bridge at Chappaquiddick

The Bridge
at Chappaquiddick

by JACK OLSEN

LITTLE, BROWN AND COMPANY · BOSTON · TORONTO

LIBRARY OF CONGRESS CATALOG CARD NO. 79-110261

FIRST EDITION

Published simultaneously in Canada
by Little, Brown & Company (Canada) Limited

PRINTED IN THE UNITED STATES OF AMERICA

This book is dedicated to the kind and patient
people who aided in its preparation:

JONATHAN AHLBUM

DOMINICK "JIM" ARENA

GEORGE ARNOLD

MILDRED ARNOLD

WILLIAM ARNOLD

DOUGLAS BASSETT

ANTHONY BETTENCOURT

WALTER BETTENCOURT

HAROLD BRIDGE

JAMES BROWN

ROBERT CARROLL

JOHN CHIRGWIN

LEO CONVERY

LEO DAMORE

RICHARD DeROCHE

ALAN DUCKWORTH

MARIAN DUCKWORTH

M. FRANCIS DeFRATES

HARVEY EWING

STEVE EWING

JOHN FARRAR

EUGENE FRIEH

STEPHEN GENTLE, JR.

JARED GRANT

ROSS HARDING

DICK HEWITT

JOHN HIKADE

ROBERT HYDE

HAROLD KELLEY

CAMILLE LAWRENCE

CHRISTOPHER (HUCK) LOOK, JR.

LAWRENCE MERCIER

DONALD R. MILLS, M.D.

ROBERT MORGAN

BARBARA NEVIN

ROBERT NEVIN, M.D.

RUSSELL E. PEACHEY

JOHN PINE

LORETTA PINE

GENEVIEVE PRADA

CARMEN SALVADOR

ROBERT SAMUEL

GEORGE L. SEARLE

EDWARD SELF, M.D.

FOSTER SILVA

DODIE SILVA

WALTER STEELE

FRANCES STEWART

THOMAS TELLER

ESTEY TELLER

WILLIAM WALL

ARTHUR YOUNG

NANCY YOUNG

NATURE hates monopolies and exceptions. The waves of the sea do not more speedily seek a level from their loftiest tossing than the varieties of condition tend to equalize themselves. There is always some levelling circumstance that puts down the overbearing, the strong, the rich, the fortunate, substantially on the same ground with all others. . . . The farmer imagines power and place are fine things. But the President has paid dear for his White House. It has commonly cost him all his peace, and the best of his manly attributes.

—Ralph Waldo Emerson, *Compensation*

Contents

Prologue   3

I. Before Chappaquiddick   7

II. Regatta at Edgartown   67

III. The Morning After   107

IV. The Wheels of Justice   181

V. The Trap   251

I

Before Chappaquiddick

Prologue

I N most respects, the incident was trivial. It involved the death of a nice girl, but nice girls die every day and this particular one—impeccable as her moral pedigree might have been —had nothing to commend her to the special attention of history. For that matter, the man most closely involved in the incident with her also appeared ordinary in most matters. Certainly he was not reputed to be an intellectual giant, an "egghead." His own name, Edward Moore (Ted) Kennedy, was not closely associated with any cultural or scientific advances, nor had he made any significant contributions in the areas of statesmanship or diplomacy. There was, nonetheless, a touch of *noblesse oblige* about him. He was that rarest of noblemen: a future king in a land that had purged kings. For millions of people whose daily lives were lacking in any semblance of high romance or grandeur, he satisfied deep anachronistic longings: to bow before purple robes, to idolize, to lift up and carry above the heads of the mob, to cheer and cheer.

Once in Massachusetts an opponent had charged publicly that the young Kennedy had never worked a day in his life, and the next morning a laborer with a twinkling Irish smile told the crestfallen young candidate: "Teddy, me boy, you haven't missed a thing." The election was a runaway. The opponent learned too late that Edward Moore Kennedy's appeal was *precisely* that he had never worked a day in his life; neither had Henry V nor Arthur of Camelot. Willy-nilly, the Kennedys and their assassins had brought Shakespearian majesty and tragedy to a political process that had been producing too many tawdry,

money-grubbing "pols," squirting their fountains of brown to-
bacco juice and accepting their white envelopes from the private interests. None could ever accuse this new nobility of such
base behavior. From the patriarch, Joseph Patrick Kennedy Sr.,
former ambassador to the Court of St. James's, to the youngest
prince, affectionately known as Teddy, they gave their public
salaries away or worked for nothing. What a contrast they
made to the pols of the smoke-filled rooms.

But was there more to the Kennedys than this appearance of
noble honesty and correctness? Under their regal sheen, did
they have a major offering to make to the country that had
given them the opportunity to go from the shanty to the White
House in three generations? Passionate partisans argued that
the family had made contributions and established standards
that would be recorded in later days as historically crucial, but
others argued that the evidence for such a conclusion was
slight. They pointed to the patriarch, Joseph Sr., a man almost
completely out of step with the times through the later years of
his life. His firstborn son and namesake, Joe Jr., was pulverized
in a mid-air explosion in World War II, leaving behind only a
minor record in the Massachusetts legislature. Nor was John F.
Kennedy ("President John," as his youngest brother called him)
vouchsafed the time to make the contributions of which he
seemed so capable, with personal charm and courage and intelligence that made him stand like a giant in the gallery of modern Presidents. Robert F. Kennedy, after a promising career as
Attorney General of the United States and Senator from New
York, had barely stumbled on his role as champion of the op-
pressed when he was cut down in Los Angeles.

Had the Kennedys made major contributions to American
statesmanship? The question could not yet be answered, for one
Kennedy remained. He was the repository of all the potential,
all the promise, that had been conspicuous in the Kennedy
brothers from Joe Jr. on. He was the littlest brother, the one
who had done the least, the one whose record had been tar-
nished by a few childish peccadilloes. But he was a Kennedy
nevertheless. "What is that?" his astute brother-in-law, Stephen

Smith, had asked. "A legacy? Partly myth, partly great expectations?" And even while he was saying it, he must have known that it was both myth *and* great expectations, and that Ted Kennedy would be expected to fulfill them.

For a time, the young senator denied the role, but then one day he left his house of mourning and announced that he was picking up the fallen standard. It was not necessary to proclaim publicly that he was running for President, nor that he would be elected. It was as preordained as the coronations of the Henrys and the Edwards and the Georges who had followed themselves century after century in England, regardless of their aptitude or their qualifications. No one dared question their capabilities, and few questioned Ted Kennedy's. The handful of observers who said he appeared immature and unqualified for high office were brushed aside. His courtiers pointed to his steady record in the Senate, neglecting to point out that the Senate is a place where one's qualifications or lack of them can easily be obscured, and where certain political bandits had hidden out for decades. Few took the time for an unbiased study of the youngest Kennedy's public record. He had the name; the name would suffice.

Then one night he went for a ride on a lonely island called Chappaquiddick, and suddenly his maturity and his intelligence were being called into question, and not only by hot-eyed partisans of the right who had abhorred the Kennedys from the beginning. Suspicions were rampant on a field of disbelief, and Kennedy's explanations only raised more suspicions and cast more doubt on his abilities and his truthfulness. Now the questions about him, heretofore begged, had to be answered. Who was Ted Kennedy? What was he?

The Bridge at
Chappaquiddick

E VEN sophisticates follow tribal custom, and the dominant tribal custom in the family of Joseph Patrick Kennedy Sr. was a sort of primogeniture, which Webster defines as "an exclusive right of inheritance . . . belonging . . . to the eldest son." Joe Kennedy's children would inherit his driving political ambition, but until the family had become entrenched as an American political power, the inheritance was to remain with the oldest.

"Just as I went into politics because Joe died," John F. Kennedy was to say many years later, "if anything happened to me tomorrow, my brother Bobby would run for my seat in the Senate. And if Bobby died, Teddy would take over for him." The reader will observe that there is nothing in the statement about qualifications, intelligence, ideals, ability. The mandate is simple and clear: the eldest shall carry the standard.

Edward Moore Kennedy (named after his father's confidential secretary and friend, Eddie Moore) was born February 22, 1932, the ninth child of Rose and Joseph Kennedy. As the fourth son, he was not tagged for greatness. Joe Jr., seventeen years older than the new arrival, was being groomed for the political stature that had slipped away from the father. Joe's next youngest brother, Jack Kennedy, did not know it yet, but if anything happened to the eldest, he would have to step in as the instrument of his father's ambition, whether he wanted the assignment or not. ("I got Jack into politics," old Joe Kennedy said years later. "I was the one. I told him that now that Joe was dead, it was his responsibility to run for Congress. He didn't want to. He felt he didn't have the ability, but I told him he had to.") And after Jack came Bobby, six years older than Teddy and two places removed from the key family role of Number One Son.

The Kennedys *père et mère* were far too skilled at the fine art of child-raising to allow the new baby to become a toy, a plaything—the function of the youngest in many large families. But they were human, and not without human stresses and human limitations. Joe Sr. was caroming about the world of finance and on the verge of beginning his own hectic career in public service. He was seldom around the house. After nine children, Rose Fitzgerald Kennedy, the daughter of former Boston Mayor John (Honey Fitz) Fitzgerald, was losing some of her enthusiasm for motherhood. "We tried to keep everything more or less equal," this remarkable woman was to say three decades after Ted Kennedy's birth, "but you wonder if the mother and father aren't quite tired when the ninth one comes along. You have to make more of an effort to tell bedtime stories and be interested in swimming matches. There were seventeen years between my oldest and my youngest child, and I had been telling bedtime stories for twenty years. When you have older brothers and sisters, they're the ones that seem to be more important in a family, and always get the best rooms and the first choice of boats and all those kinds of things, but Ted never seemed to resent it." Whether the youngest Kennedy resented it or not, he remembered; years later he was to tell writer Paul Healy that his clearest memory of his older sister Kathleen was of a day when she took him to the store to buy a pair of pants. At the time, the millionaire's son owned a single pair.

When Ted Kennedy was six years old, his father was named ambassador to the Court of St. James's, and the family moved into the three-story embassy mansion in London. There the child learned about the world of appearances, of pomp and display. He noticed that his father sometimes wore the fancy clothes of the court and was called "Your Excellency." He asked: "Is that your new name, Daddy?" He was told to be on his best behavior among his London schoolmates; he was not to get into fights, because his father was the ambassador. There was an image to be upheld. One day the hot-tempered child came home from school in a rage and asked permission to punch a classmate.

"Why?" Rose Kennedy asked.

"He's been hitting me every day and you tell me I can't get into fights!" the angry child exclaimed. That night, at the dinner table, a wise Joe Kennedy Sr. gave his youngest son permission to retaliate.

Later in that first year in London, Teddy went to Rome with the other members of his family to the coronation of Pope Pius XII and learned more about regality. The Pope already knew the Kennedys; as Cardinal Pacelli he had visited their home in Bronxville, New York, two years earlier. On the day after his coronation he received the important American Catholic family in a private audience and gave each member a rosary. The youngest child, Edward M., appeared to be the pontiff's favorite. He allowed the boy to crawl up on his knee and patiently answered questions about the papal ring and cross. "I told my sister Patricia I wasn't frightened at all," the seven-year-old Teddy said later. "He patted my hand and told me I was a smart little fellow. He gave me the first rosary beads from the table before he gave my sister any." In the competitive Kennedy family, it *mattered* who received the beads first.

When World War II threatened, the ambassador sent his family back to the United States, and young Ted was enrolled in one of the ten secular schools he was to attend in his life. The family pattern continued. Joe Jr. was in his early twenties, acting as his father's courier on important assignments, meeting the European heads of state, slowly being prepared for the political career that lay ahead. Jack was reading everything he could get his hands on and learning how to shape the English language into a usable tool. Bobby was busily trying to prove that the runt of the litter did not necessarily have to come in last—nor did he, except rarely. The younger children were learning the essential Kennedy philosophy: winning is better than losing. "Even when we were six and seven years old," Eunice Kennedy Shriver said, "Daddy always entered us in public swimming races, in the different age categories so we didn't have to swim against each other. And he did the same thing with us in sailing races. And if we won, he got terribly enthusiastic. Daddy was always very competitive. The thing he always kept telling us was that coming in second was just no good. The important thing was to win, don't come in second or third, that doesn't count—but win, win, win."

Perhaps because he was growing into the handsomest and sturdiest of all the Kennedys, or perhaps because there was less pressure on him as the baby of the family, Ted Kennedy did not become quite so competitive as his brothers and sisters. By another family's standards he might have seemed highly competitive, but he was a relatively relaxed Kennedy. Sometimes he wondered at the aggressiveness of the others in matters like sailboat races, but little of it seemed to rub off on him. At twelve, he wrote a touching reminiscence of his oldest brother:

I recall the day the year before we went to England. It was in the summer and I asked Joe if I could race with him. He agreed to this so we started down to the pier about five minutes before the race.

We had our sails up just as the gun went for the start. This was the first race I had ever been in. We were going along very nicely until suddenly he told me to pull in the jib. I had know Idea what he was talking about. He repeated the command again in a little louder tone, meanwhile we were slowly getting further and further away from the other boats. Joe suddenly leaped up and grabed the jib. I was a little scared but suddenly he zeized me by the pants and through me into the cold water.

I was scared to death practully. I then heard a splash and I felt his hand grab my shirt and he lifted me into the boat. We continued the race and came in second. On the way home from the pier he told me to be quiet about what happened in that afternoon. One falt Joe had was that he got very easily mad in a race as you have witnessed. But he always meant well and was a very good sailor and swimmer.

But being thrown out of a sailboat constituted the worst of the growing boy's problems, at least until college days. For the most part, he lived what seemed on the surface to be an idyllic existence. He was rich and knew it, even though part of his training as a Kennedy was a small weekly allowance. When he was not on a yacht or a sailboat, he was swimming in a pool or in Nantucket Sound, or playing tennis or softball or the Kennedy family game: touch football. Like many a youngest member of a large family, he quickly learned how to charm his elders, and throughout the rest of his life this easy affability and friendliness was to gain him the accolade, both in and out of his own house, of "the best politician in the family." It was all but impossible to dislike the handsome teen-ager with the smile flashing from ear to ear and the readiest handshake in the Hyannis compound. All the Kennedy young men were popular with women, but Teddy outdid his brothers. In 1951 he glided into Harvard, the fourth of the Kennedy boys to attend the school, and the one least prepared for its rigors.

The trouble began in Spanish, generally regarded as the simplest of the foreign languages. Ted was not flunking the subject, but he was averaging $C-$, and he knew this would be considered a low grade back at Hyannis Port. So, accustomed to an easy life and perhaps overly concerned with appearances, he hired a friend to take an important test for him. Both were caught and thrown out of school.

Old Joe Kennedy's reaction was peculiarly mixed. He was angry at Harvard for the severity of the sentence, and he showed his annoyance by publicly offering to finance the future educations of thirty-one students expelled from West Point, as though to show that all such miscreants deserved a second chance. But the injustice that rankled him did not change the essential fact that young Ted had blotched the family escutcheon. Kennedys were competitive; Kennedys did not come in second, but Kennedys did not bring shame upon the proud family name, either. *Kennedys did not cheat.* The father sat the son down and delivered a lecture that turned the air heliotrope. Years later, President John F. Kennedy recalled: "My father wasn't around as much as some fathers when I was young, but whether he was there or not, he made his children feel that they were the most important things in the world to him. He was so terribly interested in everything we were doing. He held up standards for us, and he was very tough when we failed to meet those standards. The toughness was important. If it hadn't been for that, Teddy might be just a playboy today. But my father cracked down on him at a crucial time in his life, and this brought out in Teddy the discipline and seriousness which will make him an important political figure."

In 1951, at the age of nineteen, a chagrined Ted Kennedy volunteered for military service with much the same attitude as a European youth joining the French Foreign Legion. He had taken his father's lecture to heart; now he was going to expiate his guilt. Significantly, he did not join the Navy, in which his three brothers had served with distinction. He chose the Army, signing the papers in such a hurry that he failed to notice that he had enlisted for a full hitch of four years. A few telephone calls by Ambassador Kennedy set the matter right and young Ted's enlistment was cut in half. He served in Europe, missing the activities in Korea, and was discharged in 1953 as a private first class.

Accepted once again at Harvard, he seemed more mature. He worked hard and brought his grades up, especially in subjects like history and government, Kennedy family specialties. He went out for football and caught the pass that enabled Harvard to get on the scoreboard—final score: 21 to 7—in the 1955 loss to Yale. He made a few speeches, as though dipping into the future, telling high school booster clubs and youth organizations that "the toughest characters aren't those who drink or smoke the most or have the biggest vocabulary, but those who block and tackle the hardest. In football, you learn the value of that little extra effort." In one of Harvard's rugby games, against the New York Rugby Club, he carried his own "little extra effort" a few steps too far, getting into three fights and being ordered to the dressing room. After the game, he apologized to the referee.

His family might have known differently, but to outsiders this rambunctiousness was a new side to Edward Moore Kennedy. In many ways, he still appeared to be easygoing, the same young lad who had allowed himself to be battered around for several days in the London school and who had suffered himself to be dunked into the cold water by his big brother without so much as a peep. But now his temper was exploding with increasing regularity. For years afterward, the Kennedys would amuse themselves with tales of young Ted's behavior, which they termed "boisterous." Joe McCarthy wrote in *The Remarkable Kennedys:*

One summer David Hackett was invited to join Bobby and Ethel, Teddy, Jean, and Red Fay and his wife, Anita, on a ten day cruise from Cape Cod to Maine. They anchored their boat, one afternoon, near Northeast Harbor and Teddy and Hackett rowed ashore in a dinghy to get supplies. As Teddy was paddling past a large and luxurious yacht, where several couples were enjoying a cocktail party, a man leaning over the rail of the costly craft called to him to row a little faster. Teddy advised him to mind his own business. "Come back here, and say that again," the man yelled.

"Teddy spun the dinghy around so fast I almost fell out of it," Hackett told Red Fay later. "The next thing I knew, Teddy was on the yacht and the man was being thrown overboard and all the women were screaming and running below to hide in the cabins. Their husbands were running with them, to see that they were safely tucked away, I guess. By this time, I'm on the yacht with Teddy. The men start to come back up to the deck to deal with us, but it's a narrow hatchway and they have to come up through it one at a time. As each guy appears, I grab him and spin him around and throw him to Teddy, and Teddy throws him overboard. In no time, all of the men—there were about eight of them—were in the water. I never saw anything like it."

This was the sort of behavior that Teddy's relatives and friends joked about and called "boisterous." If the story was true, there were others who might have called it assault and battery, and if any of the eight victims had drowned, the escapade might have gone under another name: manslaughter. But Teddy was the bumptious one—he meant nothing by his temper tantrums. Everybody knew that he was the soul of affability and charm, and the stories of his overblown behavior amused the family circle, and perhaps gained a bit with each telling.

By the time of his graduation from Harvard in 1956, a certain foolhardiness bordering on recklessness seemed to be well established in the young Kennedy's personality. He had, to begin with, a full apportionment of the vaunted Kennedy courage, which some called gall, some called verve, and some called downright lunacy. Once a close friend of the family was asked by a reporter, "Is there a gutless Kennedy anywhere in the world?"

"If there was," the insider answered, "he was drowned at birth."

In a peacetime setting, young Ted could never hope to match the documented bravado of his brother Jack on PT–109, or his brother Joe in the explosive-laden bomber, but he never seemed to stop trying. There were times when his friends worried about him. In Europe, he dived from the top of a dangerously high cliff into the Mediterranean, coming up with a smile on his face and a reddened forehead. In Canada, he insisted on racing down the steep Taschereau run on Mont Tremblant, an endeavor that would have unnerved a far more skillful skier. He surprised his new roommate at the University of Virginia Law School by insisting that they play tackle football on the lawn. The roommate, John Tunney, son of boxer Gene Tunney and now a Democratic congressman from California, said later, "I couldn't *believe* it! There we were in our street clothes, with no padding, supposed to be doing full tackles on each other!" Kennedy tossed Tunney the ball and then decked him on the spot with a bruising jolt that would have pleased his old Harvard coach.

Kennedy's boisterousness or rambunctiousness or courage or recklessness, whatever it was, soon spilled over into his driving. There had always been a certain *hubris* about the Kennedys and their automobiles; they drove as though they knew every highway patrolman personally. Even that most balanced of Kennedys, "President John," was no Eagle Scout behind the wheel. He drove too fast and took too many chances, though he slowed somewhat toward the end of his life. Once he parked his car squarely in front of a No Parking sign in downtown Washington and smilingly told an aide: "This is what Hamlet means by 'the insolence of office.'"

Ted Kennedy held no office when he first got into trouble over his driving. He was a second-year law student at the University of Virginia in Charlottesville, and he was already wooing the New York girl, Joan Bennett, who was to become his wife before his graduation. Some might have thought that he was maturing rapidly, putting aside his adolescent rowdiness, and looking toward his future as a responsible family man. But it did not appear so to Deputy Sheriff Tom Whitten of Albemarle County. Whitten was on duty when an Oldsmobile convertible rocketed by at about ninety miles an hour, ran a stoplight, extinguished its lights, and made a right turn into Barracks Road. When Whitten caught up and jumped out, he noticed that the car appeared to be empty. He walked to the driver's window, barked "Get up!" and watched as a slumping Edward Moore Kennedy rose meekly into sight. Whitten gave the chastened young man tickets for reckless driving, racing with an officer to avoid arrest, and operating a motor vehicle without an operator's license. After several postponements, Kennedy answered the summonses and paid a thirty-five-dollar fine, a bargain rate for such offenses. He was ticketed for speeding again during his stay at the University of Virginia, and then he picked up his law degree and headed back to Massachusetts.

The newly married Kennedys settled into their first home, a seventy-thousand-dollar brick townhouse on exclusive Beacon Hill in Boston, and the young husband petitioned for admission to the Massachusetts bar. "Service in public life can best be accomplished by an understanding of the legal process, its procedures, functions, and limitations," he wrote in his petition. "My ambition lies in the public service of this state." With a minimum of pother, Edward Moore Kennedy, son of an ambassador, brother of a United States senator, grandson of a mayor of

Boston, was licensed to practice law in the state of Massachusetts. Normally, this would have meant hanging out a shingle and beginning a plodding apprenticeship in such matters as divorce cases, broken contracts and accident claims, but at the Kennedy compound seventy miles away in Hyannis Port, heady matters were being discussed, and young Ted was included in the sessions. Joseph P. Kennedy Sr. was trying to talk his oldest living son, John Fitzgerald Kennedy, into running for President. Jack Kennedy was in his second term as a senator, and except for a few derelictions, such as ignoring the disease called McCarthyism, had rung up an outstanding record. His father felt that the moment should be grasped. "For the Kennedys," he said, "it's either the outhouse or the castle, nothing in between." Grandly, he offered the family's full financial resources to the Number One Son.

"Not all of them, Dad," Robert F. Kennedy cracked. "Don't forget Teddy and me!" At the time the remark was considered a joke, and everyone laughed.

Ted Kennedy had worked briefly and effectively in his brother's 1958 campaign for reelection to the Senate. His Irish charm and youthful enthusiasm had won many a voter to Jack Kennedy, and the senator wound up with the greatest plurality in Massachusetts history. But the campaign for the Presidency in 1960 would be another matter. Such Democratic leaders as Harry S Truman and Sam Rayburn were dead against the hero of PT–109; he was reckoned too young, too inexperienced and too pushy. Now, for the first time, the efficient Kennedy machine had to go into action on a national scale. Ted, twenty-eight years old, was put in charge of gathering delegates in eleven western states. What he lacked in experience and political savvy, he more than made up in hard work and gusto. In Montana, he climbed on a bucking bronco and lasted the requisite five seconds, winning more attention to his brother's cause than if he had delivered a brilliant peroration on constitutional law. When bad weather threatened to ground his private plane, he took the controls himself and steered the aircraft through the trouble and out the other side; then he returned the wheel to the regular pilot. In Wisconsin, he made his first ski jump, and landed on his feet. In West Virginia, he made a speech on behalf of his brother, who had lost his voice, and stirred the crowd so effectively that the candidate himself grabbed the microphone and croaked a reminder that Ted was not old enough to meet the constitutional age requirements for the Presidency. In Wyoming, a delegate grabbed the husky young man by the arm and said, "I wish *you* were running."

Wyoming's fifteen votes were needed to put Jack Kennedy over the top at the Democratic National Convention in Los Angeles, and when the unanimous vote was announced, there stood Ted Kennedy under the Wyoming banner, grinning his most dazzling Boston-Irish grin. It was not held against him later that ten of his eleven western states went for Nixon in the general election; the states had been accounted all but lost to the Democrats anyway, and impartial observers reported that Ted's energetic campaigning had done no harm. The youngest Kennedy rode a chartered bus to one of his brother's inaugural affairs, dancing a brisk jig in the aisles and singing "When Irish Eyes Are Smiling" in his loud, slightly off-key voice. After the inauguration, John F. Kennedy handed out engraved cigarette cases to his most important helpers. Campaign Manager Bob Kennedy's case was inscribed: "To Robert F. Kennedy. After I am through, how about you?"—another reminder of the family's stern policy of primogeniture. Ted Kennedy's case was enigmatically inscribed: "And the last shall be first."

A few weeks after John F. Kennedy took the oath of office as President, his youngest brother was sworn in as an assistant district attorney in Suffolk County, Massachusetts, which includes the entire city of Boston and three other communities: Revere, Winthrop and Chelsea. To one newspaper, the appointment showed that Edward M. Kennedy was coming out of the family cocoon, showing an "independent streak" of his own. But to others it was plain from the beginning that Kennedy intended neither to make a career as a public prosecutor nor to use the position the way other young lawyers used it: as a springboard into private practice. The first clear indication came even before the newly appointed assistant D.A. stepped into his office in Boston's courthouse: he went to Africa with two senators, Frank Church of Idaho and Frank Moss of Utah, on a fact-finding trip. At the time, some few critics wondered aloud exactly what facts could be found by the young man so fresh from an undistinguished career as a borderline student and army private, and with no particular qualifications as a specialist on African (or any other) folkways. But this was considered petty carping, especially when it was announced that Ted had paid his own way.

Soon there was more complaining among his new colleagues in the district attorney's office. To the wise political heads in that highly political Boston courthouse, there had never been any doubt about Kennedy's real motives. It was an open secret that the district attorney's office was simply a place for him to receive his mail while he learned the complex trade of politics and satisfied certain constitutional requirements about age. He emulated his father and all the other Kennedys by waiving the salary and working for one dollar a year, and some said slyly that he was overpaid. After he had been on the job a few months, one of his fellows griped: "Look, we all know what he's doing, he doesn't keep it a secret. He's running for office already. He almost never takes a case, and he's out night after night making speeches and running around the state meeting people, and who's with him all the time, whispering in his ear and giving him advice? Frank Morrissey, his father's old crony, the absolute epitome of the Boston politician. If this is the Kennedys' idea of how to prepare somebody for national office, he should never be elected dogcatcher!"

There was another objection around the D.A.'s office. It seemed to these earnest young men, many of them just out of law school themselves, that two courses had been open to the President's youngest brother: he could use his public office to build a record as a hard-working, dedicated servant of the people, deserving of election to a higher post, or he could relax and pluck all the grapes that would be available to him as the brother of a highly popular President. It was all too apparent that Edward M. Kennedy, once again in his life, was taking the easy way out. He hardly ever tried a case, and when he did he often failed to do his homework, coming into court unprepared. A retired employee of the office remembers: "He had no feeling for the job, none whatever, and he didn't try to develop any. He wouldn't work; he was listless and uninterested, and he tried cases only when he felt like it, which was seldom. I think he had certain natural talents, especially when it came to arguing cases. He could convince a jury, sway a jury, especially if there were women on it, but the pick and shovel work of the law he never bothered to learn. They said he won the moot court competition in law school, even while he was getting average grades. I can understand that. He was exactly the same here. A great arguer, a great showman, a politican all the way —and that's what you are when you're arguing a case, a politician. But the rest of the time you're supposed to be a craftsman, and Kennedy was one of the worst. He never learned the first thing you're supposed to learn, how to elicit your case in the stilted way the law demands in Massachusetts. If you see a good prosecutor do it, it looks effortless, but if you see a bohunk do it, it's like going to the dentist. He gets all screwed up and the judge gets annoyed and it's a pain in the ass for everybody. A great lawyer elicits his case so that the jury doesn't even know he's there: the whole story seems to be flowing from the witnesses. But Kennedy never learned this and never seemed to try. He was as bad on his last day as he was on his first; he learned nothing in a year and a half. He would ask a question and stammer around and rephrase the question and make long, omnibus statements and wind up convincing everybody that he had no case because he was putting words in the mouth of the witness. Still he won some cases, partly because he could argue, and partly because he was Edward M. Kennedy. I remember one little wise-guy lawyer from South Boston who came up to me one day and said, 'What the hell can I do? I've got the President's brother prosecuting me!' "

Kennedy made few friends in the courthouse. "He was not

only a Kennedy and a Harvard man," one colleague recalls, "but a prep school boy on top of it, and around the courthouse he always acted condescending toward the rest of us, as though we were all a bad influence and he'd been advised to stay away from us. He made us feel inferior. No one was unhappy to see him go."

The exact thought processes and the precise family planning that entered into Edward Kennedy's decision to run for the Senate in 1962 are not known to history in their entirety, nor have any of the family's biographies been of assistance in clearing up the muddle. If one is to accept the most commonly published version, a slightly reluctant Ted Kennedy was pushed by his father into running, against the wishes of John F. Kennedy. According to this version, JFK did not doubt his brother's abilities, but he was sensitive to charges that the Kennedys were building a dynasty, with brother Robert already in the cabinet as attorney general. The President caved in quickly, however, when he realized how strongly his father felt about the matter.

This version of Ted Kennedy's headlong leap into national politics may be accurate, but there are equally persuasive reports that the family had planned from the beginning to run Ted in 1962, when he would become thirty years old and eligible for the first time. As early as 1957, three years before John Kennedy won the Presidency, the *Saturday Evening Post* had run a remarkably prescient article. "Fervent admirers of the Kennedys," the article noted, "confidently look forward to the day when Jack will be in the White House, Bobby will serve in the cabinet as attorney general, and Teddy will be the senator from Massachusetts." There is evidence that the Kennedy family looked forward to the same day, worked together to make it come to pass, and never looked back or stopped to consider the youngest brother's qualifications. Old Joe Kennedy was widely quoted as telling his sons: "Look, I spent a lot of money for that Senate seat. It belongs in the family." And later: "You boys have what you want now, and everybody else helped you work to get it. Now it's Ted's turn. Whatever he wants, I'm going to see that he gets it."

The seat in question was the one that John F. Kennedy had been forced to vacate when he won the presidential election in 1960. Four years remained to be served, and waiting in the wings was Edward M. Kennedy, newly graduated from law school and eager to serve out the term, with only one obstruction in his way: the Constitution. He would not be thirty years old, the constitutional requirement for senators, until 1962. How to hold the seat in the meantime?

Foster Furcolo was about to retire as governor of Massachusetts, and everyone expected him to appoint himself to the Senate to serve for the two years until the next congressional elections, when the citizens of Massachusetts would have a chance to decide who was to serve the final two years of the unexpired term. But before Furcolo could even consider appointing himself, word came from the White House that the President would take care of the matter. JFK appointed an unknown, Benjamin A. Smith II (mayor of Gloucester, Massachusetts), to serve the two years. Democratic pols, some of whom had coveted the job themselves, asked who Benjamin Smith was, and learned that he had been John Kennedy's roommate in college. Further investigation revealed that Ben Smith was a man with no serious political ambitions, a man who could be trusted to keep the Senate seat warm but not develop any personal delusions of grandeur. "Ben's for the family," Ted Kennedy confided to a friend. But which male member of the family remained without a major political post? Only Edward.

Even with the handwriting so plainly on the wall, few Massachusetts politicians bothered to point out that if the Senate seat was being kept warm, it had to be on someone's behalf. And the someone, in the Kennedy mode of primogeniture, had to be the handsome young man who was showing up once or twice a week at the district attorney's office in Boston. The rest of the time, under the tutelage of the effervescent Francis X. Morrissey, Ted Kennedy was sharpening those talents which were already making people call him "the best politician in the family." Of all the Kennedys, he had the heartiest laugh, the most spontaneous smile, the most refreshing Irish humor, the gladdest hand. Women fell all over him. A beautiful woman once said to Jack Kennedy: "Your brother looks like a Greek god."

"Oh, no," the President replied jokingly. "He's a goddamned Greek!"

JFK could look at a photograph of Ted with a great bulging cheek and caption it playfully, "Honey Fitz's grandchild stores nuts for winter," but the jutting jaw and chunky silhouette of the youngest Kennedy only added to his boyish charm. Experience could come later. Early in the election year, 1962, the Kennedy family began its formal push to win back the Senate seat that had been placed on loan to the gracious Ben Smith since the presidential elections.

As an early step, even before any public pronouncement of the plans, young Ted was sent to address the Young Democrats of Palm Beach, Florida. It was Easter time. The assistant district attorney had been constitutionally eligible to run for the Senate for only two months, having turned thirty on February 22. The speech would provide a good test of his readiness to conduct a serious campaign on his own behalf.

On the morning after the address, a White House aide called a reporter who had covered the address. "You-know-who wants to know how his brother did," the aide said.

"You can tell you-know-who that it was the lousiest speech I ever heard in my life," the reporter answered. "Teddy made absolutely no sense on any subject!"

In later years he was to improve, but the formal address was never to become Ted Kennedy's forte as it was his brother John's. In many ways, he would remain the twelve-year-old boy whose big brother "zeized me by the pants and through me into the cold water." He was not at home with the English language; he could not shape it to his own ends as his brother had shaped it in both speeches and writings. He tended to speak in bits and pieces: "if I could . . . there comes a time . . . you have to be ready . . . not everyone . . . being a Kennedy . . . it's different for me." But if the Palm Beach speech was a disaster, the informal session afterwards was a success. Smiling and shaking hands, telling jokes and exhanging wisecracks, he was old Honey Fitz's grandson again; he was Frank Morrissey's eager pupil; he was a Boston pol. It was small qualification for the U.S. Senate, but it would have to do.

But not even the Kennedys were prepared for the eruption in the national press when the youngest brother announced that he was seeking the Democratic nomination for the interim seat. A group of professors from Harvard, the family's alma mater, announced: "Teddy has been aptly described as a 'fledgling in everything except ambition.'" James Reston, the Washington correspondent of the *New York Times,* the Kennedy family's favorite newspaper, wrote: "Teddy's bid for the Senate at 30 years of age, with the careful connivance of the President, is widely regarded as an affront and a presumption. In the end it is likely to cost the President more votes in the Senate than Teddy will ever give him." There was barely a word of approval anywhere for the youngest Kennedy's action, even in the press of his own state.

The newly announced candidate quickly won the endorsement of the Kennedy-controlled Massachusetts Democratic convention in the summer, but he would have to force the electorate in a September primary, and it would have been difficult to find a more formidable opponent: State Attorney General Edward J. McCormack Jr., nephew of Speaker of the House John W. McCormack and product of an old Boston political machine that, as one admirer put it at the time, "has done at least one personal political favor for every single person in Massachusetts and several in the Hawaiian Islands." Eddie McCormack had won honors at the United States Naval Academy; he was a seasoned political veteran with an untarnished record of public service. At thirty-nine, he had been near the top of his state's Democratic hierarchy—until the Kennedys had come along and deposed the McCormack machine in favor of their own. Even so, Eddie McCormack remained personally powerful. He held a basketful of political IOU's from all over the state, and now he was moving to collect them.

President John F. Kennedy announced that he was keeping hands off the election in Massachusetts, and then quietly moved to provide his brother with assistance. Certain subtle pressures were exerted on Massachusetts Democrats who knew they would be dealing with the Kennedy machine for years to come. Gifted White House artisans, such as the President's right-hand man, Theodore C. Sorensen, were dispatched to Boston to assist in the preparation of the speeches which the young Kennedy still tended to stumble through. And whenever time could be spared, the candidate himself dashed down to Washington for personal coaching by his talented older brothers. He remained a poor speaker, and some of his views on ticklish subjects were a cause for grimacing and complaining by his oldest brother, who thought they might later be laid at the White House door. One night Jack Kennedy was watching Ted on a television panel show, and at one of the answers, the President winced and turned the set off. He might be required by family loyalty to do everything possible to elect his little brother, but he did not have to sit and wriggle in discomfiture at the sight of the fledgling learning to fly.

To the voters of Massachusetts it seemed to matter little that the smiling young candidate was barely qualified to run as a member of the Hyannis Port board of selectmen, let alone as a senator from Massachusetts. The Kennedy name carried him over all obstacles. The news about his expulsion from Harvard —carefully kept quiet by the family for nearly ten years— broke into print and caused hardly a ripple among the electorate. *Boys will be boys; we all make mistakes, and look at him up there on the platform now, with that toothpaste grin and that tousled hair and that handsome Kennedy profile! A scandal at Harvard? Well, isn't it all kind of cute now? He'll be a good man. He's a Kennedy.* So went the reasoning—or the lack of it.

It was soon evident that Eddie McCormack was on his way to a staggering loss, and he knew it. Toward the end of the primary campaign, McCormack tried a desperation move, using a TV debate with the youngest Kennedy as his medium. First he took his opponent's arguments apart layer by layer; the *New York Times* later wrote that McCormack "devastated his opponent in logic, knowledge and style." But logic, knowledge and

style meant little to the typical Massachusetts voter, and now
Eddie McCormack set about turning the Kennedy name against
his handsome opponent. It was a bold move, but if it failed,
nothing was lost, since by now it was plain that the primary
had probably slipped out of reach anyway. Edward McCormack, in his own distinctive side-of-the-mouth style, pointed
out that his opponent had been pampered and spoiled and had
never worked a day in his life. "And I ask you," McCormack
said, pointing a stiletto finger in the direction of the President's
brother, "if his name was Edward Moore—with your qualifications, with your qualifications, Teddy—if it was Edward Moore
your candidacy would be a joke. Nobody's laughing, because
his name is not Edward Moore, it's Edward Moore Kennedy."
Ted Kennedy was upset, and showed it.

Shortly afterward, the political world found out what happens to those who mock the Kennedy name. The former assistant district attorney rolled up 69 percent of the popular vote;
the attorney general was left for dead, and seemed to realize it.
"If this is politics," Eddie McCormack said, "if they can get
away with this, then I don't want any part of politics." At thirty-nine, he announced his retirement.

At first, the general election appeared to present a more difficult prospect. Ted was pitted against youthful Republican
George Lodge, in what the newspapers gleefully tagged "the
battle of the dynasties." Ted's grandfather, old Honey Fitz, had
lost the same Senate seat in 1916 to George Lodge's great-
grandfather, Henry Cabot Lodge, and JFK had won the same
seat from Henry Cabot Lodge's grandson, Ambassador Henry
Cabot Lodge, in 1952. The presidential assistants who had
helped destroy Eddie McCormack now helped young Kennedy
work on Lodge. They reactivated Jack Kennedy's old Senate
campaign slogan: "He can do more for Massachusetts." The
message was not lost on the electorate; a senator whose big
brother was in the White House could exert heavy pressure on
behalf of his constituency. Some called the slogan irresponsible, but they were few.

By now, the Kennedy forces had learned what their man

could do best: the informal gathering, the face-to-face meeting, the handshake, the autograph. With a newly apparent capacity for hard, bruising political work, Ted Kennedy appeared all over Massachusetts, speaking from the backs of trucks, walking through lines of factory workers at dawn, attending carnivals and church bazaars. To the tune of Mitch Miller's "Lend an Ear," his aides belted out his campaign song:

> *Whadd'ya say mighty Bay State?*
> *Ted fills the bill.*
> *Go all the way, State. Put Kennedy on the hill.*
> *A young, strong and able, fair-minded man.*
> *He's ready and able to fight for you*
> *As only a Kennedy can!*

If the intellectuals chortled, the common folk (vastly in the majority) joined in and made the rafters shake with their support of the young nobleman whose forebears had so recently lived in the shanties themselves. In this general election, there was no longer the question of which candidate would capture the Irish vote, or for that matter, the Italian and Polish and Negro vote. George Lodge was a Boston Brahmin, descended from a long line of Boston Brahmins; he was therefore an oppressor by definition. The depth of this feeling became apparent as the campaign wore on. Just before election day, Kennedy made one of his typically opaque, prepared addresses, and two people in the audience burst into laughter at some of the clumsy phraseology. They stopped when a tall member of the working class, with County Cork etched deeply into his face, asked them in a threatening voice: "Are you laughing at Mr. Kennedy?" Two generations before, Edward Kennedy's paternal grandfather had been an Irish bartender in the slums of Boston. The factory workers had not forgotten.

When the final vote was counted, Kennedy was an easy winner again, polling 1,143,021 votes to 863,460 for his Republican opponent. Interviewed by reporters a few hours after Lodge had conceded, young Kennedy was asked if he had discussed his victory with the President. He said he had not but hoped to soon. Had he discussed the win with his other brother, the attorney general? No, he said, but he would shortly. Had he talked to his father? A broad grin broke across the senator-elect's face. "Oh, yes," he said. "I talked to *him*. He was extremely excited."

Others were less ecstatic. Jonathan Daniels, influential editor of the Raleigh *News and Observer* and an avowed JFK backer, wrote in an editorial: "The implications of Ted Kennedy's campaign will not help the President, the Democratic Party, or the country." James Reston was tougher. The election, he wrote, was "demeaning to the dignity of the senate and the Democratic process. . . . The Kennedys have applied the principle of the best man available for the job to almost everyone but themselves. Teddy's victorious headlines are resented . . . because he is demanding too much too soon on the basis of too little. What is particularly surprising about all this is that the Kennedys do not see this line of criticism at all, and in fact deeply resent it. They have invoked the new pragmatism, but cannot see that where the family was concerned, they applied the old nepotism."

Whatever they had applied, the Kennedys were ebullient. They made no public apologies, nor did they seem to feel that any were required. If there were doubts about Ted's qualifications, the family knew that they would be resolved in the excellence of his Senate record as the months went by. The Kennedys had made the assumption that they always made: that a Kennedy, whatever his qualifications, was better than anybody else, whatever *his* qualifications. Soon after the election, President John F. Kennedy smiled proudly and told an audience in Harrisburg, Pennsylvania, "I should introduce myself. I am Teddy Kennedy's brother."

The Senate of the United States, also known as "the Club," is a singular institution whose members are dedicated to the preservation of one another and obey certain unwritten laws. One senator does not attack another, on or off the Senate floor.

If a senator should slip and say something aggressive, or something foolish, his aides may return in the evening and alter the record to expunge the error. If a senator should become intoxicated by noon, and come reeling and stumbling to the floor, his colleagues of both parties will gently steer him outside, and the accredited reporters will look the other way. Thus, men of deep and abiding weakness have remained in the Senate for years on end, protected from the scorn of their constituencies by the rules of the Club. They let their white hair grow long in the back, affect black string ties and dark coats, and call themselves statesmen, and soon the public finds it difficult to distinguish between the handful of true statesmen in the Senate and the numerous impostors.

In his rookie years as a member of the Senate, Edward M. Kennedy was plainly neither statesman nor impostor. He was simply a young man trying to get by. Now that he was in, it had become necessary to alter his image, from the overly ambitious candidate to the sincere public servant. Self-depreciation was the order of the day. His staff announced that he would not allow himself to be interviewed by anyone except newsmen from his own state; he was not interested in national publicity. Just after his swearing-in in 1963, he told friends: "I was down at the White House this afternoon with some suggestions for the State of the Union Address. But all I got from him was, 'Are you still using that greasy kid stuff?' " Privately he told members of his staff to "knock off" referring to him as Teddy —he intended to establish the kind of serious, creditable record that would mark him as a more mature "Ted," and ultimately as the distinguished Senator from Massachusetts, Edward M. Kennedy. From the outset, he tried to make friends with his fellow senators, accommodating, backslapping, and praising indiscriminately. The role of organization man came naturally to him, although there were a few surprises. While he was paying an early morning courtesy call on Senator James Eastland of Mississippi, Kennedy watched wide-eyed as the Southerner poured him a stiff shot of whiskey. When Eastland turned his back, Kennedy dumped the glass in the wastebasket.

On the floor he risked nothing. His interests were provincial. Years later, one of his aides was to recall: "I'd talk to him about the national interest, and all he'd talk about was the Springfield, Mass., arsenal." His maiden speech, short and to the point, was a denunciation of the Civil Aeronautics Board's decision to shut Northeast Airlines out of the New York–Miami run. Northeast had twelve hundred employees in Massachusetts. The speech could do no harm with his constituents, and his fellow senators would not hold it against him. In off-hours, he worked hard, studying legislation, doing his homework. He immersed himself in the painful tasks that his seniors avoided: taking the chair during the hours of fustian debate, chasing down his fellows for quorum calls, showing up to vote the party line on inconsequential matters. He waited sixteen months before making his first major address on the Senate floor, and he moved slowly into areas of national moment. Every move he made, however minuscule, was preceded by letters of explanation to his fellow senators, or accompanied by visits to the other members of the establishment, "just seeking your advice, Senator, your guidance."

In any other public body, this supercautious behavior would have identified the new man as a harmless drudge, but in the United States Senate it was the surest guarantee of approval by one's peers. The other senators appreciated Ted Kennedy's thoughtfulness and deference, his eager acceptance of the new senator's mute and humble role, his willingness to "go along" and "accommodate." Senior senators compared him more than favorably with his brother the President, who had twisted and squirmed uncomfortably in his own role of freshman senator. The statesmen recalled the day in Jack Kennedy's first term when he had moved down to a front-row seat so that he could take part in a floor debate, and found himself sitting next to the Senate dean, Carl Hayden. Kennedy whispered a question: What changes had taken place in Hayden's forty years in Congress? "New members did not speak in those days," Hayden said coldly.

On November 22, 1963, Senator Edward M. Kennedy was

carrying out one of the boring tasks that he had embraced as a freshman senator: he was in the chair, in the absence of the Vice-President, presiding over a listless debate on a library services bill. In front of him was a gallery of empty seats: Senator Winston Prouty of Vermont was speaking to a small collection of senators when a press aide ran to the floor with a bulletin he had ripped off the teletype machine in the lobby. The aide handed the bulletin to the first senator he reached, Spessard Holland of Florida, and whispered: "The President has just been shot." Then he cried out to Kennedy: "Senator, your brother has been shot!"

The young senator paled. "No!" he said. He gathered his papers, hurried to the lobby, and began making phone calls. When he learned that his brother was dead, he rushed home to Georgetown and told his wife Joan, who had heard nothing. The two of them broke down together. That night Kennedy and his sister Eunice Shriver flew from Washington to Hyannis, where their father lay half-paralyzed with a stroke. They found that the other members of the family had kept the tragic news from the patriarch.

Joe Sr. seemed happy to see his son and daughter; there was nothing foreboding about a spontaneous visit from members of the close-knit family, and that night the old man allowed himself to be taken to his room at the customary 9:30. Nor did he make a complaint the next morning when the *New York Times* was missing from its usual place by his breakfast dish. When Ted and Eunice returned from mass at nearby St. Francis Xavier Church and visited their father in his room, Joe Kennedy asked that the television set be turned on. Ted said that it was not working. The old man pointed to the plug, lying on the floor below the socket. The young senator started to plug in the cord, then dropped it and told his father that John F. Kennedy was dead.

By the time Ted Kennedy was to return to the electorate of Massachusetts to ask for a full six-year term in the Senate, events had made his reelection inevitable. His Senate record was immaterial; if it was true that he had done little or nothing, it was also true that he had done little or nothing *wrong*. And the sorrow over the death of his brother—a sorrow that seemed to border on hysteria in parts of Massachusetts—had been translated into a feeling that staggering debts were somehow owed by the common people to the nobility called Kennedy. Robert Kennedy, a forceful and talented politician, moved to collect one of the debts in New York State, where he would easily defeat a well-entrenched Republican senator named Kenneth Keating. For Ted Kennedy, victory promised to come even more easily. He was flying to Springfield, Massachusetts, to accept the nomination of the state's Democratic convention when the twin-engined Aero Commander went out of control in a heavy fog and crashed in an apple orchard at Southampton, seven miles from its destination.

A broken Ted Kennedy lay in the twisted and mangled wreckage, barely conscious, unable to move a muscle or speak a word. Outside he could hear voices counseling others not to go near the plane, not to go inside. Someone was shouting that the rest were dead, that the plane might explode or catch fire any second. Then the strong arms of Senator Birch Bayh, himself seriously injured, grabbed him and hauled him away from the wreckage. Outside, Kennedy learned that the pilot, Edwin T. Zimny, had been killed instantly, and Kennedy's aide, Edward Moss, was beyond help. The young senator had a broken back and three broken ribs; a lung had collapsed. The first doctors who saw him, at Cooley-Dickinson Hospital, said that he might be paralyzed for the rest of his life, like his father. A bitter Robert Kennedy heard the news and commented: "Somebody up there doesn't like us. It's been a great year for giggles, hasn't it?" Friends said that the former attorney general's sarcastic levity covered up a deep grief, almost as deep as his grief when the President was assassinated. As children, the two younger brothers had been close; now Robert Kennedy lingered for long hours at the bedside. After a few days, doctors issued the first optimistic report: it appeared that there was no permanent nerve damage; Ted Kennedy would have to spend many months on his back, but he probably would function again as a whole man. Massachusetts Governor Endicott Peabody announced: "While our great Senator may be temporarily bedridden, the fight will be carried by us for him." A patented Kennedy-family blitz was applied to the Bay State; Ted's sisters made whistle-stop tours; Mrs. Rose Kennedy brought her own graciousness and charm into play on her son's behalf; Joan Kennedy, Ted's attractive blond wife, took to the stump; and such family functionaries as Stephen Smith busied themselves behind the scenes.

In retrospect, one realizes that the expenditure of so much political energy by so many Kennedys was redundant; the family was using a sledgehammer to kill a gnat. The young senator had been certain of victory on a wave of public sympathy and compassion *before* he himself was seriously injured. Now, as he lay face down on his Stryker frame in Boston's New England Baptist Hospital, one could almost hear the ground swell of affection that coursed through Massachusetts on his behalf. To say an unkind word about him or any other Kennedy in the Massachusetts of late 1964 was to invite instant retaliation, sometimes physical.

At the state Democratic convention, which he never reached, Kennedy was nominated by acclamation. He won the general election (against a relative unknown) by 1,129,000 votes, or more than his brother Jack's record-setting 875,000-vote plurality six years before. He also did some thinking during his long months of immobility. He was honest enough to recognize that his qualifications for statesmanship were meager; he decided to improve them. He arranged with friends on the Harvard faculty to conduct seminars on some of the subjects that had failed to gain his full attention in his hapless college years. The Harvard men found that the patient had boned up before each seminar, and had as much to contribute as anyone. John Kenneth Galbraith, who functioned as dean of the bedside cram course, said later that Ted was "first rate as a quick study— almost as good as JFK." In mid-December, 1964, the convalescent strapped on a backbrace and walked out of the hospital a wiser man, and presumably a more dedicated one. After a short holiday in the bright sunlight of West Palm Beach, he returned to Washington to take his place as a full-time senator.

No public officeholder with an electoral mandate like the newly reelected Edward Kennedy need pussyfoot around his peers, and the young senator did not. While retaining the courteous, respectful attitudes of his first two years, he moved quickly to make a record that would carry him abreast of his brothers. Hardly had Congress convened in 1965 before the thirty-three-year-old senator took dead aim on one of the South's favorite devices for depriving blacks of voting rights: the poll tax. The Johnson administration had worked up a compromise civil rights bill that deliberately ignored the poll tax in the hope that Southern members of Congress would find the bill more palatable. Kennedy was advised by Republicans and Democrats alike to let the matter lie; the poll tax could be dealt with at a later date. Instead he went ahead, starting with a deep reach into the pool of brainpower that always seemed at the beck and call of the Kennedy family. Three esteemed members of the Harvard law faculty were enlisted to draft an amendment banning the poll tax, and three esteemed members of the Howard law faculty were enlisted to drill the young senator in the techniques of arguing on behalf of civil rights. Thus armed and girded, Kennedy took his battle to the floor of the Senate and showed more eloquence than ever before in his short career as a public servant. When he was not on the floor leading the fight for his amendment, he was working effectively in the back alleys of Congress, buttonholing, cajoling, imploring and threatening in the traditional style of the august chamber.

Against both the Republican and Democratic leadership, Kennedy's amendment lost by a scant four votes, but the message of the battle was not lost on anyone. Ted Kennedy, the silent man of his early Senate years, had made his first big move; from now on, he would have to be counted in. Few senators were upset. Already, Kennedy was proving to be a gracious loser, substantiating the belief that, unlike his brothers, he was a true "Senate man." By now, his brother Robert had joined him in the upper house, but Robert quickly made plain that the Senate was a steppingstone, a tedious but necessary platform for larger plans. He showed open contempt for tradition by making a major address three weeks after the session opened; old-time statesmen sat open-mouthed, and some walked out. But the youngest brother, even after losing his floor fight on the poll tax amendment, continued to show respect for what the author Jules Witcover later called "the wheel-spinning, the empty gestures and the time-wasting procedures [that] were cherished trademarks of the Club." Ted was held in higher esteem than ever, and not only in the Senate. Lyndon Johnson, the former "Senate man" whose public feud with Robert Kennedy was beginning to break into the open, issued regular invitations to both brothers to attend White House functions, but only the younger brother arrived with regularity. Robert often failed even to acknowledge the invitations. Soon President Johnson was telling confidants that he had no respect for "that little bastard Bobby Kennedy," but that Ted Kennedy was "a nice kid, really likeable, with a great future."

Perhaps it was because of the growing rapport between the two men, or perhaps it was because Kennedy was beginning to feel his own muscle, but he soon made a glaring miscalculation. He asked President Johnson to nominate Boston Municipal Judge Francis X. Morrissey to the federal bench, and Johnson, trusting the judgment of his only friend in the Kennedy clan, compounded the error by making the nomination. All at once the United States Senate found itself sitting in judgment on a Boston politician whose qualifications for a federal judgeship were almost entirely invisible. A pro-Kennedy, pro-Morrissey book published in that same year, 1965, might have told the intelligent reader all he needed to know about the nominee. It was called *The Life and Times of Joseph P. Kennedy,* it was written by William J. Duncliffe, and it included this passage:

Every morning Frank Morrissey, his confidant for so many years, came to see him, and every morning the two of them played a kind of game. Morrissey would come into the room and exclaim: "Ambassador, I've never seen you looking better." Then, to prove his point, Morrissey would hold up a mirror to Kennedy's face. Joe would grimace and, with the one hand he could move, would motion away the mirror. No one, not Frank Morrissey or anyone else, was going to pull a fast one on him. . . . On January 8, 1962, he [Kennedy] was released from the hospital and was taken to his estate to continue his convalescence. When the big league baseball teams came south for spring training, Morrissey corralled several members of the Milwaukee Braves and the New York Yankees and brought them to Palm Beach. Warren Spahn was one of them. In Kennedy's presence, Morrissey told him: "Warren, you may not know it, but the Ambassador was quite a ballplayer when he was young. He batted .583—or something like that—one year."

Now, for such kindnesses, the amiable Boston politician who had never heard a jury or equity case as a judge, had never tried a case in court as a lawyer, and who had required three attempts to pass the Massachusetts bar examination, was to be named a federal jurist. Not even the United States Senate, with its notoriously strong stomach, could accept such a proposition, and the battle lines were drawn. To some, it was painfully obvious that the young Kennedy was risking his political life as part of a solemn promise made to his father; Ted had always been close to old Joe Kennedy, and he had tried to carry out his father's wishes. Others thought there was a different motive: it had been Francis X. Morrissey who tutored the young man with the Gaelic charm and the magic name during his stint as a nonfunctioning assistant district attorney. People said that Morrissey, the Irish politician from the Charlestown area, and Kennedy, the Irish prince from Hyannis Port, were cronies themselves, two of a kind under the skin. They had probably laid their plans for the judgeship years before.

Whatever the reason for the nomination, Ted Kennedy did not give up easily. He led a floor fight on behalf of his friend, he lobbied members of the committee that would have to pass on the nomination, and he allowed the matter to remain before the Senate even after the American Bar Association had voiced its hearty disapproval of the nomination. At the last instant, when the roll was about to be called on the Senate floor and it was clear that Kennedy and the old family retainer were doomed to ignominious defeat, the young senator stepped to the microphone and in a highly emotional manner asked that the nomination be returned to committee, tantamount to killing it. Characteristically, he emerged with a whole skin. The dominant leftover feeling among the members of the Club was that it had been decent of the young man to spare them having to go on the record in the matter. True, he had engaged in a misguided effort to place an unqualified crony in high position (and hadn't almost all the senators, at one time or another?), but when the curtain fell, it was his character as a "Senate man" that one remembered. The statesmen appreciated that. Here and there a voice was heard about the contempt for the democratic and judicial processes so clearly shown by the Massachusetts senator, the pettiness of mind that would attempt to inflict a Frank Morrissey on the thousands of litigants and defendants who would come to the bar of federal justice in the future, the arrogance and cronyism that permeated the whole matter. But these voices soon died out, and the overriding national attitude, led by the members of the Club, was that everyone makes mistakes.

After the Morrissey affair, Kennedy retreated into the cautious posture that had characterized his earlier Senate career, following the Democratic party line and striving mightily to become a member of the inner circle. As a Kennedy, he drew around him a large collection of talented people, and he tended to rely on his staff more than either of his brothers had. When Jack Kennedy had planned a speech, he would assemble his writers, outline his own ideas and put the writers to work on them. Ted Kennedy, lacking this confidence, would simply state the subject matter and give his writers free rein, later making only minor changes in their draft, and then in the direction of caution. All the Kennedys had tended to rely on task forces, but the youngest brother seemed to use them to the exclusion of his own intellectual capacities. Nevertheless, his name and his reputation flourished. Simply by being in the Senate, and by tending to day-to-day chores for his constituents, the young

Senator gained status within the Club as quickly as anyone in memory, not excluding that summa cum laude alumnus, Lyndon Baines Johnson. "[Ted Kennedy] does not have an original mind, nor a mind of large grasp," a student of the family was anonymously quoted in the press, ". . . but a Senator can be an accepted member of the Club without notable abilities. Teddy rose because he discovered a talent for using other men's talents." He was also unremittingly pleasant and polite, almost aggressively so. Only one member of the United States Senate paid a courtesy visit to Senator Thomas Dodd of Connecticut on the day that the Ethics Committee recommended Dodd's censure. The visitor was Senator Edward Kennedy, calling to tell his humiliated colleague that he would have to vote for the motion to censure, but that he was personally sympathetic and would offer any other assistance he could. "Jack Kennedy would have ignored the likes of Dodd," an observer said at the time. "Bobby Kennedy would have threatened to punch him in the mouth. Ted Kennedy paid a social call on him. That's the difference between the three."

This preoccupation with political protocol extended even to Kennedy's public speeches. He campaigned actively for men like Senator Paul Douglas of Illinois, Congressman Rodney Love of Ohio, gubernatorial candidate Pat Lucey of Wisconsin, but his addresses seldom touched on anything as important or as crucial as Vietnam or civil rights. "I don't come to Wisconsin with any easy solutions to the problems of Southeast Asia," he told an audience in a typical address. He preferred to spend most of his speaking time extolling the qualities of the candidate, wandering only rarely to such safe subjects as the need for more citizen involvement in politics, for cleaner cities, and for high levels of public morality. By February of 1967, his brother Robert had become unalterably opposed to the war in Vietnam and the President's handling of it, but in all the family councils one voice rang out louder than any of the others, urging the plainspoken former attorney general to bide his time and remain quiet. The voice was Ted Kennedy's, ever the apostle of caution and accommodation, of political peace. Robert spoke out anyway, and when Ted joined his brother in mild criticism of the war effort, he tended to do so in terms of homeless refugees, rather than American dead, and sent advance copies of his remarks to the White House, as a courtesy.

And yet there had been signs, rare but unmistakable, that underneath the safe-playing, archetypal Washington politician beat the heart of a true Kennedy, unafraid to tilt at an occasional windmill. There had been the time in 1967 when he had gone against Richard Russell and John Stennis, the two top Democrats on the Armed Services Committee, by introducing his own bill to change the Selective Service laws. He lost, of course, but not before gaining new admirers of his skillful floor management, not to mention his bravado. A year later, when he was counseling his brother to be more cautious, he defied one of the sacred canons of congressional tradition and won. The House had passed an odoriferous redistricting bill that flew in the face of the principle of "one man, one vote," and Kennedy announced his opposition. He was advised to mind his own business; there was a longstanding tradition that the Senate did not upset the House on matters of comity, because the House might later reverse the procedure. But Kennedy pushed on, and when it became obvious that he had the votes, the bill was returned to the House committee whence it had come, a clearcut victory for the young senator.

He also showed some of the old Kennedy attitudes on a visit to South Vietnam early in 1968. The generals and the diplomats had laid out a red-carpet tour for the influential senator, but Kennedy and his aides quickly stepped from the red carpet into the mud of Southeast Asia and spent twelve days slogging around seeing what they chose to see. More than once Kennedy trapped American officers in typically grotesque exaggerations and sometimes in downright lies, and more than once he showed his disgust openly. When he came home he criticized the Johnson administration and the government in Saigon for the deplorable refugee conditions he had found, and for the corruption that was rife in the South Vietnamese government.

Now and then someone would wonder publicly which Kennedy was going to reach for a Democratic presidential nomination some day, the fiery one named Robert who was busily ignoring the Senate and running around the country building up a constituency of the downtrodden, or the more cautious one named Ted who was gaining stature slowly but surely in Congress. The subject was never more than the stuff of humor for the two Kennedy brothers, both of whom well understood the family's rigid policy of primogeniture. They laughed together when they discussed what Adlai Stevenson III had once said: "It's well known that President Johnson is watching with interest the political activities of Senator Robert Kennedy. But perhaps it's not so well known that Senator Robert Kennedy is watching with more than passing interest the political activities of Senator Edward Kennedy." Once Bobby jokingly told a group of admirers that he had just received a telegram from his brother: PRESIDENT IS IN ASIA. VICE PRESIDENT IS IN MIDWEST. YOU ARE IN MICHIGAN. HAVE SEIZED CONTROL. TEDDY. Robert Kennedy told a crowd: "Before I left Washington, I asked my younger brother, Teddy, to have ten thousand Kennedy campaign buttons made up. But when I opened them on the plane, I found they all had his picture on them."

Of course, the question had never been whether it should be Robert or Ted, but instead *when* should Robert run? The forty-two-year-old senator from New York had a mind to come out against Lyndon Johnson in 1968, and announce early in the year, but he was strongly influenced against this course by several cautious voices in the inner circle. Theodore C. Sorensen, who had been President John Kennedy's closest advisor, and Pierre Salinger, JFK's press secretary, spoke for caution, and so did Ted Kennedy. Privately, the younger brother told Robert Kennedy that he agreed that the war was a disgrace, that his own recent trip to Vietnam had only reinforced this belief, but that political considerations dictated against the campaign. He argued that not even the Kennedy machine could unseat an incumbent President at a national convention, and that the only effect of Robert's candidacy would be the election of Richard Nixon. Along the way, the family name and influence would be

seriously weakened. The argument made sense to others, nota-
bly Sorensen and Salinger, and indeed there is reason to believe
that it was not mere caution, but also genuine political acumen
that made Ted Kennedy speak out. Whatever the reason, he held
his position until the day in March when Robert Kennedy,
against such advice, entered the race for the nomination.

Some argued later that Ted Kennedy served his brother's
candidacy poorly, pulling his punches and failing to show the
all-out dedication that had characterized the family's earlier efforts. Certain members of Robert Kennedy's staff wrote Ted
Kennedy off; it was plain, they said, that his main interest was
in himself, that he was looking ahead to his own candidacy, following the inscription on his inaugural cigarette lighter: "And
the last shall be first." But the men closest to the young senator
vehemently disagreed. They argued that Ted Kennedy idolized
his last remaining brother, the brother closest to him in age,
and that he was campaigning quietly and effectively in his own
style. The tough and blunt-spoken former attorney general
worked with a bludgeon; his little brother was more likely to
use the techniques of the Congress, inviting prospective delegates to have a drink with him in his suite, to sit down over a
cigar, and to work out the differences between them that might
have gone back to the JFK presidential campaign when Bobby
managed to abrade hundreds of important Democrats. This was
not a spectacular method of campaigning, Ted Kennedy's aides
pointed out, but it was effective. They argued that Ted was
working eighteen hours a day for his brother; in two months of
campaigning he was to spend exactly five nights in his new five-
hundred-thousand-dollar home overlooking the Potomac in
McLean, Virginia; did that represent letting his brother down
in favor of his own candidacy?

The arguments became moot on the night of June 5, just
after Robert Kennedy had won the most important election of
his own short life: the California primary. As usual, his
younger brother was out working for him, representing the candidate at a campaign workers' victory party in San Francisco.
Just after midnight, Robert F. Kennedy was shot in the kitchen

of the Ambassador Hotel in Los Angeles. Ted Kennedy, almost in shock himself, rushed to the airport and flew to his brother's bedside.

Jack Newfield wrote later, "[Robert] Kennedy was never to recover fully from the trauma of Dallas, the way his brother Edward seemed to." If the statement seemed unfair and harsh, it nonetheless made psychological sense; there were fifteen years between JFK and his youngest brother; as children, they had gone their separate ways to their separate prep schools and their separate careers. But the death of Robert Kennedy was a blow from which some intimates doubted that Edward M. Kennedy would ever recover. Robert was the brother he had tagged after, the brother who had wiped his nose and protected him, the brother he had needed. "With Bobby," Jean Kennedy Smith said, "he had the same thing he did with Dad. Teddy depended on his judgment. . . . It's hard to find a substitute for Bobby."

His friends had never seen Ted Kennedy in such a deeply depressed state. He wept, sometimes in public, and he fought uncharacteristically for his privacy, even refusing to see close friends who wanted to comfort him. There were Kennedy haters who said that the mourning was a grandstand act, that Ted Kennedy had been running for the Presidency the second he climbed aboard the old-fashioned observation car to accompany his brother's body back to Washington. Such remarks were irrational, cheap attacks on a man who was emotionally shattered, barely able to pull himself together to deliver his brother's eulogy at St. Patrick's Cathedral in Manhattan. Aides begged him not to go. They were afraid he would break down completely. But Kennedy opened his final speech on his brother's behalf in loud, ringing tones from the pulpit. Twice his voice broke and it appeared he could not continue. But he paused and regained control and finally approached the conclusion, his voice quivering, his eyes wet. "My brother," he said, "need not be idealized, or enlarged in death beyond what he was in life, to be remembered simply as a good and decent man."

The good and decent man was buried on June 8, 1968, and once again the Kennedys retreated to Cape Cod with their losses. Robert's widow, Ethel, was soon delivered of her eleventh child, and the brave woman was back on her feet and able to see visitors before her brother-in-law was. Ted Kennedy had drawn the protecting sands of the Cape around him. He spent days sailing, sometimes with his wife, sometimes with his children, and sometimes by himself, riding the wind far out into Nantucket Sound and tacking back alone with his thoughts. Relatives would see him lying at the end of the stone breakwater, his head turned away from the sun, and they would give him the wide berth that he so obviously needed. On those few occasions when he confided in friends, he spoke of dire events, of morbidities. He was afraid that his father, with whom he had been extraordinarily close, was nearing the end. To a few, the bereaved young senator admitted that he could not get the sight of his dying brother Robert out of his head. He confessed that he was sometimes afraid for his own life; there were unknown numbers of lunatics walking the land, and one of them might well be pondering the assassination of the last Kennedy brother. "I know I'm going to get my ass shot off," he said in the blunt way in which close friends speak, "and I don't *want* to get my ass shot off."

But there were family problems to be solved, and the period of his hermitage could not last forever. With Robert's death, Ted had become the functioning head of the sprawling family, the father or surrogate father of fifteen children. Two of Robert's boys were having the typical prep school problems; Ted took the oldest son, the fifteen-year-old Joe, off to Spain, and paid a visit to the Aristotle Onassis yacht long enough to learn that his famous sister-in-law planned to marry again. He rushed home with the news, and presided at family conferences where the problems presented by Jacqueline Kennedy's impending remarriage were discussed. Then he arranged for Robert Kennedy Jr. to visit Africa in the company of an old family friend, Lemoyne (Lem) Billings. He turned to the John F. Kennedy Library project and gave it some sorely needed attention, joined in creating a ten-million-dollar foundation for social action in the name of the fallen Robert, and busied himself in minor tasks.

As the Democratic National Convention in Chicago approached, Kennedy remained at his Squaw Island home hard by the family compound at Hyannis, knowing that political approaches were coming, and wondering what to do about them. Privately, he had decided not to accept the vice-presidential nomination; he remembered too well his father's statement: "For the Kennedys, it's either the outhouse or the castle, nothing in between." As for the presidential nomination, he had reason to believe he could get it, and reason to wonder if he was qualified for it, and the same cautious attitude toward the 1968 elections that he had tried to pass on to his brother Robert. He was not even sure that he would discuss the matter with other politicians. His grief still weighed him down, occupied almost all of his thoughts; the times were asking much of him. He alternated between periods of deep depression and periods of inner doubt. No one else in the family had been kicked out of college. No one else had a reckless driving record. No one else had committed a cheap *faux pas* like the Morrissey nomination. He acted as his own judge and jury, and almost invariably found himself guilty. In those rare moments when he could compare himself favorably with other potential nominees, realizing that no one was truly qualified for a job as complex as the Presidency, he considered other reasons why he should not run, the first and foremost being that he might lose. Richard Nixon would be the opponent, and underneath the newly powdered stubble, the fourteenth version of "the new Nixon" was the same old gut-fighting, shin-kicking politician, with a reputation for making personal public attacks. Kennedy and Ted Sorensen talked about the prospects of running against such a man; they agreed that Nixon, up for his last chance, might be more irresponsible than ever. Certainly he would accuse the youthful candidate of being raw and inexperienced, "a fledgling in everything except ambition," as the Harvard professors had described him only six years before. Nixon would not hesitate to charge that Kennedy was trying to ride public compassion into the White House, trying to cash in on his name and his tragedies. And how would Ted Kennedy answer these charges? How did one go on national television and explain that one's tears had not been faked, one's quavery voice had not been practiced in front of a mirror? How did one combat charges of immaturity and inexperience, especially when they were true?

The young senator was painfully aware of earlier criticism about the Kennedys' trying to go too far too fast. In the campaign of 1960, Harry S Truman used the medium of television to put forward the names of ten possible candidates, including his own man, Senator Stuart Symington of Missouri. Addressing himself directly to John F. Kennedy, the former President said, "Senator, are you certain that you are quite ready for the country, or that the country is ready for you in the role of President . . . ? [The country needs] a man with the greatest possible maturity and experience. . . . May I urge you to be patient?"

A few days later, the brilliant history scholar John F. Kennedy dissected and destroyed Truman's argument in a manner that served to emphasize the true differences in class and culture between the young Harvard man and the former haberdasher from Kansas City. "If fourteen years in major elective office is insufficient experience," Kennedy intoned, "that rules out all but three of the ten names put forward by Truman, all but a handful of American Presidents, and every President of the twentieth century—including Wilson, Roosevelt and Truman." If the age of forty-four had been selected as an arbitrary test of maturity, Kennedy went on, it "would have kept Jefferson from writing the Declaration of Independence, Washington from commanding the Continental Army, Madison from fathering the Constitution . . . and Christopher Columbus from even discovering America." (At Theodore Sorensen's request, Kennedy had stricken another impressive name from the list: Jesus Christ.) With such crystalline logic, JFK turned Truman's attack on him into a net gain, and by a succession of such gains, won the Presidency.

Against similar attacks by Richard Nixon in 1968, Ted Kennedy would have had a far more difficult time defending himself, and he was well aware of it. He might feel that he would make a better President than Nixon, for all his own inexperience, but he could not be sure the electorate would agree. Like other Democrats in 1968, he knew that a heavy white backlash was being directed against the party in power; there was a strong antiwar feeling that was certain to hurt the Democrats, and there was an undercurrent of annoyance at the Democratic master manipulator who had only recently announced his impending retirement from the Presidency. The times were out of joint for the Democrats, and the cautious Ted Kennedy was not interested in political martyrdom. (In the light of later developments, many argued that a man named Kennedy running on a strong antiwar platform would have trounced Richard Nixon, but everyone is a sage the day after election.)

Still, the pressures were exerted, the strings pulled. Hubert Humphrey sounded Kennedy out on the subject of the Vice-Presidency, and was told that there was no possibility. To make matters unmistakably plain, Kennedy's aides spread the word that he was not a candidate, he was not going to endorse the candidacy of anyone else for the Democratic nomination, he would not meet or bargain with any of the candidates, and he would not even attend the convention as a delegate. When the pressures continued, Kennedy slipped out of his privacy long enough to make a speech in Worcester, Massachusetts, one week before the convention was to open in Chicago, and publicly announced that he would not run under any conditions.

At the convention, the pressures continued. Key Democrats realized that there was only one way to stop Richard Nixon, and that was by exploiting the Kennedy name, the Kennedy mystique, and the Kennedy tragedies. Former Governor Mike DiSalle of Ohio launched a "Draft Ted" movement; Kennedy telephoned him and asked him to stop. DiSalle said that an informal count showed almost enough votes to win the nomination; Kennedy pondered the information briefly and stubbornly repeated his request to call off the draft. Democratic leaders like Jesse Unruh of California and Mayor Richard Daley of Chicago pushed for Kennedy to take an active role in the convention, if not as a presidential candidate, then as a candidate for the Vice-Presidency. When Senator Eugene McCarthy of Minnesota, possessor of a substantial bundle of delegates, offered to abandon his own plans and support the young senator, the convention came alive with the rumor that another Kennedy was about to arrive and lead them out of the wilderness. But Kennedy was adamant. His representative in Chicago, Stephen Smith, explained later: "If there is such a thing as a draft, that was it. If Edward Kennedy wanted to lift a little finger, he could have been the nominee. But he could foresee Nixon throwing his age and his family at him. And paramount was his determination that he didn't want to move on a wave of sympathy for his brother."

When the convention was over and Hubert Humphrey and Edward Muskie had been nominated, Ted Kennedy went to his new home overlooking the Potomac River and continued his period of self-imposed exile. He made a few campaign appearances for the party, helped to raise money to pay off the $3.5 million debt left from his brother's campaign, but generally went about his activities in a lethargic manner that reminded others of his rookie years in Washington. One day he climbed into his car and headed for the Senate Office Building. As he drove, he thought about confronting his staff, the inevitable memories of Bobby, the discussions they were sure to have about the lost campaign and the tragic murder, and before he reached the Senate Office Building he turned around and gunned the car back toward McLean. On his next attempt to return to his senatorial duties, he made it. "Today, I resume my public responsibilities," he announced. "Like my brothers before me, I pick up a fallen standard. Sustained by the memory of our priceless years together, I shall try to carry forward that special commitment—to justice, excellence, and to courage—that distinguished their lives."

What did it mean? Many hoped that the statement foretold

his candidacy in 1972. How else could he carry forward the commitment of his brothers, both of whom had sought the Presidency, one of whom had attained it? But of course it was necessary to deny such ideas, in the tradition of the men who seek the highest office. "Yes, he picked up the standard," said a member of the family, Cousin Joseph F. Gargan. "But you can pick up the standard without picking up the Presidency. The standard is the causes, the work, the poor, the blacks. . . . He's got other things on his mind than being President." Kennedy himself shrugged off any talk about the White House. "I'm just feeling my way, day by day," he said. To close friends, he confided that he wanted to make more of a record in the Senate, and to others who asked about his future plans, he insisted that he had "no timetable." And so matters stood for a few months, while the young senator grappled with his grief and tried to stabilize himself emotionally. By November, 1968, his aides had noted a quickening in his step, and a month or so later, the wisecracking Kennedy of the past had returned. "Hey, where d'ya think you're goin'?" he would call across the office to a hard-working aide who was rushing out to catch a plane. "You've worked a lousy twelve hours, *and you're leaving already?*" The little jokes resumed, the mimicry, the friendly attentions to the miniskirted stenographers, the crunching slaps on the backs and arms of fellow senators, the long chats with cronies in the privacy of his office, serving up cranberry juice and smelly Philippine cigarillos, and exchanging jokes and compliments and laughs over such displays as the yellowing letter from the fourteen-year-old John F. Kennedy on the wall: "Dear Mother: It is the night before exams, so I will write you Wednesday. Lots of love. P.S. Can I be godfather to the baby?" Ted had been "the baby."

Nothing happens as quickly or as dramatically as people would like to believe, and Ted Kennedy continued to have his moments of doubt and darkness—some intimates said he would always have them, he would never become completely accustomed to the idea that Bobby was gone, let alone Jack, let alone Joe, let alone the father who hardly recognized him any more, the father who had watched Dwight Eisenhower's funeral on television and thought it was Ted's. But plainly he was going to survive, he was over the worst, and perhaps something could still be made of the shambled tragedy called the Kennedy family. Once again the senator's office hummed. There was a vitality to the work; "great expectations," as Steve Smith might have put it, were coming alive once again.

One must assume that Edward M. Kennedy, on at least one level of his thinking, had made the decision to go for the Presidency in 1972, else little that happened after his ten weeks of mourning would make sense. To be sure, neither Kennedy nor anyone on his staff was admitting that they were looking so far into the future. All the talk was about building a career in the Senate, adding to his record of accomplishment, reaching for the chairmanship of a major subcommittee, taking on more and more Senate responsibilities. Months earlier, Majority Leader Mike Mansfield had said that Ted Kennedy would make an excellent Senate leader, that his election to a high Senate post was inevitable and salutary. This had never been said before about a Kennedy. Politically, Jack had pushed too hard and too fast for the slow-moving solons, and Bobby had given his colleagues apoplexy. But Ted's metabolic rate appeared compatible with the Senate's, and when Mansfield voiced his predictions, there were many on both sides of the aisle who agreed with him. Of course, Ted was still too far down in seniority (he was number twenty-three) to achieve any major post before another term or two. Or was he?

By the time the Senate adjourned for Christmas vacation, 1968, the senator from Massachusetts had begun to consider a high-level coup. Whatever his innate cautiousness, he had always believed in the Kennedy manifesto: if you have the votes, make the run, and develop the qualifications later. Now he wondered if he might not have the votes for a post in the Senate Democratic hierarchy. As the leadership was then constituted, the mild and balanced Mike Mansfield was the top Senate Democrat, but he was followed by three hard-rock conservatives: Assistant Majority Leader Russell Long of Louisiana, Georgia's Richard Russell, who was slated to become president pro tem, and West Virginia's Robert Byrd, who was to continue as chairman of the Democratic Conference. No one, not even a Kennedy, could hope to oust Mansfield, nor did Kennedy have anything but admiration for the elderly senator from Montana. Byrd and Russell looked to be equally unassailable—not that Kennedy would have minded taking a run at either of them if there had been the slightest chance of winning. That left Russell Long, who at first glance did not appear to be any more vulnerable than the others. But a few conversations with some of the more responsible senators convinced Kennedy that the present mood of the Senate was away from the Long style of leadership and that Huey's son could be beaten. There were many reasons, none of them having to do with Edward Kennedy's excellence, but with Russell Long's conspicuous lack of it. As assistant majority leader, or "whip," Long had done precious little whipping in four years, preferring instead to turn over the job to the next man down the line. Though he was always called "the distinguished senator from Louisiana" by his fellows of the Club, Long had in recent years distinguished himself by tying up the Senate for days at a time with more or less incoherent speeches about pet projects, by haranguing the Senate with a mawkish defense of Senator Tom Dodd for diverting campaign funds to his own wallet, by embarrassing his fellow Club members with saber-rattling justifications of the unpopular war in Vietnam, and by closely involving himself with special interests, which almost all senators did, but which almost all senators handled with more discretion than Long. A few years earlier, he had brought into the Senate an omnibus bill so freighted with baubles and gewgaws for the special interests that it had become known as the "Christmas Tree Bill."

Following style, Kennedy moved slowly until he was certain that he had obeyed all the established requirements of the Club. If anyone was to take on Russell Long, protocol prescribed that the first opportunity must go to the Lincolnesque senator from Maine, Edmund Muskie, who had received full marks for his

conduct of the vice-presidential campaign. Kennedy waited for
Muskie to make a move, then picked up a newspaper and saw
to his surprise that his major rival for the 1972 Democratic
presidential nomination had firmly decided not to challenge
Long in the Senate. Kennedy mulled over the matter on the
flight to Sun Valley, Idaho, where he was taking his wife, his
own three children, and seven of Ethel Kennedy's brood for a
short year-end ski vacation. When the party checked in at Sun
Valley Lodge, the senator's ski boots were nowhere to be
found, and while everyone else headed for the slopes, the leader
of the Kennedy delegation was left behind in his suite, busily
dialing airline baggage depots for clues to the missing gear. The
process went slowly, and while waiting around, the restless
young senator called a few of his friends back in Washington
and discussed running for whip. The reaction of senators like
Joseph Tydings, Henry "Scoop" Jackson and Birch Bayh was
the same: negative at first, but after a little thought and conversation and a few pointed questions from Kennedy, changing to
"Why not?" In the first place, they agreed, there was an excellent chance of winning, and in the second, he would gain even
if he lost; his reputation would be enhanced as the man who
had tried to throw out the rascals of the old-style, wheeling-
dealing kind of Cro-Magnon politics. The challenge was perfect: it was incontrovertibly safe, but it gave the appearance of
verve and dash.

By the time he had talked to a few more friends, Kennedy
had made up his mind. But he had to be triple-sure about Muskie. He placed a personal call and told his friend from Maine
that he would put all the resources of his own office behind
Muskie's candidacy for whip, if the senator chose to run. The
senator did not so choose, Muskie said, whereupon Kennedy responded: "Well, if you are absolutely sure you won't run,
maybe I will."

Muskie replied enthusiastically: "Do! I urge you to."

On Sunday, December 29, the vacationing Kennedy, still operating from his improvised "office" in the Sun Valley Lodge,
began a whirlwind four-day campaign among his fellows. "I

contacted people myself," he said later. "I had no campaign manager. Nearly all of my campaigning was from Sun Valley, or from my house. I suppose some other calls were made, but the people who made the calls did so on their own. . . . There was no time to write letters. There was no time for personal contacts. The telephone is not very satisfactory, but it was the only way. My argument was pretty much the same to each. It was that I felt the job of majority whip was important, that it could be effective, that although the job was not clearly defined, I would try—if I won it—to make it important to the nation, the Senate and the party."

Veteran political observers, who might have known better, predicted that he had no chance, that the Senate would go in the direction it had always gone: toward old age and seniority. Tradition held that the senior senators got the plums, so long as they could remain on their feet long enough to read the speeches whipped up by their writers and introduce the bills worked up by their aides, and so long as they were intelligent enough to play by the rules of the Club. Thus Kennedy was made to appear, in many a newspaper, as a swashbuckling adventurer challenging the entrenched powers of arteriosclerosis. "At last," a congressman was quoted in the *New York Times,* "Kennedy has undertaken something which is not guaranteed in advance." Another observer put it more succinctly: "After six years," he said, "he shows some guts!"

Kennedy's short-lived campaign ran smoothly, fetching up only momentarily on the rock of Senator Eugene McCarthy, the Senate's preeminent dove and spokesman for the so-called "new politics." Solicited for his vote, the inscrutable lone operator from Minnesota was noncommittal, but later asked Kennedy to see him in his office, where he told the hopeful aspirant: "I haven't got anything against Russell Long. I don't see any reason to strike out against him over something this unimportant." Fellow Club member Kennedy was hard pressed to counter this argument, let alone McCarthy's next one: that a victory for Kennedy would only give the *appearance* of reform, while reforming nothing, and that the cause of liberalism would be damaged far more than by the return of Russell Long to the post. McCarthy held fast to his position, and Kennedy could see that he was not going to get the vote of his fellow member of the liberal bloc.

By 10 A.M. on the Friday after Kennedy had decided to run, Democratic senators began arriving one by one for the caucus in the capitol, while reporters jammed the halls outside the caucus room and made guesses about the outcome. Argyle Campbell, aide to House Democratic Whip Hale Boggs of Louisiana, told the group, "Russell's got it. It'll be 29 to 28 at worst, 30 to 27 at best. We were all bettin' money yesterday but we aren't bettin' any today. Russell's got it, but not by much." The Louisiana senator himself, corpulent and red-faced, squeezed through the throng and entered the caucus room with a knowing smile. The other senators said little as they entered; the trick was to keep one's vote concealed so that neither Kennedy nor Long could charge treason later. "I will know and God will know how I vote," said Montana's Lee Metcalf. "But I will try to keep the man on my left and right in the caucus from knowing." Ted Kennedy arrived, looking bulgy about the waist, but not so bulgy as his opponent, and not so confident, either. "Teddy looks as if he thinks he hasn't got the votes," a reporter said. A Kennedy aide said nervously, "We're sure of thirty votes—if everyone votes the way he told us he would."

Then the doors were closed; there was nothing to do but wait. At 11:10, there was a round of applause from inside the closed doors. *Somebody* had won. A half hour later, a glum Russell Long emerged from the room and told the reporters, "I don't think I could have been defeated by anyone else in the U.S. Senate, and my guess is that I would have taken any other opponent by about a 2-to-1 margin. This happens to have been a race where it was a nationwide proposition, and while I had Senator Kennedy outgunned in the United States Senate, he had me outgunned in the United States."

The winner was gracious, as always. He said he did not view his victory as a win for an individual named Edward M. Kennedy over an individual named Russell Long. Not at all. "I view it," he said, "as expressing the sense of the Democratic senators in favor of an aggressive and creative program in the upcoming Congress." Later he philosophized to the *New York Times* about his career in the Senate. "There is a tendency to categorize me—usually in contrast to my brothers—as a 'Senate man,' " he said, "and with some justification. Bob, for example, had served in a high position in the administration before he came to the Senate and naturally his interests were broad. President Kennedy had served for a number of years in the House before he came here. For me, however, coming to the Senate at an early age, it has been a place to grow. That meant a period of learning, then chairmanship of a couple of subcommittees last year, still more responsibility this year. I have, as everyone does, my moments of frustration and anxiety with the legislative process, but, looking at the broad sweep of history and how this institution has been able to deal with the great crises of the past, I have confidence in it. Of course, it failed one time—the Civil War—but I have a healthy appreciation of its capacity to bring about change and human betterment. The Senate may very well be facing its period of greatest challenge right now. Can it be responsive to present needs? I don't know. We'll see. But we have to try."

A man who could say, without choking on his words, that the Senate had "failed one time" in "the broad sweep of history" was a Senate man, indeed. But did he intend to remain a Senate man, "to pursue a real sort of growth based on my own experience," as he put it, or did he intend to use his job as whip as a power base to steamroller the opposition in the 1972 presidential elections? "I know I will have to live with that type of question, as my brother Bob did, . . ." Kennedy said. "Now I want to give my full attention to the Senate. You go on, and you see what happens. I am not planning four years or eight years or twelve years in the future. I am planning to serve my party and my country now, to the best of my ability, in the United States Senate."

If Ted Kennedy's entire public career to that point, from assistant district attorney to assistant majority leader of the Senate, was in fact a sustained and careful march toward 1600

Pennsylvania Avenue, he could not forever remain the docile, obsequious "good companion" of his six years in the Senate; he would have to lash out, make some waves and some headlines, attempt to superimpose the public profiles of his powerful brothers atop his own, so that they would be equated together. In this attempt, he would have to keep a weather eye on the forces of the opposition, the Republicans. Whatever his intentions, the GOP had taken dead aim on his potential candidacy, he had become Public Enemy Number One to Richard Nixon and his aides. In such a setting, common citizens are left with almost no resources for judging the sincerity or insincerity of their leaders. Suppose Senator Kennedy makes a move and gains headlines; is he making the move because of the benefits it will bring his countrymen, or because it will help him become President in a few years? President Nixon's forces on Capitol Hill strongly oppose the move and attempt to block it; is it because they believe the move is genuinely harmful to the commonweal, or because they are trying to sabotage *all* efforts of the unannounced candidate? Only the most astute political observers—the ones who used to be called pundits—are qualified to judge, but the general public does not read the most astute political observers.

Kennedy's well-publicized trip to Alaska in April, 1969, quickly became a case in point. He had succeeded to the chairmanship of the Senate subcommittee on Indian education, formerly headed by his brother Robert, and now he was going to fulfill a pledge made by his murdered brother to see for himself how the Eskimos and Indians lived. On the surface, the move was nobly motivated and sorely needed. Most Americans never see an Eskimo, and most Americans are able to stand up under the hardships of others so long as they can avoid close contact with them. Ted Kennedy and his fellow senators were going to bring the sufferings closer to home.

But from the instant that the subcommittee members settled back in their first-class seats for the long flight to the northernmost state, powerful political currents eddied. For one thing, the plane was full of reporters and TV cameramen, about six

times as many as would normally have been on such a trip, and
every one of them had been instructed to focus his attention on
Kennedy. At one stop, a cameraman shouted "Out of the way!"
to Senator Walter F. "Fritz" Mondale, and the Minnesota Democrat obeyed quickly so that the camera could bore in on the
flashing smile and bright blue eyes of the senator from Massachusetts. Far in the background, where they would not interfere
with the action, stood other senators—William Saxbe, Theodore Stephens and Henry Bellmon. A little boy in the crowd
said to his friend: "Did you see the President?" In an earlier
trip to Vietnam while his brother Robert was alive, Ted Kennedy had made an appeal to the press to ignore him and his
staff so that they could travel more freely and gain more legitimate information, but this time the young senator was making
no such plea. With Robert's death, the peck order had changed:
a year earlier he had been a step down the list; now he was
"Kennedy."

But being Kennedy called for certain modes of action, and
as soon as the party arrived in a bleak Alaskan village he
began to dig for the facts in a style that reminded many of
his brother Bobby. While other members of the party stood
around with mouths agape, Kennedy bored in on such matters
as why the natives had not used the town well for five months,
preferring instead to haul water from two miles downriver. No
one would answer. The party traipsed to a nearby school run
by the Bureau of Indian Affairs and found out that the school's
well was functioning perfectly. Nothing about the situation
made sense, and finally Kennedy forced the village's wellmaster
to admit that the town well was contaminated and there was no
money for purifiers. "Why can't you use the school's water?"
Kennedy asked. When no one answered, Kennedy provided the
answer himself: the school was run by the Bureau of Indian Affairs, and the BIA kept its pompous distance from the villagers.
No one would be bold enough to ask for the BIA's water, and
if they had asked, red tape probably would have kept them
from it.

So it went from village to village, with Kennedy and a few of the fact finders ducking in and out of smelly Eskimo shanties while most of the others hung back so that the cameramen and reporters could crowd along inside. Kennedy's words were harshly critical and eminently newsworthy. He came out of one Eskimo school noting that there were no native teachers, which forced the children to solve a language problem before their learning process could even begin. Their textbooks were from the lower forty-eight states; they showed scenes that were totally alien to the children. "What do fire marshals and cows mean to these children?" Kennedy said loudly as he looked through an elementary school textbook. "They teach nothing that's really relevant to these children's lives."

Not that every minute of the trip was grim. Here and there the politicians ran into smiling people wearing "Eskimo Power" buttons, and there were hands to be shaken and backs to be slapped. Among themselves, the senators appeared to be a jolly group, taking their cue from the friendliest of all, the chairman, and another senator who seemed to enjoy a good time, George Murphy of California. The former movie actor did not trouble himself to enter many of the shanties; he had an expensive movie camera along, and he seemed to be shooting a full-length feature film of the young subcommittee chairman. Whenever the cameramen lined up to photograph Kennedy climbing out of a shack or entering a school or conferring with befurred Eskimo leaders, George Murphy would be in the rank, his camera whirring away with the others. Kennedy and Fritz Mondale ribbed him about it, and Murphy ribbed back. After a long day of puddle-jumping from one village to the next, the party arrived in Anchorage and Kennedy said to his Republican colleague: "George, I don't know how you do it. You look as fresh as if you were just starting out." Murphy, star of many a Hollywood dance epic, performed a few turns and then locked arms with Kennedy for a chorus of "Hollywood."

On those rare occasions when Murphy was asked to comment on some of the unfortunate facts that were being elicited on the trip, his answers were often lighthearted. At one school, he suggested that there would be no problems if the teacher were fired. At another, he suggested that tap dancing should be added to the curriculum. He took up most of one subcommittee session with an impromptu explanation of a major Alaskan problem: drinking. The Eskimos and Indians who sat around sipping from bottles all day were suffering from a vitamin deficiency that caused alcoholism, Murphy explained, reminding his colleagues that he was an expert on the subject. If the vitamin deficiency was corrected, the alcoholism would end. Fellow senators tried to explain that the bleak, barren lives of the people were a major factor in the heavy drinking, but Murphy did not concur.

Despite these gentlemanly disagreements, the members of the subcommittee were making the best of a difficult trip, and if the heavy attention on Edward M. Kennedy was annoying any of them, they were keeping it quiet. Then the political lightning struck. The telephone rang in Kennedy's room at the Anchorage Westward Motel early one morning, and the voice on the other end was Senator George Murphy. He told Kennedy that he "didn't like this from the start," that he was going home, and that two other Republican senators, Saxbe and Bellmon, were going with him. Said a shocked Kennedy: "Well, I hope you got some good pictures, George." Murphy said that he had.

As the splintered subcommittee stirred itself to face another long day in the tar-paper shacks of Alaska, reporters scurried about to find the cause of the Republican revolt. "He was just tired of a one-man act," a Murphy aide explained. Someone said that the public release of a subcommittee memo back in Washington had revealed that the whole fact-finding trip had been misrepresented and was strictly a publicity stunt. Others said that Murphy had received several calls from high-ranking Republicans, asking why he was taking part in a Democratic roadshow aimed at building up another Kennedy. Fritz Mondale tried to counter some of the effect of the walkout. "I deeply regret that the Eskimos' desperate need to be seen—and heard—should raise a doubt as to the intent of our efforts," he said. "I suppose the reason is to discount recommendations we will probably make to relieve conditions we have seen destroying these decent people. The conditions are tragic enough that one would think they could at least be spared being made a political football." Among themselves, Republicans laughed at the comment. It was not Murphy who had started kicking the old political football around, they told one another. They were only playing a game that Kennedy had started. In the general brouhaha, any good that might have been done for the unfortunate Eskimos and Indians was quickly lost.

Back on the C–130 transport ("this isn't Air Force One yet," a leftover Republican grumbled), there were efforts to dispel the pall that Murphy, Bellmon and Saxbe had cast over the trip. "I told you to see that Murphy got his box lunch on time," a reporter called out gaily, and Ted Kennedy smiled his appreciation of the gibe and the good intentions. Like the big kidder he was, he went to the store of box lunches and wrote quickly on several of them: "Murphy." But in the long run he was fooling none of the perspicacious members of the party. He had been seared to the quick by the outburst of partisan politics, the very sort of partisan politics that he had tried to float gently above, paring his fingernails, during six smooth years in the United States Senate. That night, grounded a hundred miles north of the Arctic Circle, he seemed to show worry and fatigue as he discussed the matter with a *Life* reporter in his typically fragmented style: ". . . Political occasions . . . these are the legitimate times . . . opportunities to take you on . . . general public will accept that . . ." He pulled out a silver flask that had belonged to Robert Kennedy. "First time I've used it," he said. Then he spoke on a favorite topic. "It's timing," he said. "You have to know when the time is right. . . . You know, it isn't enough just to be a Kennedy. There is a *time* for Kennedys . . . and you have to know when that time is. You have to know what the country is ready for."

On the last leg of the fatiguing trip, en route back to Washington by commercial jet, the anxieties and frustrations spilled over. Kennedy had a few drinks, and a pillowfight started. A staffer confided to a reporter: "I figure we lose sixty voters every time this happens, but it's worth it." The senator from

Massachusetts led a group in loud cheers: "E-s-skimo power! E-s-s-kimo power!" and the plane droned on through the skies.

Close aides expected Kennedy to draw back into his shell, to regroup and work out a careful line of defense against the next such Republican assault on his image. Indeed, some of them begged him to take exactly that course. But a month later his spirits had revived and he was ready to follow his newly developed spirit of adventurousness once again. The grape strikers, long identified with Robert Kennedy and long embraced by all Kennedys, had asked him to come to California, but aides were sternly against the trip. The very idea of striding into such an explosive setting appalled them, for good reason. The strike leader, Cesar Chavez, had been threatened and attacked, and southern California was known to be a breeding ground for the same sort of psychopaths who had murdered his brothers. Besides, there was no political gain to be made by such a trip. The Kennedys were already fully identified with the strikers.

But suddenly, at the end of a touch football game at Hickory Hill on a Saturday, the senator began slipping notes into reporters' hands: "LA nonstop—6 P.M., Friendship." "Come on, come on, run, run, run," he shouted. "Shall we go see Cesar? Can you make it? Hurry, hurry, hurry." The next day he was out among the strikers in California, shouting *"Viva la huelga!* Cesar is my brother!" He told a reporter, "Every morning this week I've woken up wanting to go . . . and then I see those guys [his aides] all day, they're at me with all the reasons for not going. And they're right, their reasons are right. But every morning I wake up and I want to go. This morning? I'm here."

What did it all mean? Students of political reality, as contrasted with students of political appearances, were withholding judgment. Some suggested that Kennedy was at last trying to make an impression, not only with members of the Club, but also with the people, to walk where his brothers had walked, to show that the name Kennedy had a genuine meaning, not only in the world of politics, but in the world of social action. But others charged that Kennedy was only being his usual shallow self, making a cynical move to wrap up his fallen brother's constituencies: the Indians, the strikers, the blacks, the downtrodden in general. Washington correspondents, who looked around them at chaos most of the time, somehow remained hopeful, at least in their public reports, and they continued to give Kennedy the benefit of the doubt. The *New York Times* took him seriously. The news magazines gave him credit for being much more than a pretty face and an honored name. To many, it appeared that Ted Kennedy might have forged from the deaths of his brothers and his own tragedies and petty malfeasances a commitment to something more than political advancement, a commitment to "pick up the fallen standard" in fact as well as in appearance. In truth, there were no overpowering reasons to believe this, beyond the reasons of need, of hope, of frustration with the whole political scene. People noticed that Ted Kennedy had been called "the best politician in the family" by his brother Jack, by his father, by Lyndon Johnson, by many another; it did not seem to matter that he had never been called "the best statesman in the family." Nor did it seem to matter that throughout most of his career he had appeared to be little more than an armature on which certain forces were trying to sculpt a statue of victory. Standing down there in the well of the Senate, whispering in the ear of his mentor, Senator Mike Mansfield, he gave a daily appearance of solidity in his conservative blue suits—the dark ties, the razor-cut hair with a slight touch of gray, the back brace that barely showed and served as a symbol of his maturity and suffering.

Did he look like a candidate? Certainly he did to the Republicans. His old friend, Senate Minority Leader Everett Dirksen, took several potshots at him before expiring in mid-1969. The White House sent an all-points bulletin to its deputies in the field that Ted Kennedy was the man to beat. William F. Buckley received an "EMK in '72" button and exploded in his column: "Really, the dynastic assertiveness of the Kennedys is a wonder of the world." By the summer of 1969, the buttons were all over the place, and one could also see placards—

HAPPINESS IS TED KENNEDY IN '72—in many a Washington office.

An even surer sign of Edward M. Kennedy's candidacy was the unsubtle campaign to move his wife Joan into the public eye, as a potential first lady, even as Pat Nixon had been pushed, and before her Lady Bird Johnson, and before her, the most conspicuous White House resident since the days of Dolly Madison: Jacqueline Bouvier Kennedy. Joan Kennedy seemed neither markedly more nor less talented than the others; she gave, perhaps, a slightly more flamboyant appearance, with her overbleached, overteased blond hair and the miniskirts which she insisted on wearing to White House functions. Music had been one of her majors in college, and she performed as the narrator of Prokofiev's *Peter and the Wolf* at several concerts, a feat accomplished years earlier by Eleanor Roosevelt with approximately equal finesse. Mrs. Kennedy's public appearances revealed that she had a somewhat harsh Westchester County accent, not unlike Nelson Rockefeller's, but at least a far remove from the cultivated tones of her family predecessor, Jacqueline, who had sounded to many like an erudite Marilyn Monroe. One could not help but compare the Kennedy women as Joan appeared on educational television, patronizingly guiding some children through the National Gallery of Art, for all the world as though Jacqueline Kennedy had not staked out that particular art form for herself, pat. pending, trademark registered.

If the television appearances and the concert performances left any doubt that the 1972 publicity buildup was on, the magazine articles made it transparently plain. One popular magazine after another wrote gushingly of the future first lady. *Coronet* set Washington insiders to cluck-clucking violently with an article that began: "Those closest to Ted Kennedy are constantly amazed at how deeply in love he still is with his wife— like a bridegroom, almost. He wants to be with her every moment he can. . . . In his eyes, Joan can do no wrong. . . . Whatever she does, and in whatever style, Ted backs her up, not bothering to hide his looks of admiration." Members of Washington's active social set did not wish to be catty (or per-

haps they did), but like the Dedalus father and son in Joyce's
fiction, they did "not recognize him from that description."
Joan and Ted Kennedy, like most young couples, reportedly
had had their share of marital troubles; that was *their* business,
but why the sudden spate of stories to the contrary? Some
thought they knew.

One could approach the subject obliquely and hesitatingly, as
the public press was obliged to do later, or one could approach
it head on, as gossips had for years. The simple fact was that
the Kennedy men appreciated pretty faces and figures and sometimes took few pains to conceal it. Whether their interest carried
them further was a matter for themselves and their wives, but
this did not keep lurid tales from spreading. When John F.
Kennedy was found sneaking down the back stairs of a hotel
in the early hours of the morning, the nation laughed good-
heartedly at his explanation that he had just been trying to elude
the Secret Service men for a breath of fresh air, but the Washington press corps chortled. John Kennedy liked the girls, and the
girls liked him, and every one around him knew it. From this
acorn of fact, a mighty oak of rumor grew during his thousand
days as President. When a pretty White House stenographer
would appear in a hotel room two thousand miles from Washington at the same time that the President was in the same town
to make a guest appearance, reporters would get together later
over their highballs and chuckle at the neatness of it all. Of
course, they would say, she could be there to take dictation, *ho,
ho, ho.* . . . No one was writing anything on the subject; the
President was entitled to a private life of his own, just as members of the press corps were. When he went to Hollywood or
Palm Springs to frolic with his friends among the beautiful
people, it was nobody's business how late they stayed up, or
how much they drank, or what went on in the small hours, or
why Jacqueline was not with him.

Robert F. Kennedy's reputation was free of such innuendo
until the last few years of his life, but then the inevitable sly
hints began. When he would leave a gathering with a woman on

his arm, as almost all men do on occasion, the cruel assumption was made that they were headed for mischief. Insiders spoke of the night he had met Marilyn Monroe, and danced her around till dawn, and others hinted that the relationship had grown from there. In 1969, a popular work of nonfiction described Miss Monroe's love affair with "a lawyer and public servant . . . a married man," and before the book had sold ten copies, gossips had spread word all over Washington and Hollywood that the man, discreetly anonymous in the book, was Robert F. Kennedy. Common decency and, later, respect for the dead had kept the rumor out of print, but there were occasional hints like the one that appeared in a question-and-answer column in *Parade,* the newspaper supplement:

Q: Is it true that the late Marilyn Monroe was in love with the late Bobby Kennedy?—V.T., McLean, Virginia
A: She knew him but was not in love with him at the time of her death.

Amateur psychologists nodded knowingly and pointed to the well-known tendency of sons to imitate strong fathers. Joseph P. Kennedy Sr. had been fond of film star Gloria Swanson at a time when he was investing heavily in Hollywood. A passage in *The Founding Father* by Richard J. Whalen was enough to confirm the theorizing. "Dazzled and drawn by this radiant presence," Whalen wrote, "Kennedy won entry to her [Miss Swanson's] circle, becoming banker, adviser and close friend. They were seen together frequently at parties and dinners in New York and California, their mutual admiration apparent to everyone."

For a time it appeared that the only male Kennedy to escape the taint of extramarital fingerpointing would be Joe Jr., lost in World War II. But a book published in 1969 wiped away even this antiseptic memory. *The Lost Prince* by Hank Searls described the valorous young Navy pilot as a sort of international Casanova, a dashing bachelor who was engaged in a romance at the time of his death with an Englishwoman whose husband was at the front.

One might have supposed that Edward M. Kennedy, highly ambitious and certainly aware of his family's reputation, deserved or undeserved, might have been sensitive on the subject, and might have gone far out of his way to avoid the same gossip. But he did not. "He loves to be surrounded by beautiful women," a member of Washington's "swinging" set reported. Others described the handsome young senator's activities at such spots as Le Club in New York and at fetes in places as far apart as Acapulco and Georgetown. *Newsweek* referred later to "his ever-ready eye for a pretty face," and *Time* was to observe: "As for women, there are countless rumors in Washington, many of them conveyed with a ring of conviction. Some who have long watched the Kennedys can say with certainty that he often flirts with pretty girls in situations indiscreet for someone named Ted Kennedy. At the same time, he and his wife, Joan, are rumored to have had their troubles. There is no question that they are frequently separated. On one journey alone last summer, he was seen in the company of another lovely blonde on Aristotle Onassis' yacht. Such incidents might be recounted about innumerable people in Washington and elsewhere."

Some said the gossip about the Kennedy brothers was unfair, that there was no connection between moral rectitude and political ability in the first place, and no proof that they had acted immorally in the second. This did not stop the tongue-wagging, nor did it change the fact that any male Kennedy, whether he was actively on the town or faithfully being the admiring husband, had to live his life with one eye on the gossip, especially if he aspired to high office. His private life had to be managed in such a manner that the most wild-eyed and malicious scandalmonger could find nothing from which to hang a rumor. Only thus could the brothers' reputation, so damaging in certain areas of the electorate, be kept pigeonholed in the social circles of the big cities, where it could do no political harm. By mid-1969, Ted Kennedy, despite some near misses, had managed to keep it there.

II

Regatta at Edgartown

For years, tourists had been coming to Edgartown to play the fool, deluding themselves into thinking that out here in the Atlantic, separated from the mainland by miles of salt water, channels and shoals, no one cared what they did; no one kept score. They came and went in self-delusion, unaware that they had been watched and studied and analyzed and discussed and finally categorized by townies who had watched all kinds of behavior and knew where to look. If there was any place on earth where nothing was secret or sacred or private, it was Edgartown, on the island of Martha's Vineyard, Massachusetts. The natives had a passion for watching, for sharing information, and for making judgments. The practice was blessed by tradition; widow's walks atop the white frame houses attested to earlier watchers. For as long as anyone could remember, the town's most respected currency had been news, tidbits of news, great gobs of news, spread by word of mouth from one end of matriarchal Edgartown to the other in eyeblinks of time, as though by instant osmosis. "I don't know why I bother to write anything," a local reporter grumbled. "By the time the paper comes out it's old stuff around here." The visitor to such a place was a focus, the immediate object of prying eyes, penciled notes stashed in vest pockets, thrummings on the island-style bush telegraph, endless conjecture. One came into such a setting at one's own risk. The natives were nosy.

In the summer of 1969, Edgartown had been hot and crowded. The mainlanders looked at their maps and saw the little town perched on the far eastern side of Martha's Vineyard and reasoned that way out there at sea the breezes must be cool and the salt spray a refreshing change from broiling Boston and Providence and New Haven. So they came by the thousands, swelling Edgartown's population from its normal fifteen hundred to four or five times that number, almost all of them united in an unspoken attitude that somehow they had been misled, that the townspeople should have told them about the humidity in this sea-sodden place. There was something called the THI, the temperature-humidity index, and it was no lower at Edgartown than back home. But at least there were sailboats to be sailed, outboard motorboats to be rented, bicycles to be pedaled, fish to be caught, and a few places where one could swim without too much danger of being carried down-beach by the strong undertows and rips. And when the sun failed to appear, there were shops to be visited: alley-front stores where daytrippers could buy overpriced whaletooth carvings called scrimshaw, and exclusive shops like Lilly Pulitzer's, where the affluent could buy jeans for forty dollars. At night the narrowness of Main Street was choked by shoppers and gawkers and sometimes by troublemakers, out to compress a short vacation into a single orgy of misbehavior.

As usual, the five-man permanent police force had been doubled for the summer, and a second policewoman had been put on duty to answer the telephones in the tiny two-room headquarters in the town office building up Main Street. But even with the extra help, Chief Dominick (Jim) Arena was finding himself hard put to keep up with the demands. He was the kind of policeman who enjoyed nothing more than strolling up and down the street exchanging small talk with the townspeople, ribbing the old men who sat for twelve and fifteen hours a day under the maple tree on the "drunk bench" by the courthouse, and counseling the younger Edgartowners in the paths of righteousness. Despite his awesome size (six feet four inches, 225 pounds), Jim Arena was a nonphysical kind of cop; in thirteen years on the highly political Massachusetts State Police he had learned the rudiments of investigation and the rudiments of intimidation, but most of all he had learned persuasion, the fine art of making one's points without force. Now that he was in his third year as chief at Edgartown, he found himself growing secure in a role that came naturally to a person who tended to think highly of his fellow human beings: the classic role of "nice guy." Edgartown was right for him. Major crime hardly existed in the place; people got drunk and they sometimes lost their inhibitions and went skinny-dipping, or slept on unauthorized beaches, but these were problems that did not require the use of the blackjack or the pistol or certain physical maneuvers that Jim Arena had learned as a staff sergeant in the United States Marine Corps. He would smile and wisecrack at the culprits, and usually the problems would evaporate. To be sure, there was one case during the summer that had taken more than a friendly grin and a handshake; it had taken skilled detective work and long hours, but now it was close to solution. Forty old whaling logs, worth about two thousand dollars apiece, had vanished from the Dukes County Historical Society on School Street. Arena learned that they had been taken by the twenty-one-year-old son of a school principal, and now he had enough proof to make the arrest and mark the theft solved. "This is your biggest case since you came here," Special Prosecutor Walter Steele had told the chief. "You'll really make a name for yourself with this thing." Despite his tendency to run himself down, the chief had had to agree. Not that he had left the state police and taken the top job in lonely Edgartown to make a name for himself, but at thirty-nine years of age, with four children and a wife to support and alimony from an earlier marriage to consider, he could not afford to become lackadaisical about his future. Perhaps a larger police department in another town might be willing to pay more than the ten thousand dollars that Edgartown was paying. One had to think ahead; on such cases as the theft of the whaling logs, small-town police chiefs built their reputations.

On the other hand, there were the less rewarding matters, the petty grievances that the chief of a larger force might not have had to confront. The townspeople had a tendency to complain about things that were beyond Arena's—or anyone else's—control. Certain Edgartowners acted as though they lived in a feudal fief, and this included most of the wealthy "summer people" who had been coming to the place for peace and quiet for decades. Every time a motorcycle rode through town, Arena braced himself for the telephone calls. "Yes, Mr. Smith, I *know* they're noisy," he would say, "but they're not against the law, that's the problem. As long as we're a public place and these are public streets, they're entitled to ride up and down on their motorcycles." On and on he would talk, promising to "see what I can do," all the time knowing there was nothing he could do, except perhaps leave Mr. Smith with a feeling that the matter was occupying his full and undivided attention. No sooner would that problem be solved, at least temporarily, than a wheezy sightseeing bus from Vineyard Haven would contaminate the air on one of the narrow one-way streets, and the telephone would jangle again. "Yes, Mr. Jones, I *know* they're a nuisance," the chief would say, "but as long as we're a public place . . ." Another citizen appeased, he would untangle himself from his undersized desk and go for a walk down Main Street, there to hear more complaints of the same nature and to amuse himself by reading one of the town's most popular bumper stickers of the summer, 1969: BAN BIG BUSES. Here and there he could see where children with paintbrushes had altered a single letter and turned the signs into pronouncements against mammary overdevelopment. Other bumper stickers read NO JETS, a message of opposition to the runway lengthening even then going on at Martha's Vineyard Airport; SAVE THE SUBSTANDARD BUMP, an argument against certain contemporary roadwork; and RUSSIA GET OUT OF ESTONIA AND LATVIA, a sticker which at this stage of history made little sense to the chief, especially since the citizen who displayed it most conspicuously was an old Yankee with deep roots in New England and no visible connections to Eastern Europe. Well, that was part of the town's charm. The people spoke their minds, whether on their telephones or their bumper stickers or at their town meetings, and Jim Arena was glad they did. There were no riots in Edgartown; the place was a police chief's dream.

By midsummer, Edgartown had become glutted with visitors; one noticed it especially on rainy days, when there was nothing to do but shop and eat. There were three steady lines at the clam bar on Mayhew Lane, and hardly enough room to move about in such fine stores as Tashtego and Avery's and the Ocean Trader. Sport fishermen walked the streets muttering to themselves about the poor fishing, and a few commercial fishermen bemoaned the fact that fluke were scarce, flounder were hardly to be found, and lobstering was far below normal. Joseph Chase Allen, the town's senior expert on such matters, wrote about fishing in the *Vineyard Gazette:* "The critters are uneasy and we understand it. Too cussed hot weather and no storms at all. A moderate shakeup with an easterly wind and all such fishing would improve." Still, there was reason for hope. Swordfishing was good; a single market had taken in twenty-five of the large fish for butchering. There were signs that the lobstering might improve; two lobstermen from Cuttyhunk had brought in five hundred pounds one day. The bluefish were beginning their summer run; Nelson Amaral of the nearby town of Oak Bluffs had taken twenty-eight on a single night, from eight to fifteen pounds. And the mackerel off Gay Head were running up to two pounds. One only had to wait for the end of the heat wave and everything would right itself, and the fishermen would haul themselves clear of the streets of Edgartown and get out to the beaches and the rips where they belonged.

Some few prophets of doom nodded knowingly when the *Roma,* Frank Sinatra's eighty-five-foot diesel yacht, put into the nearby port of Vineyard Haven for a social call on the author William Styron. Four years earlier, another Sinatra yacht had dropped anchor at Martha's Vineyard and a crewman had drowned during a midnight outing with two local girls. But this time there were no untoward incidents. Sinatra and his guests, who included Bennett Cerf, went ashore for a party at Styron's, and by the time the yacht had sailed away there was nothing for the islanders to gossip about except that Mia Farrow, Sinatra's ex-wife, had attended the affair and the two had been seen in earnest conversation. The only other indication of summertime prescience on Martha's Vineyard was a highly personal one: a general practitioner named Donald Randall Mills confided to his wife in their Edgartown home: "Esther, I have a premonition that something is going to go wrong."

"Now whatever gives you a silly idea like that?" Mrs. Mills said.

"Because everything's been going too good," the gray-haired doctor replied. Mrs. Mills laughed, but her husband did not. To him, the premonition was real.

The week of July 13, 1969, began quietly. Bird watchers across the narrow channel on Chappaquiddick Island reported seeing a short-eared owl, snowy egrets in abundance, four Baird's sandpipers, twelve dowitchers, two Arctic terns and a whimbrel. Out near the old jetties, a black skimmer was hanging around, and an immature male rose-breasted grosbeak had taken up residence near a summer cottage. A game warden named Michael A. Renahan spotted two men emptying an offshore lobster pot, and when he checked them he found that their identification cards did not match up with the initials W.W. cut into the pots. The culprits, both "off-islanders," wound up before the local district judge, James A. Boyle, and paid $525 each in fines. Judge Boyle was renowned for his fairness in sentencing, but molesting lobster pots was the local equivalent of rustling in the Wild West; it was an attack on a lifeline of the island, and stiff fines were always imposed.

Toward the middle of the week, Edgartowners had begun to brace themselves for an annual event that sometimes had been known to upset the equilibrium of the community. For decades the Edgartown Regatta had been serving the wealthy youth of the mainland as an excuse for getting away from family restrictions and throwing drunken parties in one another's yachts and hotel rooms. "Don't care whether they come in first or thirty-first in the race," an old-timer confided. "Come here to get bred and get drunk. Very seldom get bred, but they always get drunk." In recent years, the event had quieted down somewhat, attracting more dedicated sailors and fewer rowdies, and this year the *Vineyard Gazette* was hopeful. Its headline read: 46TH REGATTA IS DRAWING OUT BIG FLEET OF YACHTS. LARGEST ENTRY EVER IS SET FOR SUNDAY'S OCEAN RACE. The article noted, "If the weather cooperates, and comes forth with the brisk breezes that caused burgees to crackle yesterday, it is going to be an exceptionally good three days of racing."

By Thursday afternoon, July 17, the town was beginning to wear its "regatta look," with dozens of young men in deck shoes and red tags and yachting caps strolling about, and four or five gleaming sailboats arriving every hour. Already the harbor was crowded, with boats doubling up at each buoy, and still they kept coming: Wianno Seniors and Juniors, SMYRA's and Rhodes 19's, Gems, Ospreys, Shieldses, Wood Pussies and ten or fifteen representatives of the new class, Soling. There were sloops and yawls and ketches and even a full-rigged schooner, the *Shenandoah,* hauling tourists for a price, and the usual support vessels: the harbor master's runabout and the yacht club launch and the Coast Guard cutters that would stand watch around the racecourse out in the open water.

That same Thursday afternoon, a few sharp-eyed citizens of Edgartown noticed a white-haired man buying items like frozen steaks and hors d'oeuvres at a Main Street market called Mercier's. Soon word was out that Senator Edward M. Kennedy's local driver, a Boston bachelor named Jack Crimmins, was in town and that the senator must be planning to sail in the regatta. That was nothing new; Kennedys had been sailing in the Edgartown Regatta for more than thirty years. Indeed, the Kennedys had acquired a certain local reputation, and most of it had been built up during Edgartown regattas. It was said of them in earlier years that they used the weekend event for the same purpose as other wealthy young men of their era: to let go for a few days, just as Philadelphia boys let go in Atlantic City,

New Jersey, and Manhattan's young men in Harlem. No one had been excited about the behavior—it was normal for regatta time—but after the ascendancy of the illustrious Hyannis Port family to the top echelons of American politics, the stories about the brothers had made fascinating telling on the long winter nights. Natives chuckled slyly as they related how the teen-aged Jack Kennedy and his older brother, Joe Jr., had entertained themselves on one regatta weekend by inviting friendly young couples aboard their boat and then trying to steal the girls from the boys. According to one version of the tale, the family's hired skipper had buttressed his courage with gin and issued an order that all couples who boarded the yacht together would have to leave together, an order that outraged the headstrong young brothers and caused them to have the captain jailed for drunkenness. For the rest of the weekend they had things their own way. Later, however, the captain won his revenge. Leo Damore wrote in *The Cape Cod Years of John Fitzgerald Kennedy:*

One mid-1930 Edgartown regatta, degenerating as such events customarily did into an aftermath of drinking and rowdiness—a release from the tensions of the day's hotly contested sailboat races —provided more serious difficulties. One particular victory celebration hosted by the two oldest Kennedy brothers at an Edgartown hotel came to an abrupt end when damage prompted the management to alert police. Both Joe Jr. and Jack were taken to the village's small, cramped jail. When called to go bail for the boys, the "skipper" flatly refused, instructing the boys that they could "stay where you are" in order "to teach you a lesson." No charges were pressed. The brothers, both under twenty-one, were released the following morning.

There were fewer such stories about Robert Kennedy, eight years younger than Jack and ten years younger than Joe Jr., and hardly any such stories about Ted Kennedy, the baby of the family. There was a persistent report that the young senator had been thrown out of the Edgartown Yacht Club, but club authorities swore it was a canard, traceable to a night when Kennedy had presented himself at the door of the weatherbeaten old building and had been turned away for lack of coat and tie. They said he had taken the rejection like a gentleman. A similar story, this one set across the harbor at the Chappaquiddick Beach Club, had gone the rounds for years. Kennedy was said to have created a major disturbance when he was denied access to the private club, but manager Harold Kelly insisted that the tale was fabricated. It was true that the Kennedys had anchored the family motor yacht, the *Marlin,* just off the Chappaquiddick Beach Club dock, and that Ted had come ashore to ask permission to use the club's facilities. But when he was politely turned down, he politely went elsewhere.

Then there was the story about the time Mrs. Ted Kennedy had made a difficult dismount from one of the family boats to the Edgartown Yacht Club pier, while several elderly crustacea watched scornfully without lifting a finger to help the attractive young woman. The story was told in high glee later, as though to show that the Kennedys made no impression among the Edgartown elite, which indeed was close to the truth. Edgartown was about 90 percent Republican, and the members of the Yacht Club were politically to the right of the town. Just as they had snubbed Joan Kennedy, the club members had once allowed a guest named Dean Acheson to sit at a banquet table in silence for the better part of an hour, while they gabbled merrily among themselves. The town had hardly changed since seventy-five years before, when the *Vineyard Gazette* had reported: "There is not the slightest truth in the widely published report that Hon. Ichabod Luce, of Cottage City, has been obliged to undergo amputation of one of his legs at the knee, or that he is a Democrat."

In an area of such hard-backed conservatism, the tiniest evidence against a conspicuously Democratic family like the Kennedys was considered sufficient justification for circulation of the wildest slanders. One heard that Ted Kennedy and his cousin Joseph Gargan and their wives had been involved in a violent dispute with the personnel of the Harborside Inn over a bill. In fact, the party had overstayed the checkout time by five hours and been charged for another day, and Kennedy had lodged a mild objection. He asked if the hotel would give them four box lunches in return. The hotel manager, Arthur Young, said that he would not give them anything *in return,* because the extra day's billing was fully justified, but he would be glad to give them four *complimentary* box lunches for the trip across Nantucket Sound to Hyannis. The matter was settled amicably (although the Kennedys never returned to the Harborside Inn, perhaps Edgartown's fanciest establishment).

One also heard about a night when Kennedy had hosted a small delegation to the Seafood Shanty, on Edgartown's Dock Street, and regaled the group with songs and jokes and impressions of Richard Nixon and Everett Dirksen and other GOP luminaries until the small hours. "Drunk!" a cantankerous old man confirmed the next morning, but those who had been closest to the scene in the restaurant, including the owner himself, took violent exception to the sidewalk opinion. They protested that there had been drinking, but no drunkenness. The senator had simply been enthusiastic and ebullient in that Irish way of his, and even some of the stiffest Edgartown conservatives had had to laugh at his table remarks, and the way he went through the scullery afterward, shaking hands with the workers and cracking still more jokes.

The Kennedys had visited Edgartown in the early summer of 1968, during the period of their mourning for Robert, and a few minor attacks on them had grown out of even this innocent visit. They had stayed at the Harbor View Hotel, several blocks away from the Harborside, and with their Secret Service men and aides had filled almost a whole floor. There—according to the tongues that wagged afterward—they proceeded to wash the family dog in a bathtub, rip out television wires, bully the help, and make impossible demands for rapid delivery of food, laundry and dry cleaning. On top of this "misbehavior," they waited three months to pay the bill, which seemed to some of the oldline townies to be typical of a political party that believed in spending everybody else's money. Unfortunately, the truth never caught up with these intriguing rumors. It *had* taken the

Kennedys three months to pay the bill, but only because the hotel had made a bookkeeping error and charged them for twenty rooms instead of twenty guests. The matter was cleared up at the Kennedy end shortly after it was cleared up at the hotel end, but it was not cleared up on the street corners of Edgartown, where the name of Kennedy continued to make an impression midway between annoyance and ennui.

Several hours after the faithful retainer Jack Crimmins was seen buying groceries, another member of the clan Kennedy surfaced in Edgartown to the consternation of a family of hoteliers on Water Street. Mr. and Mrs. Thomas Chirgwin, owners of a genteel establishment called the Daggett House, were standing outside the front door of the old hotel waiting for their son John, a travel guide and international businessman, who was taking them out to dinner. As a group of four or five sloppily dressed young men approached, the elder Chirgwin whispered to his wife: "Gee, isn't it nice that we have the house full and there's not a bunch of rowdy regatta types here?"

The words were hardly out before the young men, several of them carrying sleeping bags and one of them wearing a woman's hat pulled down over his ears, strode past the Chirgwins and into the front door of the Daggett House. Thomas Chirgwin turned red and called out, "Hold everything! Where do you think you're going?"

"We're going up to our room," one of the boys answered. "We've got a room upstairs."

Young John Chirgwin came on the scene in time to see his father shaking with rage. "You don't have any room in this hotel!" the old man shouted. "Not in this hotel, you don't!"

"Oh yes, we do," one of the young men hollered back. "We've got number nine."

"Well, we'll see about that!" the senior Chirgwin said, and began to elbow his way into the lobby.

"Wait a minute, Daddy," John Chirgwin said. "Let me take care of this." He had seldom seen his father so exercised, and he momentarily feared for the white-haired man's health. There was no point in having a heart attack over a problem that could be solved easily. "You and Mother go ahead to dinner, and I'll join you," young Chirgwin said. "I'll just be a few minutes. Go on, now! I'll take care of this!" Gently he urged his parents to move away, and when they were gone he stepped inside the tiny lobby with the others. As he recalled later, he turned to the boys and said, "Now, what's going on here?"

The youth in the woman's hat said sharply, "We've got a room upstairs. That's what's going on."

"No, you don't," Chirgwin said. "You *can't*. We don't rent to kids and there's been a mistake if you have a room."

The boy tore the hat off and flung it on the floor. "Do you know who I am?" he shouted, and without waiting for Chirgwin to answer, he said, "I'm Joseph Kennedy!"

Chirgwin noticed that the boy appeared to be in his late teens, and he was wearing an ancient leather flight jacket with his name across the breast pocket. Vaguely, Chirgwin remembered that the oldest Kennedy brother, Joe Jr., had been a Navy pilot, and he supposed that the boy might be wearing the crackly old jacket out of veneration for the war hero. Chirgwin searched the face, and realized that the boy was Ethel and Robert Kennedy's son; his features proved it, and he wore his hair over his ears in the characteristic style of the Kennedys.

"Now look," Chirgwin said firmly. "Don't take it personally, but you just can't stay here. You wouldn't *want* to stay here anyway. We've got a bunch of old people living here and you wouldn't like it. There's no action here."

At that, young Kennedy picked up his hat and replaced it on his head. He seemed calmer. "I'll be happy to line you up someplace else," Chirgwin went on. "You'll feel more at home. We cater to an elderly clientele here."

Another of the young men said, "Well, we've already been up to the room. We took a shower. We messed it all up."

"That's *our* problem," young Chirgwin said. "We'll take care of that." Seeing that the boys were on the verge of capitulation, he said in a friendly manner, "It isn't that we want to inconvenience you guys. I'm not so old myself that I don't understand the position you're in. I'll help you get lined up someplace else."

"Don't bother," one of the boys said disconsolately. "We've got a place we can go." To Chirgwin's relief, they trooped out the door. Making a mental note to check later on how they reserved the room, he went off and joined his parents at the restaurant.

"Do you realize who that was you were hollering at?" he said to his father.

"No," the elder Chirgwin said. "Who?"

"Joseph Kennedy."

"Who's Joseph Kennedy?" the elderly Yankee asked.

"Bobby's kid."

"Oh? Well, he's just another kid to me."

The Chirgwins did not see Joe Kennedy III again until late that night, when John Chirgwin dropped into the Seafood Shanty for a nightcap and spotted the teen-ager with a dozen or so of his peers sitting around a big table. "Hey, look!" Chirgwin recalled hearing the boy shout. "There's the guy who threw me out of my hotel!" Chirgwin smiled and waved, enjoyed his drink, and went home. Other Edgartowners saw the young Kennedy off and on for several more hours. When the Seafood Shanty closed at I A.M. the party milled about for a few minutes, then headed for an "open house" a few blocks away on Norton Street. By 3 A.M. the affair was going full blast, with the phonograph at ear-splitting volume and several of the partygoers wobbly on their feet. Young Kennedy confided to one of the girls, "I'm so exhausted I don't care whether I drink or not." He said it had been a long sail across Nantucket Sound from the mainland that afternoon, and they had had trouble with their boat, and on top of that they had been thrown out of their hotel and had no place to sleep. The party roared on until a neighbor, Mrs. John Pine, called police and complained. Minutes later, two Edgartown officers in their flashy blue uniforms arrived, and one of them shouted, "Okay, you kids, everybody out!" The partygoers, including Joe Kennedy and a young temporary policewoman who had recently been hired, poured out the front door of the old house. No arrests were made.

The *Vineyard Gazette* of Friday, July 18, echoed the feeling of the vacationers in an R. H. Grenville quotation at the top of page one: "No duties waiting . . . no clocks crying hurry, no shadow of fall—the long day, the green day, midsummer Eden . . . when we thought we had nothing at all." It was the first day of the regatta, and even nonsailors found themselves becoming swept up in the prospect of three full days of saltwater racing. Edgartown itself looked scrubbed and polished; most of the old whaling captains' houses near the waterfront were flying flags, and porches were bedecked with rose vines and lilacs and rows of potted plants set out for the occasion. Rusty iron chains and flaking landlocked anchors set off the neat black-and-whiteness of the aging frame houses, and here and there one saw primroses and peonies and lilacs and other old-fashioned flowers growing from iron try-pots that once were used to boil whale blubber. Out in the harbor, polished yachts with freshly washed and furled sails were covered down and dressed right like good sailors on deck for inspection; all of them, from small sloops to a two-masted schooner, were pointing up the wind. Viewed from the top of the two-story Memorial Wharf, the scene looked like a rich child's bathtub, and the boats like play toys. One looked in vain for barnacles, for sea slime, or weeds. Before World War II, when Edgartown was not so prim, mud flats had sent up reeking clouds of animalculae stink, and a blind man could tell when the tide was out. But now neat docks had been built over the flats, channels and drainage ditches had been dug to carry off the standing water, and the saltwater harbor was spic and span, visited daily by strong tidal bores that scrub up pilings and buoys like a vigorous washerwoman. Where once there had been the pungent stink of wrack and littoral and untenanted scallop shells, now there was only the lightly saline scent of the sea. To the north, one could barely make out the silhouette of the Edgartown Lighthouse and its warning light that kept vessels clear of flats where small bluefish and tinker mackerel chased minnows out of the water in silver sheets. There had been a lighthouse off these flats for as long as anyone could remember. One hundred years before, the wives of whaling crewmen would stroll across a wooden board-walk, known as the Bridge of Sighs, to go out to the lighthouse and pine for their husbands. It had been replaced several times since then, and the newest version was small and neat, black and white, topped by a dull red glow that gave the whole struc-ture the look of a Christmas purchase (batteries included) at F. A. O. Schwartz. The only dissonant touch to the Disney-like character of the whole harbor was an occasional workboat chugging on its way to collect quahaugs or clams or lobsters, a grubby towny at the wheel, looking neither to one side nor the other, as though aware of his inferior social position.

By the time most of the yachtsmen were aboard their vessels and preparing for the first heat at ten minutes after noon on Friday, it was plain that the weather forecasts had been overly optimistic. A southwester had been predicted, with winds of fif-teen to twenty knots, harbinger of a good day of racing, but early in the morning the winds had slowed and slacked and started backing around to the northeast, with barely enough power to stiffen a burgee. Frustrated skippers pitched coins over the side, trying to buy a breeze from the capricious skies, but by race time the winds were still light and sporadic, and for one of the few times in its history the Edgartown Regatta opened on a windward start instead of a leeward, with fifteen yawls and sloops bearing names like *Windquest* and *Pinkletink* and *Orpheus* crossing the line on the starboard tack and disap-pearing into the fog and haze of Edgartown Bay. In this faint wind, they figured to be out for half the afternoon.

An hour or so after the starter's gun had signaled the open-ing of the regatta, a man who was easily recognizable as Sena-tor Edward M. Kennedy stepped from an automobile at the foot of Daggett Street and walked onto the ferry that ran to the island of Chappaquiddick, 120 yards across the channel. The little two-car ferry *On Time* swung out into the stream, turned around, and headed toward the slip on the other side, and as it crossed the channel in the high humidity of the hot, hazy mid-day, the senator was seen to loosen up and relax. He placed his briefcase alongside him, took off the jacket of his suit, loosened his tie and drew in a deep breath of the salty air. He smiled at those who smiled at him, and exchanged a few pleasantries with a gray-haired man who seemed to be his companion.

At the end of the three-or-four-minute ride across the chan-nel, the two men were seen to walk toward a black Oldsmobile 88 parked outside the eight-by-twelve-foot weathered ferry-house on the Chappaquiddick side. The procedure was normal; those who traveled between Edgartown and Chappaquiddick regularly left a car on each side; the barge-like ferry only ac-commodated a pair of automobiles, and if the traveler kept a car on each side he could walk onto the ferry and avoid the long waits for car space. None of the gawkers were surprised when Kennedy and the older man strode up to the black Olds-mobile that was available to take them to their destination on the tiny island. Kennedy was sipping from a paper cup, and he opened the door of the car, slipped inside, and came rocketing out as though he had sat in a bucket of hot pitch. He opened the doors of the car to let it cool off, took another sip from the cup, poured the remaining fluid on the ground, and climbed inside the passenger's side of the car while his companion moved in behind the wheel. After a few minutes, the car headed down Chappaquiddick Road and out of sight.

None of the tourists saw what Kennedy did in the ensuing hour or so, but at exactly 2:50 P.M. he showed up at the helm of his blue-hulled Wianno Senior *Victura,* inherited from his brother John, and sliced across the starting line on the tardy southwest winds that had returned after several hours' absence. Not far behind, his nephew, Joe Kennedy III, crossed the start-ing line in the *Resolute.* The course covered 11.85 miles, from the flats near the Chappaquiddick side of Edgartown Bay out into the open water of Nantucket Sound and back. The winds had quickened; the Wianno Senior heat would probably be about a two-hour affair, and soon the trim white sails of the

thirty-one entries had vanished into the light fog that was standing out to sea.

By 3 P.M., ten minutes after the start of the Wianno Senior
heat, old Captain Manuel Francis DeFrates was wondering if
he was the victim of some kind of hoax. He had been waiting at
the Yacht Club wharf for several hours, keeping his appointment, but no one had shown up. Some of the heats had already
been raced; if the half-day charter party for his thirty-foot Egg
Harbor fishing boat did not arrive soon, he would have to count
the afternoon a loss. The seventy-year-old skipper lighted up a
cigar and pondered the situation. He remembered that a man
who identified himself as Paul Markham had telephoned for the
reservation; he wanted the boat for two afternoons, Friday and
Saturday, July 18 and 19, and he was so persistent about getting
the timetable straight that he had made three different calls.
"All right, all right," Captain DeFrates had said on the third
call. "I'll be at the yacht club at one o'clock Friday, ready to go.
Don't worry about it." But now the old Portuguese-American
skipper was worried himself.

More minutes passed, and he was about to batten down the
hatches and go home, when suddenly he was immersed in
bright, loud young women. He recalled later that one of them
shouted, "We're your charter! Let's get out of here!" DeFrates
started the twin engines as the girls spilled over the rail and
into the cockpit and began passing around coffee and dough-
nuts. When he asked for sailing instructions, one of the girls
answered, "Follow the fleet!" The old man gave his sea-weary
powerboat all it would take, but it was twenty minutes before he caught up to the Wianno Seniors running down the
southwest wind toward Nantucket Sound and the open water.
Now and then he turned from the wheel to look at the bab-
bling party of females. They were peering into the murky
afternoon and passing a thermos jug of coffee around, and to
Manuel DeFrates they appeared to be a wealthy group, neat
and classy in their understated black and white dresses, their

dark slacks and white blouses and knits. He was momentarily shocked to hear one of them shout, "Let's catch the son of a bitch!" but he did not stay shocked long. The women of Edgartown, correct and churchly on the surface, used far stronger language from time to time; it seemed to go with salt water and seafarers. DeFrates was about to ask which son of a bitch they wanted him to catch when a blond-haired young woman whom the others had been addressing as Mary Jo and Emjay came forward to the wheel and asked the skipper to search out the Kennedy boat, the *Victura*. Years before, old DeFrates had worked briefly on one of the Kennedy family boats, quitting shortly after several of the children had tracked across a newly varnished deck, and he had no trouble picking out the polished blue hull of the Wianno Senior that had been in the Kennedy family for many years.

"How close do you want me to get?" he asked the excited blond girl.

"Close as you can!" she said, and DeFrates eased the *Bonnie Lisa* under the shadow of the *Victura*'s sails. As he looked across fifteen or twenty yards of water, he saw the crew hard at work, and he recognized the handsome Senator Edward M. Kennedy looking up from the helm to grin and wave at the *Bonnie Lisa*'s passengers. "Are you anything to Kennedy?" the inquisitive skipper asked the girl called Mary Jo.

"No," she said, "but I'm a great friend of Joe Gargan."

The *Bonnie Lisa,* under temporary command of its passengers, followed the *Victura* around the course and across the finish line, but all the shouts and threats and imprecations of the enthusiastic girls could not help the Wianno Senior finish stronger than ninth, six minutes behind the winner. The girls complained and griped good-naturedly. As the *Bonnie Lisa* slowed to approach the narrow neck of the harbor, they could see the sails of the *Resolute,* Joe Kennedy III, master, finishing another ten places back. The Kennedys, uncle and nephew, had maintained the family's untarnished record of never winning an Edgartown Regatta.

Manuel DeFrates eased the *Bonnie Lisa* alongside the Yacht

Club wharf and watched as the six young ladies hopped nimbly ashore with mingled cries of "Thanks!" and "Enjoyed it!" A few minutes later a tall, black-haired man in bathing trunks and spectacles ambled up, introduced himself as Paul Markham, and fished a wet fifty dollars out of his pocket to pay for the half-day charter. "Same thing tomorrow?" Markham asked.

"I'll be here," the grizzled old captain replied. He made a mental note to arrive a little later on Saturday.

Ted Kennedy was seen briefly aboard the winning yacht, the *Bettawin,* congratulating the victors just after the race. Then he went ashore and to the second floor of Mayberry House, an old whaling captain's residence that had been made into a part of the Shiretown Inn, one of the newest hostelries in Edgartown. There he seemed to be giving a small party or reception on an upstairs porch which adjoined several rooms that had been booked in the names of himself and various of his yachting friends. His cousin Joe Gargan and his Boston lawyer friend Jack Driscoll had picked up six bottles of Heineken's beer at the bar downstairs at the Shiretown, and midway in the short-lived affair a waitress was asked to bring two more beers to the porch, but otherwise there did not appear to be much drinking by the eight or ten young men who milled about on the porch. Kennedy drifted away from the affair shortly after 6 P.M. and in company with another man boarded the ferry for Chappaquiddick. When they reached the other side, the two men stepped into the usual waiting car and disappeared into the evening.

Chappaquiddick was the quintessence of privacy, at least of the small amount of genuine privacy that remained in the United States in 1969. To get there, one had to go to the remote town of Woods Hole, at the eastern edge of Massachusetts, take a thirty-five-minute steamer ride to the island of Martha's Vineyard, drive ten miles to the far eastern part of the island, and then take another ferry across the heavy-running channel of water to alight, at last, on the island of Chappaquiddick. Three miles across the miniature island was a beach that fronted on the Atlantic Ocean, and the next landmass eastward was Portugal. Chappaquiddick, or "Chappy," as it was called locally, was the end of the line.

Of distinguishing characteristics, the island had hardly any. The Indians had used it for pastureland, burning frequently to improve the ground cover, and therefore most of the fifteen square miles lacked heavy trees. Instead, a thick matted weave of vines and scrub pines and oaks and bushes grew like jungle foliage, accented by poison ivy and sumac of a special virulence. In some places, this heavy underbrush was impassable, barely changed from the description applied to it three hundred years before: "an incredible store of vines" so thick that early explorers could not "goe for treading upon them." Most of Chappaquiddick was flat, its highest point a place called Sampson's Hill, soaring ninety-four feet into the sky, a lookout site from which the old Indian Daniel T. Webquish used to boast that he could "see all over God's creation and part of Chatham." Long after Webquish's death one could climb Sampson's Hill and look down upon a Chappaquiddick that could still be described by its original meaning: "Refuge Island." Once whaling captains lived there; three houses near Caleb's Pond produced thirty children, seventeen of whom had become shipmasters. Some of the old homes remained, and there were newly built cottages here and there, many of them at the end of long, secluded roads protected by gates (one house stood fifteen hundred yards from the road and presented the visitor with four gates to solve). The people who owned property there—a few well-known authors, a distillery executive, a former governor, a newspaper publisher, several magnates of industry, a few lawyers, three or four medical doctors—were almost obsessive about their privacy, else they would have been at Bar Harbor, or Southampton, or some other place where the moneyed could go to be seen and to mingle. There was hardly any mingling at Chappaquiddick. As one drove from the ferry landing around the island's only blacktop road, winding in a potholed semicircle for about three miles, one could almost feel the angry eyes peering out from summer cottages set back in the brush. Most of the Chappaquiddick residents (seven year-round families and a hundred or so summer people) were as inquisitive and snoopy as their Edgartown neighbors across the channel, but for better reason. Outsiders were simply not wanted; they defeated the very purpose of Chappaquiddick. Extraordinarily, their *money* was not even wanted. There was only one commercial establishment on the whole island; it was called the Chappaquiddick Beach Club, and membership was severely limited. As for real estate, hardly any was available, and an organization which called itself the Trustees of Reservations had snapped up five hundred acres of wild beach lands and marked them off limits to anyone but wildlife and nature lovers. Each night a hired watchman patrolled the closed areas to make sure that only raccoons and pheasants and gulls were making use of the properties.

The remotest areas of the island sometimes attracted illicit lovers, but they seldom returned. It was a Cecil B. De Mille production to get one's girl friend across the ferry without being found out, and once on the island, petting couples were subjected to constant harassment by the locals. An Edgartown professional man who began an affair with a local housewife (and later married her) liked to tell of the ordeals of their courtship. "First I had to buy a four-wheel-drive vehicle, because there was no place we could go in a regular car without being followed. So I got a Jeep, and I filled the back of it with tarpaulins and lobster pots and stuff like that and hid her underneath. She was cautioned not to move a muscle while we were crossing on the ferry to Chappy, but sometimes in the hay fever season she'd have to sneeze, and I'd stand there making conversation with the ferryman while these peculiar noises were coming from the back of my Jeep. The only thing that was ever said was one night on the way back. I think the ferryman had had a few snorts, and he told me that one of my lobsters was sneezing."

Certain other Chappaquiddickers were more malevolent than the ferryman. In a probing sociological report about the nature of the longtime inhabitants, Professor G. William Arnold theorized that some of the residents had an "intruder" complex, that they compensated for living out their years in such a lonely place by becoming overly concerned with the activities of others. Arnold described some of them as "sanctioned peeping Toms, children outside the homes of the rich, looking in the windows . . . interlopers, watching others go off into the bush, tantalizing themselves by seeing them, and ultimately, when they could stand it no longer, interfering actively." He wrote of the two Chappaquiddickers who, driving homeward one night, "saw in a car someone they knew who should have been alone. They followed and watched, looked in through the windows. The other car went before them, bright lights streaming through the Chappaquiddick darkness, and they followed as it turned down Dike Road toward the sea. And when it parked, they parked behind it, their lights still busily beamed on what was inside, on the man and the woman. And they followed when the automobile left, and kept their lights on it, turning off one road after another, down the tar road and onto the dirt roads, again and again making turns and following, pursuing, looking in. They followed all the way back to the ferry slip and fixed their lights on the car's occupants even as they slipped aboard the last trip to Edgartown for an embarrassed getaway. And they sat inside their automobile and watched the ferry disappear, and they could not restrain their laughter. Having followed and foiled and intruded, they laughed a big Chappaquiddick laugh. They did that frequently."

This was the place where Senator Edward M. Kennedy and a man with white hair had headed down the main road in a black Oldsmobile on the hot summer evening of July 18, 1969. No one of the locals knew where the two men were headed or why they were on the remote island in the first place, but they would not be long in finding out. On Chappaquiddick, they never were.

When Foster Silva went on his inspection tour of the island that Friday night, he was accompanied by his wife Dodie. Unlike some of the others who resided on Chappaquiddick, the fifty-year-old Silva was not a snoop by inclination but by trade. He was the hired watchman for the Trustees of Reservations; Dodie was the rental agent for certain cottages on the island, and various of the summer people paid the Silvas for protecting their unoccupied homes against vandals and fire. In addition to running a construction business of his own, Foster Silva was that most necessary of citizens on a remote place like Chappaquiddick: he was a master watchman, loyal and hardworking.

That night, he drove down the asphalt road to the sharp right turn that led to the Dike Bridge, a low wooden construction that crossed a narrow bottleneck of lagoon and led to the barrier beach that faced the Atlantic. The land from the bridge to the sea was in Silva's domain, and he was pleased to see that all was under control. Except for a few surf fishermen, the place was empty. A thin sliver of moon had begun to come into sight with the setting of the sun, and there was a feathery haze over the dark water of Poucha Pond just to the south of the Dike Bridge. The tide was running out strongly, and the clammy air was thick with mosquitoes.

Driving back to the other end of the island, the Silvas saw nothing unusual. They checked the beach by Wasque Point, a place that was popular with surf fishermen, and passed through a wooded area from which Silva had routed a group of hippies recently. Relieved that all was in order, Foster steered the old red Jeep back up School Road toward his home, where the Silvas and relatives intended to relax and watch the color movie on television. As they passed a nondescript cottage about a hundred and fifty yards down the road from the Silva home, they noticed that something was going on. The place was known as the Lawrence cottage; it was owned by a Scarsdale, New York, lawyer, and frequently was rented out on weekends, either through realtors across the channel in Edgartown or through Foster's wife Dodie. This time it had been rented through an Edgartown agent, and Silva was just as glad. That meant that the responsibility for the place did not rest with him, at least until the next time his wife rented it out on behalf of the owners. He had enough to watch on Chappaquiddick; let someone else worry about the Lawrence house this weekend. The front windows of the cottage were open and the shades were up, and it appeared that a dozen or so people were standing in the big front room. A barbecue sent up a ribbon of smoke on the lawn.

The Silvas and their guests had been settled in front of the television set for an hour or so when the first transient noises began to interrupt their concentration. "Aw, it's nothing," Silva said when his wife complained. "They're just having a little party at the Lawrence house."

Soon the group could hear raucous singing from the cottage a hundred and fifty yards down the road, and then a chant began, followed by cheering and yelling. "A *little* party?" Dodie Silva said. At about 10 P.M. she stepped out into her front yard, listened for a few minutes, and came back inside. "Boy, they must be having a heck of a time," she told the others. "I hope they don't wreck the place."

Shortly before midnight, Mrs. Sylvia Malm and her college coed daughter, also named Sylvia, heard a car pass in front of their rented Dyke House, four hundred and fifty feet from the narrow wooden bridge. To the daughter, the car seemed to be traveling fairly fast in the direction of the bridge and the beach beyond. Later, Mrs. Malm was not as certain of direction or time as her daughter, but it seemed to her that the car was "going faster than usual toward the dike." Mother and daughter went to sleep around midnight.

For Christopher (Huck) Look, it had been a long and uneventful evening, and at 12:30 A.M. as he stepped into the Yacht Club's launch for the ride across the channel to Chappaquiddick, he was just as happy it was drawing to an end. For fifteen years now, Huck Look had been pulling on his fancy tan and brown deputy sheriff's uniform with the bright silver buttons and whistle and the star and the nameplate, and watching over the

people who came to the Edgartown Yacht Club for regatta affairs. This Friday night, July 18, 1969, had been the quietest in
his memory, and he wondered where the classic yachting bums
had disappeared, the ones who used to spill into the club and
dance and drink and make passes at the rich girls and get into
fights with the rich men and wind up on their backsides in the
alley. There had not been a single such incident this year, and
the craggy-faced deputy sheriff had exchanged a few remarks
with club officials about it. "Won't be needing me if things stay
like this, right?" Huck had said, and the club officials had
laughed and agreed.

At forty-one years, six feet two inches and 235 hard pounds,
Huck Look was ready for anything that might erupt at the club,
although he was not the aggressive sort of deputy sheriff who
gloried in cracking skulls. He was a businessman by day, selling
fuel oil to his fellow townsmen, and in his off hours he was a
law enforcement officer three times over: a deputy sheriff of
Dukes County, which embraced all of Martha's Vineyard; a
special officer for Edgartown Police Chief Jim Arena; and a
special officer for the Edgartown Park Department. As though
these three jobs had left him with too much free time on his
hands, Look had been a $200-a-year lieutenant in the Edgar-
town Fire Department, but he had quit when his company
began selling oil to the department and he was afraid he might
be accused of conflict of interest. Huck Look, whose ancestors
had been on Martha's Vineyard for more than three hundred
years and who numbered Captain John Paul Jones among his
distant relatives, was scrupulous about such matters. He was
equally scrupulous about his behavior in uniform. "You're either in uniform or you're not," he told his confidants, "and if
you're in it, you don't drink, you don't act silly, you remember
who you are and what you're representing." Bartenders at the
Yacht Club often teased him about his abstinence in uniform;
they would mix drinks and offer them to him and watch the
look of horror, part sham and part real, cross his face. One
night when Huck was relaxing at home the sheriff had called
him to come and help out at the jail; a quick raid had just net-

ted several dozen narcotics suspects. Huck Look refused to assist, explaining to his superior officer: "I just had two beers. I can't put my uniform on." When the sheriff had insisted, Look compromised; he went to the jail in uniform to help book the prisoners, but he refused to wear his star.

All in all, it would have been difficult to find anyone in Edgartown with a better reputation. Look had been a star basketball player and a good student at the local high school; he had worked his way up from driver of an oil truck to owner of the small business; he had taken time out to serve in the Korean war as a sergeant first class; he was active in civic groups and a lay reader at St. Andrew's Episcopal Church, and he had a personal reputation for helping others in trouble. So far as the townspeople were concerned, there was only one blot on his record: Huck Look was an avowed Democrat, and a particular admirer of the Kennedys. He could be counted on to attend Democratic fund-raising dinners, to canvass voters, and even to give a small check to the party on occasion. The townspeople overlooked this strange aberration; they reckoned that nobody was perfect, and in all other departments Huck Look was a thoroughly praiseworthy person. It was true that he enjoyed a certain reputation for inquisitiveness, but who in Edgartown did not? It went with the place. Inquisitiveness was both recreation and security.

Crossing the channel back to Chappaquiddick in the Yacht Club's launch that night, Huck noticed that the tide was running in strongly, and the operator of the boat, Assistant Harbor Master John Edwards, was having more than an average amount of trouble controlling it. Usually the launch deposited Huck at the end of the ferry landing, near the spot where he had parked his 1967 Pontiac station wagon, but this time the tide carried the boat right on past and Edwards had to throw the engine into full reverse to creep back to the slip. Just as Look was stepping on the shore, Edwards said, "Look there!" Both men watched a tiny sailboat, a Sailfish, beating up the channel, and both remembered that a boat of the same class had been stolen earlier in the day from the Harborside Inn dock. "Go get 'em!" Look shouted, and Edwards gunned the engine of the launch and took off. "Good night!" Look called, and trudged up the landing toward his car. He figured it was about twenty-five minutes to one, early for him to be headed home from the regatta weekend job, but he had been on his feet all day, first at the oil company and then at the club, and he was thoroughly ready for bed. He started the car, backed it away from the tiny gray ferryhouse, and headed east on Chappaquiddick Road toward his cottage on the far side of the island near Wasque Point. The road made shallow S curves along walls of black underbrush; the night was especially dark now that the sliver of moon had set in the west. Huck and an old employee of the Yacht Club, Claude Wagner, had stepped outside to look at the thin slice of moon earlier, and the eighty-two-year-old handyman had said, "When the moon's standing up like that, Huck, it means good fishing." Driving along the rutted island road, Huck said to himself that he hoped so. He liked nothing better than to grab his surf fishing equipment and walk seven or eight miles on the beach stalking the schools of feeding bluefish or striped bass. He thought he might take the old man's advice and give it a try in the morning. He was thinking such thoughts when he came to a place on Chappaquiddick Road where the blacktop made a sharp right turn of about 110 degrees and changed its name to School Road as it continued south toward Wasque Point. The corner was tricky, and if there was any oncoming traffic, Huck always slowed to let the other driver negotiate the curve ahead of him; tourists had a bad habit of veering across the center line, and Huck would rather lose a few seconds than risk a head-on collision or a sideswipe. This time, as he slowed routinely to begin making the curve, he noticed that another car was coming along School Road at a moderate speed, and he slowed almost to a stop. But instead of continuing around the curve, the oncoming car drove straight across the sharp elbow and poked its grill into a narrow sand road that led north to a forgotten cemetery. As the other car passed full in front of his headlights, Huck saw that it was a black sedan, that there appeared to be a man and a woman in the front seat, and either another person or a suit of clothes or some kind of projection showing as a dim shadow in the rear.

Now barely rolling, and consumed with his customary twin feelings of benevolence and curiosity, Huck drove around the curve and looked into his rearview mirror. The other car seemed to have stopped after traveling its own length into the primitive road to the cemetery. Huck knew that there was a no-trespassing sign on a post there, and the people in the car might be sitting there studying it, or then again they might be just plain lost. Huck eased his station wagon to the side of the road, about sixty feet from the other car, and stepped out. "They're confused," he told himself. "They want to know which way to go." Hitching up his belt, he walked along the center line toward the rear of the stopped car. As he approached, he saw the backup lights of the car flash on, and he noted an L and some 7's, his favorite number, on the license plate. Now he was about thirty or thirty-five feet away, the brightwork on his uniform reflecting the backup beams, and he was going to call out to offer assistance when he saw the other car do a quick reverse turn and head into the fourth arm of the peculiar intersection, the dirt-and-sand road that led east to the Dike Bridge and the beach. Before Look could call out or get a better look at the occupants, the car had disappeared behind a wall of dust. "Well," he said to himself, "I can see they don't want to talk to *me!*" As he walked back toward his own vehicle, he thought momentarily of giving chase. It was plain to him that the driver of the black car had seen him clearly and had raced away for a single reason: to avoid contact with the law. Normally, the thought would have inspired Huck Look, the triple cop, to sprint to his car and roar down the road in hot pursuit, but as he walked toward his parked Pontiac he reminded himself that this was a regatta night and normal standards did not prevail. And anyway, what had the driver of the black car done wrong? He had driven into a private road, seen his error, reversed himself and turned instead into a public road. It was true that he had sped out of there pretty briskly, but there was no Massachusetts law against acceleration. "The hell with 'em," Huck said aloud. "I'm going home."

He was continuing along School Road, shaking his head at the rudeness of certain people, when his lights silhouetted some figures a few hundred feet ahead, down near Foster Silva's house and the lilliputian Fire Station No. 2, with its single wheezy engine inside and its tiny red bulb that burned all night. From a distance, the figures seemed to be doing some kind of dance in the road, a hootchy-kootchy or a conga. As Look drove up and illuminated the scene with his headlights, he saw that there were two young women, one shorter than average and one taller than average, and a man of about five feet nine or ten inches, and now they were walking single file along the shoulder. He tapped his brakes and called out the open window, "Would you like a lift?"

The tall girl at the rear said sharply, "Shove off, buddy! We're not pickups!"

Huck Look was not usually quick to anger, but he felt the blood rushing to his face and his pulse rising. He knew that summer people were not always as friendly and easygoing as the permanent islanders, but he thought that at least they should learn some of the niceties of rural courtesy. This was not South Boston or the Bronx. He touched the door handle and started to press it, but just then the man at the front of the procession said softly, "No, thank you, sir, we're only going right over here." He pointed toward the Lawrence cottage, a few hundred yards down the road. "He probably saw my patch," Look said to himself. It was a hot and humid night, and he had been driving with his left arm resting on the open window ledge; to anyone outside the car the brown and white shoulder patch and its message, "Sheriff's Department, Dukes County," would have been highly conspicuous. Still, Huck considered getting out and conducting a short interrogation, if not about the possible disturbance of the peace at nearly one in the morning, then about the proper responses to kindly people who drive up and offer rides to strangers. But once again he restrained himself. "What good could come of it?" he said to himself. "I'll get out and I'll say to that woman, 'That's a heck of a way to talk when I'm trying to be nice to you. What are you, loaded or what?' And then I'll probably wind up in a big argument and have to lock somebody up and go to court Monday for a lousy two dollars and sixty cents." He eased the car away, biting his tongue to keep from saying anything. At last he reached the small cottage where he spent summers with his wife and five children. "Gee, you're late tonight," his wife said as she rose wearily from the couch in the living room.

"No, I'm not late," Huck Look said, studying his watch. "It's only a couple of minutes to one." His wife poured him a glass of milk, and in deference to her sleepiness, Huck said nothing about his nettling experiences on the way home. A short time later, his head full of remarks that he *could* have made, he dropped off to sleep.

Foster Silva did not know how long he had been dozing when he was awakened by a familiar sound. Red, his Irish setter, had begun to bark, and now the two beagles were bugling and cater-wauling, and soon they were joined by the collie and the golden retriever and the Newfoundland. Normally Silva would ignore his dogs—somebody must be walking along the road, and the noise would end soon—but on this regatta weekend he knew that the island was fully occupied by the summer people who paid his wages, and he did not want to be blamed for anybody's sleepless night. He tumbled out of bed cursing softly to himself, saw that it was 1 A.M., and told the dogs to shut up. When the barking had stopped, he listened for party noises, but all he could hear was the faint sound of voices raised in song. He assumed that the affair had just about wound down, and returned to his bed. He had barely fallen asleep when the dogs opened up again. Silva rubbed his eyes in puzzlement. He knew that old Red and the rest did not bark at passing automobiles, only at pedestrian traffic, and he wondered why there would be so much pedestrian traffic in the middle of the night. But then he remembered again that it was regatta time, and nothing would be normal till the weekend sailors had had their fun and re-

turned to their homes on the mainland. Wearily he climbed out
of bed to hush the dogs, and this time his wife Dodie joined
him. As they stood in the darkness, surrounded by their wild-
running herd of New Zealand white rabbits and their overen-
thusiastic dogs, Mrs. Silva remarked on what a calm and peace-
ful night it was, and Foster said that he would be able to appreciate the nighttime more if people would stop walking along the
road and setting off his dogs. From the general direction of the
blacktop, the Silvas could hear the voices that had disturbed
their pets, but the sound trailed away, and soon the couple went
back inside for another crack at sleep. It was 1:30 in the morning.

Twenty-nine-year-old Jared Grant, current owner of the little
ferry *On Time,* was no more impressed by Senator Edward M.
Kennedy than most of the other Yankees of Edgartown, but
nevertheless he had spent the whole evening of Friday, July 18,
1969, looking for the senator to return from Chappaquiddick.
When he had taken Kennedy across at around 6:30 P.M. and
deposited him on foot at the slip on the Chappaquiddick side, it
had occurred to Grant that perhaps the young senator was going
to do some sightseeing, or maybe walk down to the beach,
where he could enjoy himself without being ogled or asked for
autographs. But by midnight that theory no longer made sense,
unless Kennedy was on some kind of marathon around the island. Now it was time to close the ferry down for the night, but
there were still a few cars and people waiting to cross. It was
regatta night, and since the ferry rates automatically tripled for
postmidnight service, Grant figured he would turn a few more
dollars before tying up till the first crossing of Saturday morning at 7:30. Besides, he had heard that the steamer from Woods
Hole to Vineyard Haven had docked late, and some of its passengers might be rushing to the ferry right now, depending on
him to get them to their summer homes in Chappaquiddick. So
he stayed in service till 12:45, until not another soul waited to
cross, and then shut down. Briefly, he pondered the disappearance of the senator, and concluded that he must have returned to

Edgartown by another means, or perhaps was someone's guest on the island. Grant puttered around the ferry landing, repairing lines and tinkering with the *On Time*'s 120-horsepower engine and talking to a couple of young boys fishing for mackerel off the end of the slip. The harbor was still and calm. Most of the dinghies and prams that had been scooting around like water bugs had stopped, and gradually the lights had gone off from yacht to yacht, signaling the end of the typical regatta night social crawling. There was a light haze on the water, and ribbons of gray fog had formed in the salty air and now wound among the boats that jammed the harbor. The moon had been gone for hours, and the only illumination came from lights left on by yacht owners and the night lights of the Edgartown waterfront, reflected dully in the gathering gloom. Jared Grant took a final look toward the slip a hundred and twenty yards away on the Chappaquiddick side, saw that no one was waiting, and left at 1:20 in the morning.

Joseph P. Kennedy III had spent a typical regatta evening, behaving himself in a manner that had the implied sanction of a previous generation of Kennedys and thousands of other rich young men who customarily used the regatta to unwind. Young Kennedy's boat, the *Resolute,* had finished nineteenth earlier in the afternoon, but at least there were twelve Wianno Seniors that were even slower than the *Resolute,* and his Uncle Ted had made a commendable ninth-place finish before heading ashore for his own leisure-time activities. Joe III and his crewmates and several of his friends from the posh Milton Academy had been bunking in the Shiretown Inn, not in the fancy part of the inn (the two refurbished homes that fronted on Water Street and had been gussied up for such guests as Senator Edward M. Kennedy), but in a long barracks-like building in the rear that had been converted into a motel and for ten dollars per person per night offered a bedroom and bath. A few of the young men in Kennedy's group were registered there, and the rest, including Joe III, simply tossed their sleeping bags on the floor and joined the party. Such doublings-up were a standard part of the regatta scene, and none of the hotel owners grew excited about it, since most of them were booked to capacity anyway.

After the race, the boys and young men of Joe III's group repaired to one of these Shiretown Inn motel rooms for the libations that seemed a valued tradition of the regatta, and then they wandered about town for a few hours looking at the sights and making noise. There was a brief encounter with the man on the door at the Edgartown Yacht Club; Joe Kennedy had announced his name and tried to get in, and the man on the door had commented sarcastically, "Oh, you must be one of the Iowa Kennedys?" At that early hour of the evening, not much had been going on at the Yacht Club, and the boys did not mind being turned away. But later there would be a dance, and shortly after 10 P.M. the boys went to the restaurant and bar of the Colonial Inn, where a few of them were acquainted with the waitresses. Dates were arranged, and after the girls left work at 10:30, they changed their clothes and walked next door to the Shiretown Inn motel to sip drinks with the boys in their rooms for an hour or so. Then the whole group—eight or ten young men and girls—walked three blocks to the Yacht Club, where a regatta dance was in progress. They lacked enough red tags to get inside, but that problem was solved by passing the tags back and forth through the gates. A few of the older boys bought drinks at the Yacht Club bar, but those who were underage, like Joe III, took no chances; there was a uniformed deputy sheriff hovering around and he seemed to mean business. The dance was a dull affair, and no one was sorry when midnight arrived and the deputy called out, "All right, drink up, the party's over!" There was still a long night ahead.

When no one could decide exactly what to do next, the revelers returned to the Shiretown Inn motel for a few more rounds of drinks, and by then it seemed a good idea to sneak into the patio of the Harborside Inn for a dip in the heated pool. But there were too many tourists still up and around, and the plan had to be abandoned. Then someone remembered a party that was going on aboard a yacht, and the young people borrowed a friend's small boat and rowed energetically around the harbor trying to find the party. This occupied the restless group for a half-hour or so, and by 1:30 they returned the boat and abandoned the fruitless search. Two of the waitresses said they were tired and went off to "the bunker," the old house where employees of the Colonial Inn were quartered for the summer. The young men went their separate ways into the night, some indefatigably looking for action and some headed for bed, and young Joe Kennedy and two of the girls began a slow stroll about the darkened streets. One of the girls snatched his fleece-lined flight jacket with the name Kennedy inscribed on it and stashed it in a hiding place, but no one seemed to care. Such wrongs could be righted in the morning. Sometime after 2 A.M. the threesome decided to return to the Shiretown Inn motel; Kennedy's gear was in the room of a young man named Robby, and he told the girls that he intended to collect it and sleep with some other boys that night.

The noisy youngsters walked along the driveway that ran outside the long motel building, and before they had reached the door of Robby's room they saw that a man was approaching rapidly from the direction of the inn's office, about fifty yards away. They kept on walking, and when the man drew close, they recognized him as one of the functionaries of the place. He told them that they were making too much racket and asked them to go to their rooms, if they were registered, or leave, if they were not. Kennedy and the two girls turned around and disappeared into the shadows along Summer Street.

Russell Peachey, co-owner of the Shiretown Inn, walked back toward the little office after talking to the noisemakers. At forty-one years he was, by nature, a shy and retiring person who did not enjoy confronting people and telling them off. But the house was full, and the guests deserved a good night's sleep, and Peachey and his partner, Bill Parker, were struggling to retain the genteel image that had characterized the place from its opening three seasons before. Regatta nights, of course, were always a special test, and that was why Russ Peachey was up and about long after midnight. There was a sign on the fence by the driveway, QUIET PLEASE, but some of the regatta rowdies did not read such signs; it took the personal touch to subdue them. Earlier in the evening Peachy had had to ask several parties to hold down their noise. He had been in his office working on the Shiretown's books when the loud outcries of the three young people, the boy and the two girls, had attracted his attention to the far end of the motel area. Otherwise, he still would have been inside the office working. But now as he walked back and started to open the office door, he heard another sound, this time coming from the second-story porch that opened off the rooms booked to Senator Edward M. Kennedy and his party. Only the slightest glimmers of indirect light shone over the small yard that lay between Peachey and Mayberry House, whence the noises emanated. He peered into the darkness and saw nothing, but he could make out the distinct sound of footsteps coming across the upper porch.

If there was anything that Russ Peachey and Bill Parker were careful about, it was the attraction that their Shiretown Inn seemed to hold for the young senator, whose party had stayed at the place for three consecutive regattas. Like the canny businessmen they were, the two innkeepers recognized the publicity value of the arrangement and hoped that it would last forever. Besides, they admired Kennedy, politically and personally. Every member of the staff was alerted to the importance of giving the senator and his party a royal welcome, and the desk clerks remained on the *qui vive* for the call from Joseph Gargan that signaled another Kennedy booking each spring. " 'Gargan' means 'Kennedy,' " the desk staffers were told, "and when Gargan calls for rooms, make sure he gets exactly what he wants." This year the call had been late in coming, and it had been necessary to move several parties out of Mayberry House to give Kennedy and the six others in his group the adjacent lodgings they desired. It had been done. Others around Edgartown could mutter that the Shiretown was a strange choice for the rich Kennedys; it had no hard liquor license, no telephones, hardly any room service, a tiny restaurant with a limited menu, and no particular distinction, as yet, in this town of colorful old hotels. Nevertheless, the place seemed to attract the Kennedys, and the two owners intended to keep it that way. If there was someone snooping around the porch outside Kennedy's room, he would have to be dealt with, and fast.

Peachey stood in the shadows by the office door and fixed his gaze on the Mayberry House porch and the short flight of steps that led to it. As he watched, the footsteps began coming down the steps, and Peachy could make out the silhouette of a heavyset, tall man outlined against the wall at the bottom. Later he recalled the scene vividly:

"Oh my God," he said to himself. "What now?" He called out, "Can I help in any way?" and the voice that answered from the shadows carried the unmistakable Boston accent of Senator Edward M. Kennedy. Peachey could not be certain, but it appeared that the senator was fully dressed, wearing a jacket and trousers, and spoke calmly and soberly as though he were neither upset nor disturbed.

"I was asleep," Kennedy said, "and something woke me up. Maybe it was that loud party next door." Peachey cocked his ear and noticed that noises were coming from the Colonial Inn, immediately adjacent to Kennedy's quarters in Mayberry House. He made a mental note to call the Colonial and ask them to quiet the noisemakers.

"Say," the soft voice remarked from the shadows, "I seem to have misplaced my watch. Could you tell me what time it is?"

Peachey looked inside the office to the clock on the wall and said, "Certainly, it's twenty-five after two, Senator."

Kennedy thanked him and turned to remount the staircase, and Peachey, slightly flustered by his encounter with the inn's most important guest, blurted out, "Would you like to borrow a TV? I have a little Sony here if you want it."

"No, thank you," Kennedy said. "Good night."

"Good night," Peachey said. As the figure disappeared across the porch, he told himself how clumsily he had acted, offering to lend Kennedy a portable television set in the middle of the night. Everybody knew that there was nothing on TV at that hour, at least nothing that could be picked up on a tiny portable set on Martha's Vineyard. But he had acted reflexively, and he knew that the senator would understand. The idea was to make it plain that at any hour of the night or day, even at 2:25 in the morning, all the Shiretown Inn's facilities were at its guests' beck and call. Russ Peachey realized that he had acted a trifle stagestruck in the august presence of a United States Senator, but at least he had managed to get his message of courtesy across clearly. That was what brought people like Kennedy back to the Shiretown Inn.

For a few minutes, Peachey walked around, checking that everything was in order. He strolled out between the two white houses that fronted on Water Street and constituted the elite portion of the Shiretown Inn, and standing on the sidewalk under the towering elms and maples he noticed that the loud party next door was growing even louder. He returned to the office and telephoned the switchboard at the Colonial Inn—a task he did not enjoy—and asked for relief on behalf of his guests. Not long afterward, he noticed that the noise had stopped. He worked on the books for a while, made a few more tours of the property, and finally went to bed in the converted barn that he shared with his partner Bill Parker on the grounds of the inn. One regatta night was over; he would need his sleep for the next.

When Joe Kennedy and the two young waitresses were asked to leave the Shiretown area, they headed in the general direction of the Harbor View Hotel, three or four blocks north on Water Street. Joe III knew the hotel well; a year earlier, he had stayed there with his widowed mother and a large group of mourning Kennedys shortly after the death of his father, Robert. The Harbor View pool was slightly more secluded than the busy pool at the Harborside, where the revelers had intended to swim earlier, and now the three discussed the idea of taking a quick dip if all was clear at the Harbor View. When they reached the pool, the general giddiness of regatta weekend took over, and the two girls and the sixteen-year-old boy took turns pushing one another fully clothed into the pool. Soon the girls announced that they were chilly, and that they were leaving for "the bunker." The three companions said their goodbyes; the girls headed for their apartments, and Kennedy wandered off into the night.

It was nearly three in the morning when a sometime yachtsman from Watertown, Massachusetts, steered his car into the darkened environs of Edgartown and noticed a forlorn-appearing figure walking in the opposite direction on Main Street, headed for the outskirts of town. The yachtsman pulled up and recognized a youth he had crewed with in previous years. "Joe?" he called out. "Where you headed?"

Joseph P. Kennedy III muttered something that the driver did not understand, and slowly walked to the car. He was in shirtsleeves, and drops of water fell from clothes that appeared to be soaked. "Come on, get in," the yachtsman said. "Where do you want to go?"

Kennedy's voice was almost inaudible and the yachtsman had to ask him to repeat several times. Finally he made out the answer: "The Shiretown Inn." Within a few minutes the car pulled up to the front door of the place, and the yachtsman let Kennedy out. "You okay, Joe?" he asked. The youth nodded his head and disappeared into the shadows.

III

The Morning After

THE *On Time* was not due to begin operating until 7:30 Saturday morning, but the two fishing buddies from New York
State were happy to see the ferryman at the dock when they
pulled up at 7 A.M. and parked by the landing. Their destination was the ocean beach at Chappaquiddick, and they knew
they were too early to get across on the ferry from Edgartown,
but they also knew that the little two-car boat and its operators
ran on a friendly, informal schedule. Within a few minutes
they saw a man in a baseball cap and dark glasses stride out of
the drab ferryhouse and beckon them aboard.

"We're lucky!" Robert Samuel said. The driver, he was a
twenty-two-year-old teacher of high school physical sciences.
His companion was Joseph Capparella, a fifteen-year-old student. Samuel's younger brother, also fifteen, was supposed to
have made the weekend fishing trip with them, but he had
changed his mind, to the annoyance of the others, and they had
decided to go to Martha's Vineyard anyway. They had fished
from the ocean beach the night before, but the tides were wrong
and the night was black and both of the eager fishermen had
bumpy arms from clouds of saltwater mosquitoes that seemed to
find the weather conditions perfect. By 9:30 or ten o'clock, Samuel and Capparella had been forced to quit. This morning they
would get revenge.

A few raindrops began to spatter on the windshield as Samuel eased the Ford sedan off the ferry on the Chappaquiddick
side and headed east on Chappaquiddick Road, past the fancy
beach club on the left, the dark weedy water of Caleb Pond on

the right, and into the jungle-like midsection of the island, where thick growths of young trees and bushes closed in both sides of the narrow asphalt road. The rain held off. Capparella slumped back in his seat to get a better look at the sky. "Overcast and squally," he said, "but I don't think it'll rain for a while."

"I don't care if it does," Samuel said. "It won't stop me from fishing."

"Me neither," Capparella said.

"Won't stop the fish, either," the schoolteacher said. "A little dirty weather never hurt surf fishing."

United in their high hopes, the two companions reached the place where the blacktop veered sharply to the south, toward Wasque Point, another good surf-fishing area, but instead of turning they went straight ahead onto the dirt-and-sand road that led to the Dike Bridge and the ocean beach. That was where they had fished the night before, and they had liked the looks of the place. If the bluefish were not biting in the surf of this barrier beach, the two anglers could drive back to the big lagoon and try the place called Poucha Pond.

Samuel slowed down to negotiate the humpbacked wooden bridge. Once there had been an earthen dike across this narrow neck of water, breaking the lagoon into two halves: one saltwater and one freshwater, but pressure by commercial scallopers had caused the townsmen to batter an opening in the middle of the dike and return the water to its original state: a single elongated tidal pond, choked in the middle by the narrow bottleneck opening in the dike, and open to the sea at the far northern end. The wooden bridge had been built across the gap in 1949, for the benefit of those who wanted to continue on to the beach and the Cape Poge Wildlife Refuge, a popular spot for surf fishermen, bird watchers, and lovers. There are low sand dunes, some of them sheltered by squat and sprawling wild rose bushes, with hips full of vitamin C, and fields of eelgrass that sway like Kansas wheat.

As the two eager fishermen crossed the narrow bridge, they tried to see down into the water below, but there was so little light in the early morning that they noticed only that the tide seemed to be running out heavily. The water rushed through the channel almost like a mountain stream, eddying and rippling and churning ominously, spattering against the barnacles and mussels that clung to the pilings at either end of the bridge. Samuel made a mental note that bluefish and striped bass sometimes take up stations on the seaward side of such openings, to pick up morsels of food as they sweep through. If the beach fishing did not pay off, they might try this exact spot.

Just across the bridge, the schoolteacher parked the car. Four-wheel-drive vehicles and dune buggies could negotiate the soft sands ahead, but it was a treacherous place for an ordinary car. Tourists were always getting themselves stuck in these soft sands and calling Foster Silva or Captain Tony Bettencourt or some other island functionary to pull them out.

It was two hundred yards to the beach, and it seemed like an hour's walk to the two breathless fishermen, but soon they were casting their lures far out into the low surf of the humid, windless, sunless morning. They tried popping plugs and got no strikes; they switched to swimming lures, but did no better. When metal spoons and feathered squids produced no action, they decided to go elsewhere, maybe down to Wasque Point, or maybe to try a few casts in the pond, where the tide was still ebbing.

"Don't worry, Joe," Samuel said as they stowed their rods back in the Ford and started to drive off. "We'll hit 'em. They've got to be someplace."

As they drove across the Dike Bridge, the schoolteacher slowed to see if there was any action in the water. An hour had gone by since they had crossed the bridge for the first time that morning, and the tide had dropped a few inches, and now Samuel thought he could make out something shiny on the south side of the bridge, ten or twelve feet out. "What's that out there?" he said.

"Gee, I don't know," Capparella said.

Samuel stopped the car at the top of the bridge, and the two companions stepped outside for a better look. They peered into the distorting corrugations of the tidal rush and made out the dim form of an automobile, lying on its roof with its front end facing toward the bridge. The shiny part that had caught Samuel's eye was the bottom of the gas tank.

"Maybe it's a junker," Joe Capparella said.

Samuel walked a few feet down the bridge and squatted on his haunches. "No," he said. "It looks like a pretty new car, and it's not a junker 'cause I can see a license plate."

"Probably stolen then," the fifteen-year-old said. The companions got back into their car and drove across the bridge to the western (landward) side, where the road had been widened into a parking area. There they got out and headed on foot toward a small gray building about a hundred and fifty yards away. They noted the misspelling on the mailbox—Dyke House—and knocked on the door. A middle-aged woman answered; she identified herself as Mrs. Pierre Malm, and asked the two fishermen what she could do for them.

"Do you know anything about a car in the water at the bridge?" Samuel asked.

"No," Mrs. Malm said. "They run boats through there all the time."

"Well, gee," Samuel said, "they're not gonna run too many boats through there today. There's a car right in the middle of the channel."

"Oh, there's a car in the middle?" the surprised woman said.

"Sure is," Joe Capparella said. "We saw it plain as day."

"Just a minute," Mrs. Malm said. "Let's run up to the Smith house and see if they know anything about it. They have boys that are always playing down by the bridge."

The threesome trekked fifty yards to the gray bungalow occupied in the summer by the family of the Reverend David Smith. There they learned that the Smith boys had been playing around the bridge all the previous day but had seen no such car. It must have gone into the water during the night. "I'll call the police," Mrs. Malm said.

Joe Capparella and Bob Samuel walked back to the bridge and took another look at the car. "I guess we'd better wait till the police come," the schoolteacher said, "before we go back to our fishing." Just then there was a familiar splashing sound from the seaward side of the bridge, and the two companions turned away from the car to see a shadowy school of bluefish cleaning up on a frantic run of tinker mackerel. Without a word, the fishermen dashed to the car, extracted their casting rods, and nervously snapped small silvery Rebel lures to their lines. While they waited for the arrival of the police, they stood on the Dike Bridge and hauled in bluefish till their arms ached.

As was his custom, Edgartown Police Chief Arena had reached the tiny police station in the town office building a few minutes before his appointed hour of eight, to set an example of promptness for his men. He relieved the night shift officer, Victor Danberg, greeted a pair of arriving summertime "specials," Patrolmen Roy Meekins and Robert Bruguiere, and said good morning to the daytime policewoman, Carmen Salvador, who took up her post at the desk in the outer office while the chief studied the log in the privacy of the inner one. He saw that the night had been relatively quiet. A storekeeper had inquired about the whereabouts of a woman who had run up a big bill and apparently skipped town. A car had parked across the liquor store's driveway and blocked deliveries. Someone had turned in a brown wallet and address book. An elderly resident had been carried to Martha's Vineyard Hospital in the police cruiser. A stolen car had been found outside Ralph's Cafe. A fight had been quelled at the Colonial Inn at 1:50 A.M. Eighteen cars had been tagged for overnight parking. Those were the only police matters that had been worth logging since the chief had gone off duty at four o'clock on Friday afternoon. He uttered a relieved sigh. For a regatta night, this was almost a clean sheet.

At ten minutes after 8 A.M., one of the patrolmen had gone for coffee and the other had started on his rounds, and the custom of the personable Jim Arena at this slack time of the morning was to walk across the street and exchange banter with the old-timers who sat on the two gray benches at the near corner of the courthouse lawn. Men had been sitting on these benches since long before Jim Arena had come to Edgartown three years before; some of them might have been considered ne'er-do-wells, but others were respected citizens with long pedigrees going back to the Vineyard's whaling days, when an author named Herman Melville had gone to sea on a ship commanded by Captain Valentine Pease of Edgartown and returned to write a book about it. Some of the old men merely sat and gabbed like Queequeg and Ishmael, and others nipped at "medicine" bottles hidden in the folds of their old clothes. There were only one or two who remained at the maple-shaded post all day long, but itinerants would arrive for shorter or longer stints, and there were always three or four men on the benches. Their main object was companionship and gossip (or exchange of information, depending on how one looked at it). From their vantage point directly across Main Street from the town offices, catty-cornered from the courthouse, they could see almost every car that entered the town, and as various citizens brought their own nuggets of news to the bench during the day, like reporters returning to the city desk, the store of news and gossip built up, until the bench-sitters knew more about what was going on in Edgartown than Jim Arena or the selectmen or anyone else. It was said that news traveled from one end of Edgartown to the other at two and one-half times the speed of light, and much of the credit (or blame) went to the bench-sitters. The police cruiser's reserved parking place was squarely in front of the benches, and every time the blue station wagon went on an emergency call, one of the old men would detach himself from the bench and rush a half-block down the street to the Colonial Drug Store, there to pass the word to those on the premises before going to the wall phone to disseminate the news even more broadly. Sometimes the policemen would trick the bench-sitters by sprinting out the door of the town offices, jumping into the car, flipping on the blue Mars light on the roof and speeding away. Once out of sight, they would slow to normal speed, and for the rest of the day news would crackle back and forth across Edgartown that the cruiser had rolled "on a hot one." It

was a point of pride with the old men that they never asked
Arena or the other policemen directly what was going on; everything was done sideways, like a sea crab approaching a dead
clam. "Seen you pull out purty fast," old Ellie Simpson would
say to Arena. "Must have been something important."

Sometimes Arena would feign ignorance, but most often he
would come clean after a few minutes of joshing. He enjoyed
his chats with the old-timers, and they kept him on top of
events. Long before a frightened female would telephone police
headquarters to report that her husband was threatening her,
Arena would know that the marriage was going poorly, and by
the time any shady outsiders had set foot inside the limits of
Edgartown, to attempt to peddle marijuana or goofballs or en-
gage in other nefarious pursuits, Arena knew their names, descriptions and itineraries. The old men on the bench had their
uses.

It was about twenty minutes after eight when Arena closed
the log and stepped from behind his desk to pay his morning
visit to the sitters. A meticulous man, he carefully smoothed
out the wrinkles of his uniform and put his cap on at exactly
the right angle, and as he stepped into the outer office, with its
bulletin boards showing missing persons and color pictures of
prescription and nonprescription drugs and shift schedules and
lookout notices, he saw that Policewoman Carmen Salvador
was on the telephone. From the conversation Arena could tell
that she was taking a message from the central communications
desk run by the county sheriff at the airport. When anything
went wrong on the island, whether it was at Edgartown or Tisbury or Gay Head or wherever, the citizens telephoned
693–1212, and sheriff's dispatchers took the proper action.
There was no two-way radio in the Edgartown police office,
only in the cruiser, but the island-wide emergency system had
performed perfectly.

"Well, what is it, Salvador?" the chief asked in the gruff
manner that he affected with his efficient assistant. "Murder?
Kidnap? Assault? A dog without a license?"

The dark-haired, plumply attractive policewoman did not

laugh. "Communications said a lady just called and there's a car in the water by the Dike Bridge."

"That's all?" Arena said.

"That's all. Do you want to go, or do you want to send somebody?"

"Oh, I'll go," the chief said. It was a dark and dreary morning, and perhaps a trip to Chappaquiddick would cheer things up. As he dashed across the street and into the cruiser and pulled briskly away with the blue light spinning, he thought momentarily that the bench-sitters would think he was tricking them again; perhaps, in a sense, he was. Although he was rushing, like a good cop, he doubted that there would be much of genuine news value in the car in the water. Probably some fisherman had backed too close to the pond and stuck fast, or maybe somebody had deposited his car in the lagoon rather than drive it to the nearest junkyard, on the mainland. It did not occur to Arena that anyone had gone off the bridge into the water. Although he had long regarded the Dike Bridge as an abomination, with its abrupt angle to the left and its low caplogs, he was also aware that the bridge had been there for twenty years and not a soul had ever driven off it.

No other cars were waiting in the ferry line, and the *On Time* was at the Edgartown side of the harbor when Arena pulled up. He recognized Dick Hewitt, the ferry operator, and drove aboard, and within seconds was on his way across the channel.

"What's up?" Hewitt asked.

"There's supposed to be an accident or something at the Dike Bridge," Arena answered. "You heard anything about it?"

"Not till now," Hewitt said.

Backing the cruiser off on the Chappaquiddick side, Arena took off at high speed toward the peculiar four-way intersection. Once there, he continued along the sandy road toward the dike, and when he was about eight hundred feet from the bridge he could dimly make out two or three people standing on its peak. He slowed for the deep ruts in front of the bridge, made the sharp turn to the left, drove across the narrow span

and parked. Two young men were busily fishing, and one of
them pointed into the water on the south side of the bridge.
Arena looked down and saw the unmistakable shape of a dark
sedan, overturned. It appeared that the weight of the engine
had tipped the car forward, so that it rested upside down on the
top of the grille and the top of the windshield at an angle that
thrust the rear of the car up toward the surface of the water. It
was hard to tell the depth of the channel, but Arena guessed it
would be six to eight feet. He peered into the water with a sense
of foreboding. The tide was running at full speed, and whirlpools
and rips sucked at the rear wheels, barely awash. The water
was fairly clear, and Arena could see down to the bottom,
where rocks and vegetation of a sickly mottled greenish yellow
gave the same menacing appearance as ocean shoal water, conspicuously different from the solid blues and greens of deeper
places. Arena shuddered when he realized what he would have
to do.

"How long's it been there?" he asked one of the fishermen.

"We don't know," the man answered. "But it must have been
here when we started fishing an hour or so ago."

Arena walked back toward the other side of the bridge and
saw the telltale marks of the accident. There were a few scrapes
and nicks in the caplog along the south side of the bridge, and
he figured that the largest of the indentations must have been
made by the car's differential as it ripped across the caplog.
There were tire tracks leading off the bridge, and light scuff
marks, across the grain of the wood, indicating the possibility of
last-minute braking. Arena, with thirteen years' experience as a
Massachusetts state trooper, took in all this in seconds, and
when he looked up, a woman was approaching from the direction of the Dyke House. He recognized her as Mrs. Pierre
Malm, of Lebanon, Pennsylvania; she rented old Tony Bettencourt's former gunning cottage. "Do you have any idea how
long this has been here?" Arena asked, pointing to the car in
the water.

"No," Mrs. Malm said. "I heard a car go by last night
around midnight."

"Gee," Arena said, "did you hear it go in the water?"

"No, I just heard it go by. My daughter heard something, too."

If the Malms had heard this particular car go by, Arena said to himself, then there was certainly no rush about diving down to see if anyone was in it. But there was always the chance that this was not the same car, and he asked Mrs. Malm if she happened to have a pair of swimming trunks in the house. "Yes," the pleasant woman answered. "My husband's. You're welcome to borrow them if you'd like."

Arena walked back to the police cruiser and radioed to the Communications Center. "Have the Fire Department's scuba man stand by," he said, and then he realized that the order was too vague. "No, the hell with it," he said to himself, and snapped the hand microphone back on. "Send him right over. And call the Edgartown station and have another officer come over here to help out." When acknowledgments had been exchanged, the six-foot-four-inch police chief jogged to the Malm house and changed into a pair of plaid swimming trunks that fitted him perfectly, to his great surprise. He left his T-shirt on against the early morning chill of the tidewater, stepped onto the narrow beach that extended into the rushing water, and began to wade toward the car. He had taken only a few steps when the bank started to drop off sharply, and he realized that he would have to push off and fight the current in a swimming position. He paused to consider the problem for a final time. The car was about forty more feet out, just on the far side of the channel, a short and simple swim under normal conditions for a man as strong as Jim Arena. He would be stroking crosscurrent, and if he did lose control, he would be swept under the bridge and into the pilings, where he could gain a handhold and wait for assistance. He took a deep gulp of air and kicked out toward the car.

Mrs. Frances Stewart, a stylishly dressed middle-aged woman with silver-gray hair, had just come on duty as day clerk at the Shiretown Inn when she looked up and saw a man approaching from the direction of the restaurant. It was 8:30 Saturday morning, and the attractive woman had just finished counting the daily money and secreting it in the cashbox. "May I help you?" she called out.

As Mrs. Stewart recalled the incident later, the man stepped inside and she recognized the inn's priority guest, Senator Edward M. Kennedy. He had been registered since the day before, but she had not seen him, and now as he walked up to the counter she realized that he was both handsomer and taller than she had imagined. He was dressed in knockabout yachting clothes, and it pleased Mrs. Stewart somehow that he did not look like a dude; his clothes were slightly faded and he looked ready for a day's racing, unlike so many of the other guests, who decked themselves out in fancy yachting clothes and never went near the water.

"Yes," the senator said. "I wanted to ask about the New York and Boston papers. Do you have them for sale?"

"No," Mrs. Stewart said, trying to conceal her slight nervousness at the pleasure of his company. "What we do is send the bellman over to the paper store around nine, and he picks up two *New York Times* for us."

"Well, could I order a *Times* and a *Boston Globe?*"

"You certainly may," Mrs. Stewart said. "I'll see to it that the boy brings them over for you."

"Thank you," Kennedy said, and turned toward the door. As he put his hand on the latch, he spun and said, "By the way, could I borrow a dime? I seem to have left my billfold up in my room."

Mrs. Stewart found herself musing about the wonder of it all. "He's got millions," she said to herself, "and he's borrowing a dime from me!" To Kennedy, she said, "Of course." She handed him a dime from the cash drawer and watched as he walked outside to the inn's single pay telephone about thirty feet away on an outside wall. She could see him through the screen door, and she heard him telling the operator, "No, no, no! It's M. M. M!" It sounded as though the operator was having trouble getting the name. The call was short-lived; perhaps the senator had not been able to reach his party. Mrs. Stewart busied herself behind the counter as she saw him returning. "Here," he said, handing her the dime. "Thank you very much."

Mrs. Stewart had made a positive identification already, but she found herself saying, "Are you Mr. Kennedy?" and wondered, as the words came out, why she had called him Mister instead of Senator.

"I am," Kennedy said calmly.

"I'm Mrs. Stewart," she said, and held out her hand. She was surprised that Kennedy's handshake was so weak for such a robust-appearing young man; he barely gripped her hand at all, and his own hand felt cold and clammy to the touch. "Was the trip over pleasant?" she asked.

"Yes, thank you," Kennedy said.

"Did you have a good race?" Mrs. Stewart went on.

Kennedy seemed to peer sideways at the woman's name card on the counter, and then said softly, "I'm not sure how I did, Mrs. Stewart. I think I came in sixth or seventh."

"What kind of boat did you race?"

"A Wianno Senior," Kennedy said.

The name meant nothing to the woman, and she could see that the senator was preoccupied and eager to leave. "I won't forget your papers," she said. Kennedy thanked her again and disappeared out the door.

As soon as Jim Arena pushed off into the swirling waters under the Dike Bridge, he realized that he had underestimated the force of the current. Simply to hold his distance from the pilings, he had to swim at a forty-five-degree angle to the onrushing water and pull with every ounce of his strength. He had always reckoned himself a good swimmer and he knew that he was in excellent physical condition, but there were a few seconds as he beat his way across the swirling water when he doubted that he was going to make it. When he finally reached the overturned vehicle, he found that he was still in trouble. He was panting and tired, but simply to maintain his position over the car was a difficult task. Then he noticed a turbulence around the rear end of the automobile, eight or ten feet from where he was energetically treading water, and he remembered that the car was resting at an angle, with the weight of the engine holding down the front, and the rear end poking upward. With a final burst of energy he propelled himself almost straight upstream to the rear, and felt relieved when he found a handhold under water. There he rested for a minute or two, and when his breathing had returned almost to normal, he flattened out his body, gripped the rear of the car tightly, and propelled himself with a mighty heave into the depths of the water. The current hit him like a fist, and for an instant he went completely out of control. Then he kicked hard with his feet and clawed at the heavy-running salt water with his hands, but all he could see through burning eyes was the dim silhouette of the car, slowly receding. He kicked up to the surface and found that he had been carried almost to the pilings, and once again he had to swim straight upstream against the current to regain his old position at the rear of the automobile. "I'll never make it!" he said to himself. "This is awful!" As his breath slowly returned, he pondered what he had seen on his dive. In those brief seconds below the surface, it had seemed to him that the automobile was peculiarly compressed, as though the top had been mashed down. Earlier, the last possibility on his mind had been that a body would be in the vehicle, but now he had to wonder. If the car had taken such a powerful thump, it was very likely that its occupants would have been injured, probably seriously, and they never would have been able to get out and swim ashore. Besides, if there had been survivors, the police would have known about it long ago. The survivors would have beaten their way ashore and told somebody, and inevitably the police would have been called. So Jim Arena, holding tightly to the rear of the damaged automobile, reached two conclusions: that the accident had happened sometime during the night, when no one would have seen the car go into the water, and that whoever had been in the car was dead a few feet beneath his hands. The chilling realization made him kick down into the water again, and once again he had to spend so much energy holding his position that he was barely able to glimpse the car through reddened, burning eyes. He popped to the surface, grabbed the handhold, rested momentarily, and made a third dive on the car, and this time he realized that he was wasting his time; his eyes could not focus properly in the briny water, and he could not maintain control in the current. Back on the surface, he noticed two of the Reverend David Smith's young sons standing on the bridge watching. "Hey!" Arena shouted. "You boys know where there's a face mask around?"

One of the boys said, "I think there's one over in the boat. I'll get it and row out to you."

"Don't row out!" Arena ordered, fearing that the boy would not be able to control the boat. "Just get me the mask." He swam across to shore.

The short wait gave Arena another chance to consider the situation, and he told himself that he was beating his brains out for nothing. Against the tricky, powerful current of Poucha Pond, an unequipped swimmer could accomplish nothing. Even if he could summon the strength to reach one of the car windows, he would never be able to swim inside. "If I tried to get inside," he said to himself, "I'd just become another casualty." He stroked back to the car, put on the face mask, and made a final, desperate dive, and once again the current slapped him around and sent him spinning out of control. "The hell with it," he said to himself as he came to the surface spouting water and gasping for air. "I'll wait for the experts." By now the car's rear bumper and tires were just beginning to protrude in the outgoing tide. Arena groped around and finally managed to pull himself into a sitting position on the undercarriage, nicking his foot and drawing blood in the process, and from this undignified position astride the car he saw the station wagon of Fire Chief Antone (Tony Cocky) Silva come into view down the Dike Road. It was 8:45 A.M., a scant twenty-five minutes since Carmen Salvador had taken the first report from the island communications center.

Arena watched as Silva, two firemen named Lawrence Mercier and Antone Bettencourt, a scuba diver named John Farrar, and one of his own Edgartown policemen, Robert Bruguiere, piled out of the station wagon. "Bob!" Arena shouted. "See if you can get a listing on this number." He leaned over the bumper of the automobile and called out the reading: L 78 207. Bruguiere disappeared into the parked police cruiser to radio the number to Communications, and within a few minutes the summertime policeman called to his chief, "It's registered to Edward M. Kennedy."

"My God!" Arena said to himself. "Another tragedy!" It did not enter his head that there might be more than one Edward M. Kennedy. Earlier in the week he had heard that the senator was going to sail in the regatta, and on Thursday he had seen John Crimmins shopping on Main Street. Arena *knew* whose car this was. His memory flashed back to a night five years before when he had been on duty with the state police contingent at Boston's Logan Airport, and word had come by radio that Senator Ted Kennedy's airplane had crashed and he was believed to be near death. Arena remembered other scenes: standing proudly as he had been photographed with John F. Kennedy, and the tightening in his stomach when he learned about the assassination, and the same sick feeling again when he heard about the murder of Robert Kennedy in Los Angeles. Now he was sitting atop still another Kennedy tragedy. "Jesus!" Arena whispered to himself. "That poor family!" He watched as the scuba diver lowered himself into the water.

John Farrar, thirty-three years old, graduate of Milton Academy and Brown University, had been talking to a customer at the Turf 'N Tackle Shop in Edgartown when word came that a car was submerged at the Dike Bridge. Farrar was manager of the shop, but if there was a single demand that took precedence over all others in his life, it was his job as captain of the Edgartown Volunteer Fire Department and head of the Scuba Search and Rescue Division. Shouting to a helper to take over, the lean six-footer was out the door and driving to the fire station for his gear within seconds. In company with Fire Chief Silva and a few others who had heard Arena's radioed call for assistance, Farrar made it to the scene of the accident in twenty-five minutes flat, portal to portal, and just as he was finishing strapping on his double-length blue flippers and his red oxygen tank with E.F.D. painted across it, he heard someone shout that the car belonged to Senator Ted Kennedy. The name Kennedy meant even more to Farrar than it did to most Massachusetts citizens; there was money in the Farrar family, and the two families had rubbed shoulders a few times. Farrar, a strong conservative, had nevertheless exchanged recent letters with the liberal young Senator Kennedy; he had congratulated him on opposing Richard Nixon's appointment of Walter Hickel as Secretary of the Interior, and had received a friendly letter in return. No one could call John Farrar a Kennedy man even after this warm exchange of letters, but he had told himself that at least the senator was showing promise.

None of these fleeting memories slowed John Farrar in his task, which was to get into the water and down to the car in the least possible elapsed time, whatever the occupation of the vehicle's owner. The Edgartown Fire Department had technical skills and an *esprit de corps* that would have done credit to departments in major cities, and Captain John Farrar was one of the most conscientious members. A few years before, when the department had laid in the oxygen tanks and scuba gear at a high cost and certain members of the community had made the predictable objections, the proud firemen had held a meeting and agreed that any cost would be worthwhile if a single life was saved. As he waded into the water and inserted the oxygen tube into his mouth, John Farrar thought that this might be the time.

A few kicks of his plastic flippers carried him into the stream and next to Jim Arena, who sat half covered with salt water and half with perspiration on the tail end of the car. Farrar handed Arena one end of a long rope and flung himself straight down to the rocky, sandy bottom. The current tried to shove him into the bridge, as it had shoved Arena, but Farrar had been diving for nearly twenty years; he was skilled and strong and equipped, and while he said to himself that the cur-

rent was making his task more dangerous, his first thought was
that there might be a life to save. It was not exactly a normal
scuba diving assignment, but he had seen worse.

The water was clear, but visibility was poor; there was an
overcast and a light mist in the sky, and the blanket of moisture
blocked out the sun and caused a delay of a few seconds while
Farrar's eyes adjusted behind his face mask. Then he saw that
the car had apparently executed a complex maneuver before
settling to the bottom. It had rolled completely over, and the
front end had turned through 180 degrees, so that it was facing
almost exactly opposite to its initial path of travel. As he took
a grip on the side of the car to begin searching the interior,
Farrar said a single word to himself: "Speed." To the young
diver, there seemed to be no other possible explanation for the
aerial maneuvers that had caused the car to wind up in such a
peculiar position some thirty feet from where it left the bridge.
As he worked, he realized that his hopes of saving a life were
severely diminished. A car gyrating into the water in such a
fashion would be likely to smash its occupants into uncon-
sciousness, or at least to disorient them thoroughly, before settling to the bottom. Still, Farrar followed his instincts and his
training. Without losing an instant, he ducked his head to the
driver's side of the upside-down car, saw that the window was
rolled down almost to the bottom, and peered into the gloomy
interior. The front seat was empty. He pulled his head out and
began working his way around to the back. The rear window on
the driver's side was closed tight; Farrar inched around and saw
a flash of white through the rear window. He swam closer and
looked at two sandaled feet, close together and heavily wrinkled
from immersion in the salt water. "My God," he said to himself. "There's somebody in there!" He kicked twice against the
long fins, doubled up to change direction, and propelled himself squid-like around the back of the car. He could not afford
to draw any conclusions; he had read that people had been submerged in automobiles for as long as five hours and survived.

Both windows on the passenger's side were blown in, and
only tiny fragments remained around the edges. Farrar stuck

his head in the rear window and saw a young blond woman. He reached out and touched the thigh and realized that she had been dead for hours. The leg was like iron; rigor mortis had set in. Apparently she had lived for a time before the water had risen over her head; Farrar noted that her head was cocked back as though to reach the last available oxygen in the car. Her body was in a sitting position, her head in the footwell, her thighs along the upside-down seat, and her feet reaching back against the rear window. As Farrar maneuvered his head inside for a better look, he saw that the young woman's hands were molded stiffly around the front edge of the seat. It seemed to the diver that the position could not have been assumed unconsciously, that she must have been holding the edge of the seat and craning her neck upward in the last seconds of her life. Hours later, rigor mortis had fixed her in that position.

Now that he knew the girl was hopelessly lost, Farrar slowed down and considered his own safety. He took another good look at the girl and cursed softly to himself. "God damn it, I've got my hand on a dead body," he said, "and I wasn't even on an emergency call. I thought I was, but I was never on an emergency call!" The thought somehow annoyed him as he worked to free the rigid body and carefully steer it limb by limb through the smashed window. The girl's lips were parted; he could see that she was slightly buck-toothed. Her hair was yellow and long, and her light-colored eyes were open. "My God," Farrar said to himself. "This girl is staring at me and her hair is flowing and there's something rotten. *There's something really rotten.*"

When he had inched the body slowly out of the car, he realized that the current might wrench it from his grasp, and he passed a pair of half-hitches around the neck as a safety precaution. Then he lifted the girl above his head and guided her body toward the surface.

At a few minutes after 9 A.M., while John Farrar was working under the bridge, ferry operator Dick Hewitt and his sixteen-year-old assistant, Steve Ewing, were preparing to shove

off from the Edgartown side when they noticed that Senator
Edward Kennedy and two male companions—a tall man with
slightly receding dark hair and a shorter man in sunglasses,
both about the senator's age—stepped aboard. "Hi!" Kennedy
said jovially to the young Ewing. The three men paid their fif-
teen-cent fares and sat on the side benches for the short trip,
and when they reached Chappaquiddick, they strode up the
landing and into the ferryhouse, where there was nothing but a
few wall benches and a pay telephone. Hewitt and Ewing figured the men were waiting for a ride.

Perched on the rear end of the overturned automobile, his
legs dangling sideways in the stiff current, Police Chief Arena
held the rope end in his hand and waited for something to happen below him. The arrival of the fire chief's car with its red
Mars light had attracted sightseers. Arena recognized old Tony
Bettencourt, who once had fished for a living in these same waters; Dr. Edward Self, a prominent New York surgeon who
summered on Chappaquiddick; Ralph Harding, the elderly
caretaker for a rich man's grounds, and ten or twelve others, including a couple of knockabout townies from the Edgartown
side. The Smith children were playing around the bridge, as
they did daily, and a few other children had joined them. "All
right, you kids," Arena called out. "I want you to go down the
road and get away from the bridge. That's right! Get out of
here and give us a chance." He was not sure what was going to
come up at the end of the rope, if anything, and he did not
want the youngsters to be shocked.

When the bridge had been cleared, Arena felt the rope go
taut. He interpreted this as a signal to haul up, but before he
could apply any pressure he saw what appeared to be a blond
wig floating out of the depths toward him. Then he saw the
body of a young woman slowly rising to the surface, its arms
sticking out grotesquely. Jim Arena had been a law enforcement officer for sixteen years and a United States Marine before
that, and he still had developed no inner hardness about such
sights. When John Farrar surfaced alongside the body, and Arena

reached out and pulled the woman to his side, he was deeply moved. Something about the neatness of her attire touched him. "She looks like a child's doll," he said to himself as he peered into the open eyes. "Look at her. She's dressed for a party. Neat and nice. Buttons all buttoned, everything in place, like a child going to a party." But then he remembered the automobile's registration, and he called out in a trembling voice to the firemen and policemen standing above: "Is she one of them? Do you recognize her?"

Farrar had taken his mouthpiece out. "I don't recognize her," he said.

No one spoke from the bridge. Arena cradled the body in his arms and took a closer look. He said to himself that the victim could well be one of Ethel and Robert Kennedy's children, or the daughter of someone else in the family. Demure and petite in her black slacks and white blouse, the blond-haired girl looked barely in her twenties, and hardly more than five feet tall.

Arena pulled himself together. "Bob!" he called to Bruguiere. "Go into the routine, will you?" That would mean notifying the medical examiner, the Massachusetts Registry of Motor Vehicles, the wrecker, and the undertaker. "And see if you can find out where Ted Kennedy is and get him down here!" Arena shouted. He watched as Bruguiere went into the police cruiser and picked up the microphone. Farrar had disappeared into the water again, and now the diver came up alongside the chief and handed over a fancy gold chain and a brightly colored purse. "The chain was around her waist," he said. "It fell off when I was bringing her up. The pocketbook was on the headliner of the car."

"Do you need the boat?" one of the firemen yelled.

"Yeh," Arena said. A small rescue skiff was pushed out toward Arena and Farrar, and the two men gently placed the body inside and dropped the chain and the purse in after it. The firemen on shore pulled the boat back, put the body on a stretcher, and removed it to the rear of the police cruiser. It had been drizzling, but when the body was lifted into the police car, the drizzle stopped.

Back on shore, a thoroughly fatigued Jim Arena studied the purse. It was "one of a kind," shaped like a worker's lunchbox and covered with hand-painted flowers and faces and bright psychedelic designs. Arena let the water trickle out and began to grope among the contents. There were two keys to rooms at the Katama Shores Motor Inn (popularly called the Dunes, after its restaurant), two miles outside of Edgartown. There were ample supplies of cosmetics, a few items of feminine hygiene, some bills and change, and an automobile registration and pass to the U.S. Senate. "Well, at least we know who she is," Arena said as he studied the documents. "Her name is Rosemary Keough. She must work for the senator."

Having solved the identification problem, Arena slipped inside the police cruiser and radioed the Communications Center. "Call the Dunes and see if Rosemary Keough's registered," he ordered. Within a few minutes an efficient dispatcher reported that a Miss Keough was one of six girls who had checked into the Dunes; they occupied three rooms, and none of the beds had been slept in last night. "Thanks," Arena said.

"This is bad," he confided to Bruguiere. "Some other girls were registered with her. Maybe they were in the car when it went off the bridge." He motioned to John Farrar, standing by in his scuba suit. "Check downtide, will you, John?" Arena asked. "It's possible somebody was thrown from the car. Probably they'd still be in the pond somewhere." Foster Silva had appeared on the scene, and Arena dispatched the island's premier watchman to row around the frothy edges of the pond to look for anything that might have been thrown from the car in its dive off the bridge. "Tony!" he called to old Captain Anthony Bettencourt, standing at one side watching the proceedings. "Take your Jeep down to the ferry landing and wait for the medical examiner, will you? He'll probably need a lift." The seventy-year-old man, a fire captain himself, walked spryly to his blue Jeep station wagon and drove off. As Arena watched, he saw an Edgartown tow truck coming into sight, and he recognized his friend Jonathan Ahlbum at the wheel. "Don't pull the car out of the water till the guys from Motor Vehicles get here," Arena told Ahlbum. "They get kind of touchy if you move a car before they make their investigation." He looked at the gathering crowd of spectators. "On second thought," he told Ahlbum, "go ahead and pull it out. We're drawing too many people already."

"What's going on?" Ahlbum asked.

"Jesus, it's something," Arena said. "That's Ted Kennedy's car in the water."

"That *is* something," Ahlbum said. "Funny thing, we saw him standing down by the ferry landing when we came over."

"Just now?"

"Just now."

"On the Edgartown side?"

"On the Chappy side," Ahlbum said, "right in front of the ferryhouse."

Captain Tony Bettencourt, nicknamed Midge because he was barely five feet tall, was happy to be of assistance. Once he had been as active on Chappaquiddick as his nephew Foster Silva, but the years were catching up with him, and he had had to abandon such activities as duck-shooting and commercial fishing and running to fires. Now he tended the tiny Chappaquiddick dump and the property he owned on the island, which included the little driftwood house rented by Mrs. Malm. Indeed, it had been Tony's late wife who had painted "Dyke House" on the mailbox, thus perpetuating the innocent misspelling. Tony knew Chappaquiddick intimately; he had lived there for sixty years. Three decades before, the author Irma Friedrich had written in a delightful children's novel about Chappaquiddick, *The Separated Island:* "Tony the ferryman was short and merry with beautiful white teeth flashing smiles from his good brown face." He had changed little.

As the old man drove west on Chappaquiddick Road to pick up the medical examiner for Jim Arena, he said to himself that he might never again get a chance to snap a picture of such a bizarre scene at the Dike Bridge, one of the familiar loci of his life, and he turned off the main road long enough to run up to his house and get his camera. He reached the ferry around

9:30, parked near the landing, and walked straight out to meet the *On Time* when it came over from the Edgartown side.

"Mornin', Dick," he said to Hewitt. "Hear about the accident at the dike?"

"Yeh," the taciturn ferryman said. "I saw Arena go over."

"It's Ted Kennedy's car," the old man said. "They know that much. And there was a dead girl in it."

"Oh?" Hewitt said. "Well, Kennedy's standing right over there by the ferryhouse with a couple of guys." Bettencourt looked and saw some men on the tiny porch of the shack.

When the *On Time* pulled out, the little dump keeper walked to where the three men were standing. As he remembered later, he said to Kennedy, "Senator, they just took a dead girl out of your car. Do you want a ride up to the bridge?"

"No," Kennedy said. "I'm going over to town."

"Okay," Tony said, and returned to the ferry landing. The *On Time* was churning back toward Chappaquiddick by now, and Tony thought he could recognize the medical examiner aboard. He started the engine of his station wagon and prepared for the return trip to the bridge.

Five or ten minutes after Tony Bettencourt, the medical examiner, and the undertakers had disappeared down Chappaquiddick Road toward the scene of the accident, ferrymen Dick Hewitt and Steve Ewing noticed that Ted Kennedy and his two companions were still hanging around the ferryhouse. "That's odd," young Steve said. "You'd think they'd want to go to the scene."

"I think they're using the pay phone inside," Hewitt commented as he prepared to gun the ferry back toward the Edgartown side. After a few more round trips of five or six minutes each, the two ferrymen decided that Kennedy must be in the dark about the accident. "Let's go up," Hewitt said to his young assistant as they lashed the vessel to the Chappaquiddick landing at about 9:45. "Let's at least make sure he knows about it." They walked briskly up the inclined ramp and across thirty or forty feet to the shack, and as they approached, Kennedy seemed to sidle away from his companions and drift toward a line of parked cars. While the senator was still within earshot, Hewitt said loudly, "Senator Kennedy, are you aware of the accident?"

Kennedy disappeared between parked cars, but one of the other men said, "Yes, we just heard about it."

Ewing and Hewitt returned to the ferry and prepared to cast off, and they were quickly joined by the senator and his companions. There were no cars on the trip, and the three passengers took seats side by side on the bench reserved for those on foot. Kennedy sat quietly, his head slumped, while the tall man with the receding black hairline spoke softly but emphatically, sometimes waving his arms to make a point. When the *On Time* nuzzled its nose against the landing on the Edgartown side, Kennedy jumped off even before the cables were hooked up. Hewitt and Ewing watched as the heavyset figure headed straight up the middle of Daggett Street, moving so fast that the tall, dark man was plainly having difficulty keeping up, and a photographer with a camera had to swing his body in a rapid arc to hold the vanishing image in his viewfinder. Two men strolling in the opposite direction jumped aside to keep from being bumped as Kennedy pushed doggedly on, his eyes fixed on the pavement and his deck shoes flashing in a style reminiscent of the Olympic walking event. Hewitt and Ewing watched until the senator reached the corner of Daggett and Water streets and turned left and out of sight, his companion still bringing up the rear.

Donald Randall Mills, "Doctor of Physick" as he cheerfully described himself, drew on his pipe and watched the underbrush of Chappaquiddick pass on either side of the car. All things considered, he told himself, he was just as happy to be riding in the front; his companions were Eugene Frieh and David Guay, "Licensed Funeral Directors and Embalmers," and the vehicle was a 1962 gray Buick service wagon, used by the morticians as a working hearse. The three men had met at the Edgartown ferry landing, and in typical islander fashion had decided to double up and go to the scene of the accident in a single car. Tony Bettencourt's offer of a ride to the Dike Bridge was declined with thanks, and now the little task force of death followed the old man's blue Jeep along the road toward the dike. Not that they had any doubts as to the location of the bridge, but it had been nice of Tony to wait and they did not want to deny the old man his role.

For Dr. Mills, sixty-three years old and possessed of unlimited amounts of patience, the case was one of the routine interruptions that came with the territory. He did not complain about the 3 A.M. phone calls for medical advice or the rush trips to Martha's Vineyard Hospital rubbing sleep out of his eyes, and he did not complain about being the on-duty medical examiner when there was a "fatal" at the Dike Bridge. There were only five physicians on the whole island, more than enough for the full-time population but not nearly enough for the swollen population of summer, and on one day of each week the regular medical examiner rested and Dr. Mills, the associate medical examiner, took his place. There was hardly any money in it, nor was there much money in certain other responsibilities that Dr. Mills had taken on: contract physician for the U.S. Public Health Service, medical examiner for the Federal Aviation Agency, and various board memberships and advisory positions. In a small place like Edgartown there were certain professional vacuums that had to be filled, and if one lived there, and had the qualifications, one filled them. Mills had practiced in Edgartown since 1935, with four years out for service with the Army Medical Corps in the Pacific, and in that time he had come to be one of the most admired figures on the island. A modest man almost entirely devoid of ego, he answered questions with consummate patience, and when he did not know the answers he came out flatly and admitted it. He was similarly cautious with his diagnoses; he knew his own limitations, and if there was the slightest doubt in his mind he would advise his patient to "check in at Mass. General for a few days and see what the experts have to say." In his spare time, he hooked rugs and played the organ and dug littleneck clams and scallops.

This Saturday had started, like many another, with an interruption. At 7 A.M. Dr. Mills was up, shaved and dressed, and about to sit down to breakfast when the front doorbell rang and he admitted a woman in labor. To the gray-haired general practitioner the woman was a friend, like all his patients, but she was also a multipara, a female who had borne children before, and under the circumstances he knew that she could give birth on short notice. As a general rule Dr. Mills accompanied his multiparas to the Martha's Vineyard Hospital, six miles away in Oak Bluffs, and stayed with them until delivery, but the woman was in an early stage and he thought he would have time to eat breakfast and take care of the few patients who would soon begin collecting in his office. The hospital was only a ten-minute drive, and Dr. Mills told the woman to check in and he would join her later.

By eight o'clock, the start of office hours, there were people waiting in the outer office of the little surgery that adjoined his house on Summer Street. He gave vitamin shots to a pair of fishermen who were heading out to sea for the day, and a flu shot to a "summer person." He treated two or three cases of sore, inflamed throats; it seemed to Dr. Mills that he had looked at a thousand such throats over the summer. He gave a man a shot for severe ivy poisoning, and prescribed a healing salve.

By 9 A.M. the secretary-receptionist, a native Vineyarder named Mrs. Thomas Teller, had arrived for the day and called the doctor aside. "Don't be surprised if you get a call to go over to Chappy," she said. "I understand there's been a drowning over there." Dr. Mills had smiled knowingly behind his hand. He was technically an off-islander himself, with only thirty-four years' longevity in the place, and he could never hope to understand the islanders' system of instant news-gathering. He was tempted to ask, "When did you find out, Estey, before or *after* the drowning?" But he did not want to sound sarcastic, and anyway he was grateful for the tip. If he was called to examine a body at Chappaquiddick, he would have to do some fancy juggling of his schedule. "I hope you're wrong," he told Mrs. Teller. "I just sent Betty Haynes to the hospital."

"I don't think I'm wrong, Doctor," the woman said pleasantly. "I know for sure there's a fatal of some kind over there."

A few minutes later the telephone had rung and Central Communications had advised Dr. Mills in his capacity as associate medical examiner that he was needed at the Dike Bridge. Quickly he called the hospital and learned that his patient was still in the early stages of labor. "I don't know, Estey," he said to his secretary. "I hate to go over to Chappy at a time like this. I should be with Betty." He made another call and double-checked that a resident was on duty at the hospital. "Well," he said to Mrs. Teller, "maybe there's time for me just to run over to Chappy and back. If Betty should precipitate, she'll be in good hands." He had driven two blocks to the ferry, and there he had run into the undertakers, en route to the same place.

The morning was damp and overcast, and Dr. Mills wondered what would be waiting for him at the Dike Bridge. As associate medical examiner, he was seldom called to a fatal, and almost never to the remote areas of Chappaquiddick. The only other time he remembered going to the dike had been to validate the death of a man named Kent Avery, who had walked out to the beach, downed a jarful of sleeping pills, affixed a sunshade to his forehead, and studied a book from the Edgartown Public Library until his death. It had not been a pleasant sight. The corpse had lain in the dunes for twenty-four hours, and Dr. Mills had been puzzled by the fresh cuts all over it until he heard a strident sound and looked up to see a flock of herring gulls wheeling overhead. Even now, seven or eight years later, the thought sent shivers through him.

"Looks like quite a few people down there," Gene Frieh was saying as the Buick topped a slight rise and came into sight of the bridge, a few hundred yards ahead.

Dr. Mills peered into the morning haze and made out at least two rotating cartop lights, one red and one blue. "Yes," he

said. "I think I see the police cruiser and the fire chief's car."
As they drove closer the doctor could see that the blue Edgartown police cruiser had been parked just on the far side of the
bridge, where it had the effect of blocking off the view of the
road to the beach. Eight or ten spectators stood about, and the
wrecker and the fire chief's car were parked to one side. Several
rowboats poked around the edges of Poucha Pond, as though
searching for something, and a scuba diver with a tank on his
back stood like a creature from space. To the doctor, there was
a dream-like quality to the scene; the faces were expressionless
and pallid through the bluish haze, and everything seemed to be
in slow motion.

Frieh parked the service wagon, and the three men stepped
out into the warm, salty air and began clomping across the
bridge, picking their way among bystanders. When they reached
the high point in the middle, Dr. Mills looked over the side and
saw four tires and the underpart of an automobile in the water.
He stopped momentarily for a better look and then hurried toward the other side, where he could see a small group of firemen and policemen engaged in conversation. As he walked
through the spectators, the doctor spotted the unmistakable
six-foot-four-inch frame of his friend Jim Arena approaching
from the other direction. Arena seemed totally immersed in his
own thoughts, his face pale and his hands nervously adjusting
his plaid bathing trunks and soaking T-shirt, and Dr. Mills
passed him without speaking.

To Jim Arena, the news that Senator Edward M. Kennedy
was standing around the ferry shack on the Chappaquiddick
side had come as a mild shock, and he was finding himself hard
pressed to understand a sequence of events that was fast becoming illogical. He had held the dead girl in his arms and felt the
rigor mortis himself, and that meant that she had been dead for
at least several hours, and possibly for as long as the whole
night. There was no question that the car was the senator's, but
no accident report had been filed, at least as of 8:20 A.M., when
Arena had left the station, and now Kennedy was hanging

around the Chappy ferryhouse. "Mrs. Malm!" Arena called out. "May I use your phone?" The younger Sylvia Malm walked with Arena as he crossed back over the bridge and ran the gauntlet set up by the family's two watchdogs. Inside the tiny house, he dialed 627–4343, the Edgartown police headquarters number. Later he recalled the conversation. "Carmen," he said, "listen, send somebody down to the ferry and see if Ted Kennedy's there, will you?"

"He's in the station right now," the policewoman said. "He wants to talk to you."

"Oh, okay, good," Arena said, surprised once again, but also relieved. "Put him on the phone."

A deeper voice said, "Hello?"

"Hello, Senator," Arena said. "Gee, I'm sorry, but I guess there's been another tragedy. Your car's been involved in an accident over here and there's a girl, you know—a girl died in the accident."

"I know," Kennedy said.

"Do you know whether there were any other passengers in the car?"

"Yes, there were."

Arena shuddered. "Well, do you think they might still be in the water?"

"Well, no," Kennedy said. "Say, could I see you?"

"Sure," Arena said. "Over here? Or would you like me to go over there?"

"Over here if you don't mind," Kennedy said.

"I'll be right there," the chief said, and hung up the phone. He looked at a clock and saw that it was a few minutes past ten. He thanked Sylvia Malm and hurried outside to look for a ride to Edgartown. He did not want to take the police cruiser, parked across the wooden bridge, because the body was in the back of it and the radio was tuned to Communications. He called to the vacationing surgeon standing alongside his Jeep at the bridge, "Dr. Self, how about giving me a lift to Edgartown?"

"Certainly," the doctor said. "Get in."

"I've got to get back in a hurry," Arena said. He was pondering Kennedy's words, and he was having trouble deciphering their meaning. He thought that perhaps some other member of the family might have been driving the sedan, maybe one of Ethel Kennedy's older sons, Robert Jr. or Joseph III, out on a date in his uncle's car. Or maybe someone else in the clan, a close friend or another relative, had been at the wheel. Obviously it had not been Ted, safe and sound back at headquarters—at least the idea never occurred to Arena as he prepared to return.

A Pontiac station wagon drove up and Arena recognized the familiar face of Special Officer Christopher Look and a few members of his family. Look jumped out and said, "What the hell's going on, Jim?"

"A car went in the water," Arena said, gesturing toward the uptide side of the bridge, where two wheels had come plainly into sight and two others were visible below the surface.

"I saw a car last night," Look said. "A man was driving. I hope to God that isn't the car I saw, because I think I hurried it a little, down the road."

"Well, I just had a call from the station, Huck," Arena said. "The owner of the car's over there waiting for me."

"Anything I can do to help?"

"Yeh," Arena said. "This is a bad accident. Stick around and help handle the traffic, will you? See what you can do." He sped away with Dr. Self.

Edgartown policewoman Carmen Salvador, crisply efficient and blooded in police department matters, had been on the telephone all morning long, relaying calls from the Communications Center and dispatching officers and trying to maintain the logbook in front of her, when to her shock and surprise she looked up from her large desk and saw the husky form of Senator Edward M. Kennedy looking down on her. "Hello," he said. "How are you?" Before she could answer, he asked, "Could I use your phone?"

"Sure," the policewoman answered. "You can use the

chief's." She stepped from around her desk and ushered Kennedy into the tiny adjoining office. She thought briefly about asking him what was going on, but then she realized that it might seem presumptuous. "There," she said, motioning to the wall phone that hung just behind Arena's littered desk. "Use that."

Just as she returned to the outer office, a dark-haired man entered and introduced himself haltingly as Paul Markham. He seemed to be almost out of breath, and Carmen could hardly understand him as he asked to use the phone on her desk. She nodded her head, and the man thanked her politely and began dialing the operator, while the policewoman sat back in her chair and tried to figure out the sudden demand for the station's telephone facilities.

Carmen Salvador was not entirely out of the picture, but, like her boss on Chappaquiddick, she had immense blanks in her knowledge of the situation. When Arena had bolted out of the office at 8:20 to check on the immersed car at the Dike Bridge, Carmen had switched on a pocket-size portable receiver that Arena had recently purchased. It had not answered the department's crying need for a two-way radio system, but if the antenna was pulled all the way out and situated at exactly the right angle and the volume was turned on fully, one could sometimes intercept portions of the messages that crackled back and forth between the Communications Center and the various radio-equipped cars on Martha's Vineyard. Carmen had had the miniature receiver going ever since Arena left, and slowly she had gained the information that a young woman was dead in the car at the Dike Bridge and that Senator Ted Kennedy was somehow connected with the case. Then there had been a telephone call from Communications, asking her to send an officer out to look for Kennedy and take him to the bridge. Carmen had barely made a note of the call when Kennedy walked in.

Now she tried to look busy as the senator and Markham tied up her only two means of telephone communication. A radio message started to crackle over the receiver, but she quickly shut it off. If Communications needed her badly enough, they could use the telephone, and if they could not get through, they could call someone else in the town offices and give them the message. She stole a glance at Markham, talking frenetically to the operator and apparently failing to reach his parties. He was tanned and healthy-looking, but like Kennedy he had about him an air of nervousness, of upset. He misdialed once and tried to dial again, and then he said to the policewoman, "Excuse me, would you mind giving the operator a couple of numbers for me?" Carmen tried about five numbers—one in New York, one in Pennsylvania, a few in Washington, D.C., and one in Massachusetts—and made contact on several of them. Markham spoke briefly and in low tones, and nothing that he said made sense to her.

From the inner office, Kennedy was speaking calmly but louder, a slight overtone of urgency in his baritone voice. It sounded as though he, too, was failing on most of his calls. Later Carmen recalled hearing snatches of conversation from the other room. "He's out sailing? When do you expect him? I see. . . . You say he just left the office? Well, where was he headed? . . . When will he be back? . . ." Then a few calls went through, and Carmen could tell that names and information were being exchanged. She heard Kennedy say, "Well, we'll have to notify her parents," and later, in a choked voice, "I have some sad news to tell you." Then he seemed to be talking to an aide, delivering explicit instructions on returning a body to the mainland, and after that he seemed to be relaying a message to his mother, recommending that she cancel a public appearance scheduled for later in the day. In the middle of the long sequence of calls, Markham had walked into the chief's office and pulled the door shut, and a few seconds later Arena himself had called and spoken briefly with Kennedy. A few minutes after that conversation ended, Kennedy's voice came loud and clear through the closed door. "Carmen!" he shouted. "Somebody wants to talk to you!" She picked up the phone and heard the voice of Special Officer Roy Meekins explaining that he was down at the foot of Main Street and he still was unable to find Kennedy.

Carmen told him to call off the search and go to the ferry landing to pick up the chief.

"The chief?" Meekins said.

"Yes," the policewoman told him. "The senator's here, and the chief's on his way over from Chappy to talk to him." Before she could put down the telephone, she heard a telltale click on the extension. Kennedy was dialing again.

Jim Arena jumped from Roy Meekins's car in front of the Edgartown town offices and dashed quickly inside, his mind whirling with apprehension. The prospect of a nose-to-nose confrontation with a United States Senator was not pleasant, although it would be nothing new. In his career, Arena had escorted such dignitaries as Presidents Kennedy and Johnson, Senators Hubert Humphrey and Leverett Saltonstall, and many another. He had been on the personal staff of two attorneys general, and he had carried the attaché cases of several Massachusetts governors. Once he had been shy and nervous around celebrities, but those days were gone. He was not going to fall over in a faint at the sight of Ted Kennedy. On the other hand, he would have felt better if his attire had conveyed more of the majesty of the law. In his bare feet and clammy swimming trunks, he felt slightly reduced in dignity.

Carmen was sitting alone at her desk when he entered the office; she nodded her head almost imperceptibly toward the closed door that led inside, and Arena stepped forward and pulled it open. Ted Kennedy was sitting at the chief's desk, talking on the telephone, and a man Arena recognized as Paul Markham, former United States attorney for Massachusetts, sat on the bench on the other side of the room. As Kennedy quickly hung up the phone, Arena stretched out his hand and said, "Hello, Senator. Jim Arena."

"Hi, Jim," Kennedy said, and shook hands. Markham walked out the door as though to give the two men privacy, and Arena took a good look at the senator he had not seen in several years. To the practiced eye of the chief, Kennedy looked clear-eyed and normal, although a bit down in the mouth, which seemed natural for the circumstances. Arena reconstructed the conversation later:

"I'm sorry about the accident," Arena said, still standing on the visitor's side of the desk.

"Yes, I know about it," Kennedy said. "I was the driver."

Arena tried to conceal his surprise. He blurted out, "Well, do you happen to know where Rosemary Keough comes from? I think we'd better notify her next of kin."

Kennedy began to move around from the chief's side of the desk, and as the two men hesitantly exchanged places, the senator said, "Well, it wasn't Rosemary Keough. It was Mary Jo Kopechne. I've already notified her parents."

Arena took his place behind his desk and pulled out a pencil. "Could you tell me how to spell that?" he said.

"I don't know," Kennedy said. "I only know how to pronounce it." He repeated the name and Arena jotted down "Mary Jo Copachini." He asked if there had been any other passengers in the car, and Kennedy said there had not.

"Well, what do we do next?" Kennedy asked, and Arena was relieved to see that the reasonably calm young man seated across from him appeared to be interested only in helping out, instead of trying to throw his weight around. "We've got to do what's right," Kennedy was saying, "because if we don't, we'll both be criticized for it."

"Well," Arena said, "as far as I can see it's a motor vehicle accident. The first thing we're gonna have to do is I'd like to know what happened. Maybe you could give me a statement?"

Kennedy paused. "Is it okay if I write it out?" he said.

"Sure, it's all right by me. But why don't I let you in the back office, so we'll be out of your way? I saw a reporter hanging around outside and the rest of them'll be along any minute. This way you'll have privacy, and anyway I have to go back to the scene. They're still hunting for bodies over there, and I have to go back and clean up the turmoil."

As the two men walked down the hall toward the town accountant's office in the rear, Kennedy said that he hoped the wrecker would not have to tow the car through the center of Edgartown. "The people will all be staring at it," he said. "They'll make a big thing out of it."

"I'm sorry, Senator, but I don't know what we can do about that," Arena said solicitously. "There was such a crowd forming out at the bridge that I told the wrecker to bring the car right back. They're probably on their way through town now."

Paul Markham had joined the procession, and Arena let the two men into the small office and discussed the accident briefly.

"Anything else I can do?" the chief said at last.

"No, thanks, that's fine," Kennedy said. "We'll be fine right here."

Arena shut the door noiselessly, looked at a clock, and saw that he had been gone from Chappaquiddick for thirty minutes. He headed back to quiet the turmoil.

"Hi, Doc," the young summertime officer said. "It's a girl. The body's in the cruiser. We'll take her out for you, Doc."

Donald Mills watched as a policeman and a fireman opened the back of the Edgartown police cruiser and lifted out a litter with a blue wool blanket on top of it. From all sides of him, he could hear murmured conversations: "I don't know, maybe about midnight. . . ." "Are there any more? . . ." "Pretty . . . blond . . . maybe twenty-two, twenty-three years old. . . ." He heard somebody ask, "Do you suppose there'll be more bodies?" And he heard old Tony Bettencourt answer, "There might could be some more. That time of the night, the tide was running out like a bullet. The bodies could be miles from here by now, out Cape Poge Bay, or even in the Sound."

Now the litter was placed on the seaward side of the police cruiser, providing a measure of privacy from the fifteen or twenty pairs of eyes that watched from the Dike Bridge and the other side. Scuba diver John Farrar came up as the doctor removed the blanket, and he said, "We took her out of the car in the water, Doc. We were too late."

"I see," Mills said softly. He looked down at the stiffened body of an attractive woman in her late twenties, fully clothed and neatly buttoned, dressed in black slacks, a white long-sleeved shirtwaist, and sandals. Her hair was upswept and slightly disheveled; there were three gold bracelets on her right wrist, and her color was a pale, chalky white.

"Golly!" he said to himself. "What a shame! This lovely young person. What an absolute shame!"

There was white foam about the woman's nose and mouth; Dr. Mills knew that the foam and the tiny web of blood at the corner of her nose were signs of death by drowning. The body lay on its back, and the arms were sticking almost straight upward; the doctor noticed that the hands were peculiarly cupped, almost in a claw-like position, as though they had been gripping something with a curved edge. He pulled the mouth open and saw a water level inside. He undid the buttons on the woman's blouse and laid it back, exposing a dressy blue brassiere, and percussed the chest lightly. With each tap of his fingers, water came from the mouth, and when Mills pressed hard on the rib cage the water spurted out both nose and mouth, washing away some of the foam. Whatever had happened in the car, he told himself, the girl had not been dead when she reached the bottom of Poucha Pond. She had stayed alive long enough to inhale water and die by drowning. She was *full* of water. "Why, she's the most drowned person I've ever seen!" he said aloud.

He looked and probed around the body and could find no visible signs of injury, marks or obvious lesions. The neck was white and unblemished. There were no apparent bruises on the face or upper body. The major bones were unbroken. Under the nails, there was a small amount of foreign matter, but the nails themselves were unbroken and nicely manicured, and Dr. Mills could see no significance to the debris. He ran his hands across the scalp; it was smooth and regular. The woman had not bumped herself in going off the bridge. He pulled down the slacks and observed that the woman had been wearing nothing underneath. The abdomen was flat. He pushed against the abdominal wall and noted that the uterus was normal, unenlarged. It was not impossible that the victim had been in the early months of pregnancy, but looking at her small white belly and feeling the uterus, Dr. Mills doubted it. As he tipped the body to examine the back for signs of injury, more water gushed forth, and one of the undertakers, standing alongside, said, "That probably came from her stomach."

"No, it didn't," Mills said. "I'm pressing on her chest. There's definitely water in the lungs." The rigidly extended arms made it difficult for him to turn the body completely over, so he tipped it first to one side and then the other, saw nothing unusual on the back, and returned the body to its prone position. "Death by drowning," he said to a young patrolman standing nearby. "Not a question about it." He saw old Tony Bettencourt, and to himself he said wryly, "They didn't need me on this one. Tony could have made the diagnosis!"

"What now?" Undertaker Eugene Frieh said.

"Well, I'm finished," Mills said, pulling the blue blanket over the body. "You can transfer her to the hearse."

The gray Buick was backed slowly across the bridge until it was within ten or twelve feet of the body, and the remains of the young woman were put inside in a large carrying bag. Mills turned to chat with the bystanders, many of whom he had treated in the past. "Say, who is this girl?" he said.

"Nobody knows for sure," one of the firemen said. "But she has something to do with Kennedy."

"Kennedy?"

"Senator Ted Kennedy. There's a search going on for him right now."

When Dr. Mills heard that there was a Kennedy connection in the case, he stiffened. He had never made a more routine or certain diagnosis, but now there were other considerations. Anything touching on the Kennedy family, pro or con, was potentially explosive, and one never knew whether the blast was going to come from the Kennedy backers or the Kennedy haters. For an instant he said to himself that a drowning death was a drowning death, and no political considerations could change that fact, but then he realized that certain decisions were not in his area of expertise. These included the matter of an autopsy for political purposes. "Gee," he said to Gene Frieh, "if there's any Kennedy connection here at all, this is too big for me to handle alone. I'll call the D.A.'s office and ask about an autopsy." He started to add, "Hold the embalming for a while, Gene," but he realized that such an instruction would be an insult to the undertaker's professional competence. Gene Frieh had been in the business for many years; he would know to hold the embalming.

The chief had headed back toward Chappaquiddick to "clean up," and Carmen Salvador was alone once more in the two-room police headquarters. The two frantic telephoners, Ted Kennedy and Paul Markham, were down the hall in the town accountant's empty office, and Carmen was not sure what they were doing there. The chief had left quickly and said nothing about the two men. She wondered what she was supposed to do if they calmly strolled out the door.

From the front door of the town office building, Carmen could hear the sounds of a crowd assembling outside, and once she peeped out to see what was going on. The inhabitants of the "drunk bench" across the street were firmly in place, enjoying their box-seat view of the extravaganza. In the crowd of fifteen or twenty people standing just outside the doors, Carmen recognized two or three newspaper reporters huddled together; she knew they were not making complimentary remarks about the Edgartown Police Department. Just before he left, Arena had politely but firmly ushered one of them, Bob Hyde of the New Bedford *Standard-Times,* out of the town offices and told him to stay out until further notice. Hyde and his fellow New Bedford correspondent, Harvey Ewing, must be wondering what had come over the chief; normally he invited them into his office and treated them like old friends. For her own part, Carmen *knew* what had come over Arena. The answer was Ted Kennedy, possessor of the magic name in Massachusetts. Where the Kennedys were involved, one stepped carefully.

Carmen reconstructed the subsequent scene and conversation later. She said she stepped back to her desk just in time to hear footsteps in the hall, and saw that Senator Edward M. Kennedy was taking a constitutional. After he had paced up and down the hall two or three times, he stepped into her office. In the few minutes since she had seen him last, he seemed to have become more nervous; to the policewoman, he looked like a man hopelessly trying to juggle a half-dozen thoughts at once, and coming to grips with none of them. "Do you think the people know?" he said.

Carmen tried to speak soothingly. "Well, they probably know *something,"* she said, "but maybe not the whole story." She laughed to herself. Who *did* know the whole story, except perhaps for the man in front of her?

"Are there many people outside?" Kennedy asked.

"Well, you know how a small town is," she said. "News travels fast."

Kennedy disappeared into the hall and returned almost immediately. He said nothing, but continued his pacing in front of the policewoman's desk, and Carmen began to get nervous. He seemed to be silently soliciting comfort, some friendly words, but she was ignorant of the protocol involved in calming a United States Senator. "I wouldn't worry about those people outside," she said finally. "In a small town when people hear something like this, that some celebrity's involved with the police, well, they come to take a look, that's all. I wouldn't worry about it."

Kennedy smiled weakly and went back into the hall. He returned several more times, and each time the compassionate policewoman gave him a few comforting words. He was a suffering fellow human being, and she felt it was the least she could do.

Back at the Dike Bridge, the wrecker operated by Jonathan Ahlbum proved to be too big and heavy to be moved into position on the narrow beach, but a jury rig was devised for pulling the damaged car from the water. A fully equipped Land Rover belonging to Dr. G. W. Sands, a Chappaquiddick summer resident, was driven down to the water's edge and its winch hooked to the left side of the rear axle of the submerged car. Then a cable was run from the wrecker, upon higher ground, to secure the Land Rover, and the winch was turned on. The car flipped over, and then the rear end came around toward the shore until the whole vehicle was parallel to the bridge. "Hold it!" Ahlbum shouted. "We don't want the tide to fetch it up in the pilings."

Tony Bettencourt, the lifelong expert on the waters of Poucha Pond, was consulted, and the old man said that the tide would be slack in less than an hour, at about 11:30 A.M. After a short wait, the power of the outgoing tide seemed to diminish, and the winch was put into action again. This time the car rolled smoothly and evenly across the bottom of the channel and up the bank on the west side. Even before the Oldsmobile sedan had come completely ashore, John Farrar was wading alongside studying the interior. When the car reached the strip of sand, Farrar opened one of the doors and went inside. He saw that there was glass all over the floor, indicating that the windows had blown inward on impact with the water. Of the six major windows, the one on the driver's side was wound down to within an inch or so of the bottom; the back window on the driver's side was up and intact; the rear window was undamaged; the two windows on the passenger's side were blown in, and the windshield was shattered but hanging on its safety layer.

Farrar saw that the door on the driver's side was locked; the headlight switch was in "on" position, the automatic gear shift was in "drive," and the ignition key was turned to "on." There was a hairbrush on the seat, but it was so old and battered that it appeared to be for pets instead of humans. A soaked copy of the *Boston Globe* for the previous day, Friday, July 18, 1969, lay on the driver's seat. The top headline announced: EARTH WORLD JOINS ASTRONAUTS IN FANTASTIC MOON SHIP VISIT, and a weather story promised that cool air was en route from Canada after a temperature climb into the nineties had produced Boston's hottest day of the year. Farrar opened the glove compartment and found a small package of facial tissues, an automobile registration for a 1967 Oldsmobile 88 sedan, made out to Edward M. Kennedy of 3 Charles River Square, Boston, and a few papers.

Ever since Huck Look had learned that a car was in the water below the Dike Bridge, he had been hoping that it would not turn out to be the car he had seen the night before. He did not want to be involved in any way, but if the cars proved to be the same, he would *have* to be involved. He suspected that the black car might have sped down the Dike Road in direct response to his own actions. He had not intended it that way; he had only been trying to help, but apparently the driver of the car had not waited to find out; at the sight of the bulky uniformed figure approaching, he had stepped on the gas. "Jesus," Huck said to himself as he paced back and forth on the bridge and waited for Ahlbum and the others to finish pulling the car out. "It could be partly my fault. Maybe the guy had an argument with his wife or something. Maybe he was driving *mad* in the first place. Then I come along. . . ." He rapped his forehead with the palm of his hand. "Damn! Maybe I should have gone down the road after them. Maybe I could have saved a life." Then he remembered the peculiar threesome on the School Road, dancing out on the center line but quickly returning to the shoulder at the first sign of approaching headlights. "I wonder if they had anything to do with it," he said to himself, but if there was a connection, it was not obvious to the troubled deputy.

Now Huck watched with grim fascination as the rear end of the overturned automobile was pulled around and the whole car began inching on its own wheels toward the bank. When the license plate came into sight, he whispered, "Holy Jesus!" and went over to Edgartown Patrolman Robert Bruguiere. "Gee, Bob," he said, "I saw that car last night."

"You did?" the summertime policeman said.

"Yes."

"Who was in it?"

"A man and a woman in the front seat and another person or some kind of object sticking up in the back."

"Well," Bruguiere said, "I'll tell the chief when he gets here."

A few minutes later, Jim Arena, still wearing the same outfit, drove up with Dr. Self, and Look and Bruguiere walked quickly to the doctor's Jeep. The patrolman said, "Chief, Huck says that's the car he saw last night."

"The one you said that a man was driving?" Arena demanded.

"That's right," the deputy sheriff said. "It was about quarter to one in the morning."

Arena emitted a soft exclamation and climbed out of the car. "Huck," he said, "do you know who the man was?"

"No," Look said, "I haven't the slightest idea."

"It was Ted Kennedy."

The deputy's first reaction was disbelief, but he knew Jim Arena well, and he could see that the chief was serious. "Holy Jesus," Look said facetiously. *"I didn't see a thing!"*

"Huck," the chief said, "how sure are you that this is the same car?"

"How sure am I?" Look repeated. "I'm positive. That's how sure I am."

Jim Arena did not want to spend a second longer than necessary back at the Dike Bridge. He summoned Fire Chief Antone Silva over and told him that there was no longer any need to sweep the pond and the lagoon; it was definite that no one else had died in the accident. He started to make his own search of the black Oldsmobile, but then he remembered that Ted Kennedy was preparing a statement at headquarters and he did not want to inconvenience the senator by making him wait. "Come on, Bob," he said to Bruguiere. "Let's go!" Bruguiere took the wheel and backed the blue police cruiser over the bridge, and the two policemen returned to Edgartown.

When Arena entered the room where he had left Kennedy and Markham, he saw that the Senator was pacing and Markham was seated at a desk, writing in longhand. "How's it going?" Arena asked.

"Coming along," Markham said.

Arena checked into his office, and a few minutes later Markham walked down the hall and sat on the wooden bench across from Carmen Salvador. He made a few last-second adjustments to the report, which he handed to the chief. "Maybe we ought to have it typed," Markham said, glancing toward the police-woman.

"I'll be glad to try," Carmen said, "but these phones are keeping me hopping."

"Don't you bother," Arena said. "I'll type it." He peeled off his damp T-shirt, exposing a mass of curly black hair, and sat down at the typewriter. The handwriting was legible and neat, but Arena paused when he saw that the victim was not identi-fied. "Why the blank?" he said to Markham.

"We're not sure of the spelling," Markham said. "We can fill it in later."

When Arena had finished typing the statement and a carbon copy, he yanked them from the typewriter and read to himself:

On July 18, 1969, at approximately 11:15 P.M., on Chappaquid-dick Island, Martha's Vineyard, I was driving my car on Main Street on my way to get the ferry back to Edgartown. I was unfa-miliar with the road and turned onto Dike Road instead of bearing left on Main Street. After proceeding for approximately a half mile on Dike Road I descended a hill and came upon a narrow bridge. The car went off the side of the bridge. There was one passenger in the car with me, Miss   , a former secretary of my brother Robert Kennedy. The car turned over and sank into the water and landed with the roof resting on the bottom. I attempted to open the door and window of the car but have no recollection of how I got out of the car. I came to the surface and then repeatedly dove down to the car in an attempt to see if the passenger was still in the car. I was unsuccessful in the attempt.

I was exhausted and in a state of shock. I recall walking back to where my friends were eating. There was a car parked in front of the cottage and I climbed into the back seat. I then asked for some-one to bring me back to Edgartown. I remember walking around for a period of time and then going back to my hotel room. When I fully realized what happened this morning, I immediately contacted the police.

Arena took the original down the hall and handed it to Ken-nedy. "This is the statement, Senator," he said. "Is it okay?"

Kennedy said, "Wait a minute," scanned the paper, and said, "Okay."

Walter E. Steele, a skinny forty-three-year-old Boston lawyer with a Humphrey Bogart lisp and manner, looked out the window of his Edgartown fishing "chalet" and called to his wife, "Hell of a day for a barbecue. It's cloudy and overcast. Well, maybe it'll cool down a little." The Steeles were going to leave their Martha's Vineyard *pied-à-terre* to pay a social call on the mainland, but first they had to go downtown to the police station. Six weeks earlier, the Dukes County authorities had examined Walter Steele's record of fourteen years as a top assistant in the Boston district attorney's office and had hired him as "special prosecutor" at five thousand a year. At the time, Steele had told his wife, "In the summer it means court maybe two days a week maximum, but we're in Edgartown in the summer anyway. In winter it means going to court once a week or maybe even less." There were other reasons why Walter Steele cherished his new part-time job. Since leaving the Boston D.A.'s office, he had been teaching criminal prosecution at Boston University and running a private practice in Boston, but his main interest in life—the one that surpassed every other interest except his wife and four children and the Boston Bruins—was surf fishing. Standing in swirling, cold, salt water at all hours of the day and night, rigging smelly eels and extracting no. 2 hooks from his ears and his fingers, the owl-eyed prosecutor was a man at peace with everything except bluefish and striped bass. Any excuse that took him to Martha's Vineyard, where the surf fishing was justifiably famous, would suffice, and if there was a five-thousand-dollar stipend attached to it, so much the better. As he yanked on his clothes in the little cabin five miles up the sound from the Edgartown courthouse, he looked back on his new job with satisfaction. Here it was the heart of the summer, the time when his work on Martha's Vineyard should have been at a peak, and he had been in court only four times in six weeks, prosecuting such matters as a skinny-dipping party at Oak Bluffs, a fisherman with short lobsters, a scalloper with underage clams, and a case of disorderly conduct. Of course, he had spent several hours working on the whaling-log case with Jim Arena, but otherwise his summer had been a pleasant saga of blues, stripers and mackerel, interspersed with an occasional beer.

Shortly after 11 A.M., the Steeles piled into their creaky red Land Rover and headed for Main Street. "Don't worry," Steele said to his wife from behind his brown-rimmed spectacles, "I only have to see the chief for a few minutes, and then we'll be off."

He parked in the lot behind the Dukes County courthouse and rushed across the street and into the station, elbowing his way through a crowd, and before the doors had closed behind him he realized that something extraordinary was going on. Whatever was happening, it was not a case of short lobsters or skinny-dipping. To begin with, the usually immaculate Jim Arena was dashing up and down the log corridor in bare feet and swimming trunks. On one of the trips, Steele stepped in front of the chief and said, "What the hell is this, an early-morning swim?" The preoccupied Arena brushed by as though he had not even seen the prosecutor. Then he stopped and pointed to the closed door of his office. "Senator Kennedy's in there," he said.

"You don't mean Senator Edward M. Kennedy, Democrat of Massachusetts?" Steele asked, jokingly.

"Listen," Arena said in his most businesslike tone, "do you know him?"

"Sure, I know him," Steele said. "I used to work with the guy in the Suffolk County D.A.'s office."

"Well, listen, Walter, stick around for a while, I might need you."

"What for?" Steele asked. "What the hell's going on?" But Arena opened the door and ducked inside without another word.

Steele looked up and down the empty corridor and tapped his foot. He had not been a crack Boston prosecutor for fourteen years without learning a few of the practicalities of the business. He considered how Arena had acted, and he considered the conspicuously closed doors leading to the police station, and he told himself that a small beef was at this very moment being squared, being "cooled and broomed," as the procedure would have been described back in the Boston courthouse. Probably somebody in Kennedy's party had committed a minor indiscretion, sassing a cop or getting drunk in public or making a pass at a meter maid. No police chief liked to make arrests in such cases, and no prosecutor liked to prosecute such cases; they were not even as important as short lobsters, least of all in a resort at the height of the season when certain behavioral lapses were to be expected. Probably the chief was inside trying to cool down an annoyed cop, and Ted Kennedy was smoothing things over, and before long the door would open and several smiling faces would emerge and the case would be closed.

Walter Steele had only one objection. He wanted to get inside and join the party. It annoyed him that he had been shunted aside. If there was a small beef, he said to himself, who was better qualified to "cool it and broom it"? And could it hurt his future career to have the eminent senator, Edward Moore Kennedy, ever so slightly indebted to Walter Edward Steele, attorney-at-law? He thought not. But for the life of him he could not figure a way to intrude his own skills into the situation. The doors were glaringly closed, and even if he was the Vineyard's special prosecutor, he had no intention of breaking them down.

Just then he saw the friendly face and stark crewcut of his steady fishing companion, District Court Clerk Thomas Teller, at the other end of the corridor. The two men came together and Teller said, "Jesus, Walter, Kennedy's in the jackpot."

Steele recognized the criminalistic jargon—it meant that Kennedy was in serious trouble—but it did not make sense to him. "I heard that Kennedy was driving a car that was involved in a bad accident," Teller went on. "He's *really* in trouble."

"No, no, Tommy," Steele said to his friend. "That's a lot of crap. He wasn't driving the car, I'm sure of that. Things just don't happen that way. It must have been one of his flunkies."

"I heard different," Teller said.

"Oh, Tommy, cut it out!" Steele said. "Kennedy's in there with the chief right now, for Christ's sake. It was probably somebody in his party."

Teller said that he had to go across the street to the courthouse, and disappeared out the front door into the crowd. Steele stepped into the outer office of the police station, where Carmen Salvador sat at a big desk, and as he did so, he saw the side door to the chief's private office swing open and Ted Kennedy sitting behind Arena's desk making a phone call. Reflexively, Steele waved at his nodding acquaintance from the past, and to his surprise Kennedy waved back with his free hand. Steele was pleased. Even though he was a Democrat, he was not the type who swooned in the presence of the Kennedys, particularly in the presence of a Kennedy who had lounged around the D.A.'s office for more than a year while others picked up his case load, but it was always nice to be recognized by a celebrity. He started to step inside, now that he had been recognized by the party of the first part, but before he could cross the threshold the door had been slammed shut once again by a nervous-looking Jim Arena. "What the hell's going on here?" Steele said to himself, and as he turned to discuss the mystery with Carmen, he saw a tall, good-looking man slumped on the bench across from her desk. The man looked up through reddened eyes and said, "Hello, Walter."

Steele pushed his hand through the thinning wisps of brown hair that remained on his head, and did a flash inventory of his circle of friendship. The answer came to him just as he was sticking his hand out to return the morose greeting; he was in the presence of the Honorable Paul Markham, former U.S. attorney for Massachusetts and a longtime friend of the Kennedys. "Paul!" Steele said with enthusiasm that belied his momentary confusion. "How've you been?"

Arena stepped into the office and said, "Oh, Mr. Markham, I'd like you to meet our county prosecutor, Walter Steele." The two men continued to shake hands like old pals, and in the confusion it occurred to Steele that Markham had not even heard the chief's words, and probably would not have comprehended them if he had. Steele was the only county prosecutor in Massachusetts; there were city and town prosecutors, but the job of county prosecutor was new and unique. It also occurred to Steele that the former U.S. attorney did not seem to be at his most alert. As soon as the friendly greeting wore off, Markham returned to a hangdog expression and began wringing his hands nervously. Like the good prosecutor that he was, Steele did not want to jump to conclusions, but he would have been willing to bet that Markham had had very little sleep.

As Steele recalled the incident later, Markham said peremptorily, "Say, I'm going over to the Shiretown Inn to get my clothes," and just as peremptorily, Walter said, "I'll come with you and give you a hand." The two men ducked out a side door, circled the growing crowd, and headed down Main Street to the inn. The prosecutor waited for Markham to speak, and nothing was said for a few minutes. Then Markham began muttering, and Steele leaned closer and heard his companion saying, "Oh, my God! Oh, my God!" and then, "The poor guy! It's terrible. She's dead! She's dead!"

Markham looked to be on the verge of tears, and Steele did not know how to comfort him. He listened as Markham raised his voice a little. "You know, the senator almost drowned himself," he said. *"He almost drowned himself!"*

"Oh?" Steele said.

"Yes, he did," Markham went on. "Jesus, it's awful. The poor guy! He almost went. The girl was drowned." Over and over he kept repeating the same phrases, and Walter Steele kept listening and saying nothing, until after about five minutes they reached the front entrance of the inn.

"Come on up," Markham said, and led Steele to a short flight of stairs that took them up to a second-story balcony opening off several rooms. Markham walked straight ahead and entered a room with two single beds. Still wringing his hands and appearing close to tears, the tall lawyer began to pick things up and throw them into a tired old zippered bag. Steele noticed that the two beds were neatly made, but otherwise the room appeared to be a typical weekend bachelor's haunt, with socks and shoes and other articles of apparel strewn about. Trying to help, he picked up a pair of large yachting sneakers that lay damp and dirty between the beds.

"What about these sneakers?" he asked Markham. "Do you want these?"

"Yeh," Markham said, motioning toward the bag. "Throw them in."

Steele picked up a heavy comb that was eight or nine inches long and had teeth about two inches deep. "Want this?"

Markham looked across the room. "No," he said.

When the satchel was just about full, the door opened and a husky man who appeared to be in his late twenties entered the room in tennis shoes and shorts. "Can I help?" he asked, and Markham answered, "No, thanks."

The young man appeared to be composed and sober, but aware that something was going on. He had thick dark hair, and Steele told himself that the young man looked enough like the Kennedys to be a Kennedy himself.

"How's everything going?" the newcomer asked.

"Fine, fine," Markham muttered as he stuffed a pair of socks into the bag.

"Is there anything I can do?" the young man asked.

"No, no," Markham said. "Thanks anyway."

"I'm sorry," the young man said, and slipped out of the room.

Markham spoke in a slow stream of consciousness as the two companions left the inn and headed down the driveway to return to the police station, and by the time they had retraced their steps to the Edgartown town offices, the prosecutor had become aware that Ted Kennedy had driven off the Dike Bridge in his car, that a young woman was dead, that Kennedy had almost drowned, and that nine hours had gone by before the accident had been reported. When it appeared that Markham was going to say nothing more, Steele said, "Jesus Christ, Paul, nine hours! This is gonna be a tough one. I feel sorry for

the senator, but Paul, nine hours is a long time." He was thinking that something was amiss, but based on Markham's skimpy
narrative, he was not sure what it was.

By the time the pair came abreast of the crowd in front of
the building, Markham had settled down, and for a brief few
seconds the two men stopped and faced each other. "Paul,"
Steele said gently, "your problem is not with me, and it's not
with the chief. We have that district attorney in New Bedford
to think about. You know who the D.A. is down here." Edmund Dinis, the flamboyant district attorney of the area, had a
widespread reputation for unpredictability. "You know, they
say he's kind of an intractable guy," Steele told Markham.

"Oh, my God," Markham said. He pressed his hands together again, and then the two men stepped inside.

Robert "Bobby" Carroll, Edgartown's only Democratic se-
lectman, a real estate agent and a major owner of various business establishments like the Harbor View Hotel and the Seafood Shanty, was driving down Main Street shortly before noon
when a man stepped off the sidewalk almost in front of his car.
"Hey!" Carroll shouted, and then he recognized Joseph Gargan,
a lawyer and Kennedy confidant from Hyannis Port. The pug-
nacious little Carroll had campaigned for various Kennedys
going all the way back to JFK's Senate days; he reckoned that
he knew Gargan and Gargan's cousin, Senator Edward Kennedy, fairly well, certainly better than anyone else in the little
town, and he was slightly miffed at both of them. He had heard
earlier that Kennedy and his entourage were around, and that
they were staying at the Shiretown and had rented another
piece of property somewhere in the vicinity, and he wondered
how they had managed to avoid him so completely in the process. Not that he needed the business; the Harbor View was
full, and most of the cottages on his rental list would be occupied for the rest of the summer. But he *knew* the Kennedys,
and for the life of him, he could not understand why they had
come to Edgartown and snubbed the area's single most prominent Democrat. With those thoughts in his mind, Carroll did

not feel particularly warm toward Joseph Gargan, and he called out the window of his car in a half-serious, half-sarcastic manner, "Look out, for Christ's sake! I don't want to run over any big shots this morning!"

To Carroll's surprise, Gargan did not acknowledge the remark. He continued rushing up the street toward the police station, while another Kennedy equerry, Jack Crimmins, struggled to catch up.

"Well, how do you like that?" Bob Carroll said to his companion. "Maybe I'd better check my bath soap!"

He parked the car near his real estate office on Kelley Street, and as he stepped out a female acquaintance walked up and began talking rapidly. "Did you hear about your friend Teddy Kennedy's secretary?" she said. "She went off the bridge in his car and drowned over at Chappy and he's at the police station."

Now Carroll realized why Joe Gargan had been so distracted, and he said to himself, "Well, you'd think he'd have enough sense to say to me, 'Bob, we're in trouble,' and see how I could help out." He rushed inside and dialed the Police Department number. "Jim?" he said. "I understand somebody went off a bridge in Ted Kennedy's car."

"Yeh," Arena said in a hushed voice. "But the worst thing is that Teddy was driving."

"Oh, Jesus," Carroll said. "Well, if there's anything I can do to help, let me know."

Not long afterward, the telephone rang and Carroll recognized Arena's voice again. "Bob, you *can* help," the chief was saying. "Teddy wants to get to Hyannis as quick as he can, and he's trying to charter a plane. Can you fly him over?"

"Sure," Carroll said. "Who all's going?"

"Well, I'm not sure. There's the senator and Paul Markham. Joe Gargan just walked in a little while ago, and Jack Crimmins is hanging around in the hall. So there may be four, there may be one, I don't know. How many places does your plane have?"

"Six," Carroll said. "It's a Piper Comanche. No problem."

Arena paused. "Let's see," he said. "Teddy wants to drop by

the Shiretown to pick up some stuff. We're gonna sneak him out the back door to avoid the press and the crowd, and one of the guys from the Motor Vehicles Registry is gonna use his own car to drive them around. So by the time you get out to the airport and get the plane warmed up and everything, they should be there."

"Right," Carroll said. He made a call to Martha's Vineyard Airport to check on the weather, found that there was an overcast but generally adequate visibility, and left.

Kennedy and a man Carroll did not recognize met him at the airport, and as they walked out to Carroll's white, black and gold airplane, Kennedy said, "Bob, I'd like you to meet Paul Markham." They shook hands, and Carroll noticed that Markham appeared to be much the more upset of the two men. The conversation was desultory, and Markham contributed not a word to it.

As they took their seats in the plane, Markham in the back and Kennedy in the copilot's place, Carroll said, "Gee, Ted, I think the first time I ever met you was when you came over to the island in this same kind of plane, right?"

"Yes," Kennedy said in a flat monotone. "That's right."

Carroll could see that both men were deeply preoccupied, and he abandoned any further effort at conversation. "It's like somebody's mother died," he said to himself. "What's the use of trying?"

The wind was from the east, and he took off on runway six and landed ten minutes later at the same numbered runway at Hyannis, flying on a straight course northeast all the way. He taxied the Comanche up to the apron, and as the two men stepped out, Carroll said, "Look, if there's anything I can do for you over on the Vineyard, let me know."

"Thanks, Bob," Kennedy said. "I appreciate your help." The two men got into a waiting car, waved once, and drove away.

A party of young women boarded the *On Time* on the Chappaquiddick side and huddled together along the rail for the short trip to Edgartown. Several of them were red-eyed, as though they had been crying, and one of them was sobbing softly to herself. On the Edgartown side, the girls got into a cab and told the driver to take them to the Katama Shores Motor Inn, a reconverted naval barracks two miles out of town. As the party drove along the marshes and salt flats toward the remote motel, the driver tried to make small talk, but there was no return comment from the rear, and when one of the girls said impatiently, "Yeh, yeh, yeh," he shut up. The girls were nicely dressed, and he figured they were probably rich snobs.

For the second straight day, Manuel DeFrates waited at the yacht club deck for his half-day charter, but this time the girls did not arrive. Instead, a man who introduced himself as Joseph Gargan drove up in a car with another man and paid the old skipper fifty dollars in cash. "Say, what's going on over at Chappy?" DeFrates asked as he stuffed the bills into his wallet. Gargan looked at him blankly, said nothing, and stepped back into the car. DeFrates started to repeat the question, but then he realized that the man must have heard. He watched as the two companions pulled out of the parking lot and headed up Main Street as though they were in a rush.

Later Saturday afternoon, the real estate agent who had rented the Lawrence cottage to the Kennedy party answered his phone and heard a man who identified himself as Joseph Gargan explain that everyone had checked out and the place was vacant. When the agent went across to Chappaquiddick for an inspection, he found some leftover snacks in the refrigerator, but except for small amounts of sand on the floor the cottage was immaculate. Something puzzled the agent as he went from room to room. The cottage had been occupied for two or three full days, but there was not the slightest indication that anyone had taken a drink. All the highball and cocktail glasses were neatly in place, and there were no empty bottles in the trash cans. He scratched his head. He had not thought of the Kennedys as drunks, but he had not thought of them as teetotalers either.

When Dr. Donald R. Mills had left the hectic life of his native Providence, Rhode Island, it had not been for the sole purpose of re-creating that same hectic life on the island of Martha's Vineyard. He recognized that somewhere beneath his placid approach to life there was a threshold of volatility, and he tried to manage his affairs in such a fashion that the threshold was not reached. Of course, there were times when the pressures built up and he found himself approaching a state of nerves, just like the big city M.D.'s back on the mainland. At such times, he sat at his desk, smoked a few Pall Malls in chained succession, gazed fondly on the genuine antique Flügelhorn and other horns and ship models and maritime paintings and family photographs and the facsimile of an original Wagnerian script that decorated his office, and relaxed. Sometimes, he walked around the corner to St. Andrew's Episcopal Church, where he had carte blanche to sit at the organ and play for all he was worth. These were the gentle physician's tranquilizers, and they never failed him.

On this particular Saturday, the pressures were piling up, and Dr. Mills was working to relieve them. When he had returned to his office from the Dike Bridge, his main preoccupation had been his multipara, Betty Haynes, and he had called Martha's Vineyard Hospital to see how she was. He was told that the pains were more frequent, but that the final stage had not been reached. "Tell her I'll be over soon," he said. Then he turned to the problem of Edward M. Kennedy.

If there was a single trait that was firmly established in Dr. Mills's personality, it was his cautiousness, which he did not regard as a passive inability to make decisions but rather a healthy awareness that there were plenty of matters that others knew more about. This included the subject of forensic medicine and the subject of politics. As associate medical examiner in the Edgartown area, the sixty-three-year-old general practitioner handled perhaps six public cases a year. He had perused the *Handbook for Massachusetts Medical Examiners* many times, but since the public medical examinations were such a minute part of his total case load, he had paid more attention to other technical subjects, such as obstetrics and gynecology. Now, rather than pull out the handbook and spend half a day looking for the applicable portions, he decided simply to leave the question of an autopsy up to the experts. "If it were only a medical matter," he told his secretary-receptionist, Estey Teller, Tom Teller's wife and Huck Look's sister, "I'd close the case right now. But whenever the Kennedys are involved, you have to walk on eggs. Get me the state police barracks at Oak Bluffs, will you?" This was the routine method for communicating messages to the district attorney's office across the channel in New Bedford.

"Hello," Dr. Mills said. "There's a traffic fatality over on Chappaquiddick and I'd like you to notify the district attorney about it."

"Yes, sir," a trooper replied. "What else can we do for you? Do you need any help?"

"No, no," Dr. Mills said. "Everything's taken care of. Just one thing. The body that was found in the car—I think it might be one of the Kennedy crowd."

"Okay."

"And I'd like you to call Mr. Dinis's office and find out whether they want an autopsy done. I'm completely satisfied myself that it was a death by drowning, but I thought I should notify the D.A.'s office because of the political repercussions. Do you understand?"

"I think so, Doctor," the trooper said.

"Let me repeat just to make sure," the physician said, and explained the situation all over again. ". . . And please make the point quite clearly," he said at the end, "that the name Kennedy is mixed up in this, because this is more than I want to carry alone."

"You'll hear back from us," the trooper said.

"I've got to go and see another patient," the doctor said, "but I'll leave the number with my office."

Now only one task lay between Mills and his multipara. A woman who lived nearby had called to report persistent bleeding. Dr. Mills had treated her earlier for the same problem, and he drove to the woman's house to provide solace and medication. He had hardly walked in the front door when the telephone rang; another state trooper was on the line with a message. "Doc," the officer said, "we finally reached Lieutenant Killen—he's the D.A.'s chief investigator—and he said that if you're satisfied that the cause of death is drowning and there's no evidence of foul play, they don't want an autopsy. As far as they're concerned, they don't need an autopsy." Dr. Mills was relieved, because there was still a baby to be delivered and he would have had to be present at an autopsy on the body. "By the way," the trooper went on, "Lieutenant Killen suggested that we take a routine blood sample and send it to the state labs for testing, and he said if you have any questions, you can reach him at home."

"Fine," the doctor said. "I'll take care of it." He dialed the Martha's Vineyard Funeral Home and asked to speak to Eugene Frieh. "Gene?" he said. "There'll be no autopsy. You can go ahead and embalm. But first take a blood sample for the state lab, will you? . . . Fine. I'm glad it's all over with."

He treated the bleeding case, drove to Martha's Vineyard Hospital, called on a few bedridden patients, and delivered a fine baby boy, without complications, early in the afternoon. Now he was looking forward to a light lunch, a few minutes of rest, and a return to routine. Maybe he would even have time to work out on the organ.

Jim Arena and Walter Steele had been considering some of the ramifications of the "Mary Joe Copachini" case when the telephone rang and Carmen Salvador announced that Lieutenant George Killen of the district attorney's office was on the line. The two men knew Killen mostly by reputation; he was a balding, taciturn Boston Irishman who dressed sharply and

looked as though he had just stepped out of a crime movie from
the mid-1930's. They knew little about Killen's skills in criminal investigation, but they both remembered that District Attorney Edmund Dinis, a man who seldom dealt in understatement,
had once described his number one cop as "the best detective
investigator in the country." Later, Arena remembered the short
conversation:

"Hello, George," the friendly police chief said. "What can I
do for you?"

"Jim, on that accident case," Killen said, "the doctor called
and he's a little bit worried about whether we should have an
autopsy or not. What do you think?"

"Gee, I don't know, George," Arena said. "You know, it's
up to the doctor, and he says it was a drowning. Whatever he
wants to do is okay with me. I looked at the girl and I couldn't
see anything else wrong with her. Looks like a drowning all the
way. I don't see why we'd need an autopsy."

"Okay," Killen said. "Then there's no problem."

"Fine," Arena said. "I'm cleaning up things at my end. You
know, the Kennedy involvement and all."

"Yeh," the Boston-accented voice came across the line.
"Well, you're the guy who can handle it. I feel sorry for you.
You've got a real tiger by the tail there. Lots of luck!"

"Thanks," Arena said. "But everything's coming along
okay."

When the conversation was over, the chief looked at the
signed statement from Kennedy again. Three or four representatives of the press, including the *New York Times* and *Newsweek* and the local newspapers, had been banging on the outside door demanding to be briefed on the case, but Arena had
promised Markham and Kennedy not to release the statement
until he received a clearance from them, and in the meantime
he was keeping the reporters at bay. It bothered him that the
statement contained a blank for the girl's name, and then he remembered Rosemary Keough's water-soaked purse and the two
keys to rooms at the Katama Shores Motor Inn. He picked up
the telephone, dialed 627–4747, and asked to speak to Rose-

mary Keough. "This is Chief Arena," he said when a female voice came on the line. "I wanted to let you know that we have your pocketbook here at the station. I'd also like to know if you can tell me how to spell Mary Jo's last name."

Arena heard a voice in the background ask "Who is it?" and the girl's muffled answer, "The police." Another voice asked, "What do they want?" and the girl's voice said, "They want to know how to spell Mary Jo's name"; then directly into the phone, "It's Kopechne. K-o-p-e-c-h-n-e."

"Do you know how old she is?" Arena said.

"Twenty-eight, I think," the voice said, and Arena thought he could detect a slight break, as though Rosemary Keough was trying to hold herself together. He decided that the girl must be aware of the accident.

"Okay, Rosemary," he said gently. "Remember, we've got your purse here whenever you want it."

Walter Steele, who had wandered into the outer office, wandered back in just as Arena was hanging up. "Chief," he said, "let me see that statement, will you?" Arena handed it over, and after the prosecutor had studied it carefully, he emitted a long whistle and pulled the door shut behind him. "Jim," he said in shocked tones, "this is a goddamn confession! I'm not sure to what, but I *am* sure it's a confession!"

"I know it," Arena said calmly. "The senator asked me to hold it while he tried to get in touch with Burke Marshall."

"Who the hell's Burke Marshall? The name's familiar, but I can't place the guy."

"A lawyer, that's all I know. Kennedy said if we'd wait till he gets in touch with Burke Marshall, he'd call us and we can release the statement."

"Release it?" Steele said, pacing to the wall of the tiny room and waving the statement in his hand for emphasis. "What do you mean, *release it?* I never heard of releasing a confession or an admission to the press. Chief, are you kidding me?"

"No, no," Arena said. "Kennedy *expects* us to release it."

"Well, let's hold up. I'll tell you what's gonna happen. He's gonna get in touch with a lawyer who knows which end is up, and then they're gonna call us and tell us *not* to release the statement, and that'll be it."

"Well, I'm just trying to do what he told me to do," Arena said.

"Okay," the prosecutor said. "Let's wait and see what develops."

Steele walked over to the chief's skimpy bookcase and pulled down a dog-eared copy of the Massachusetts motor vehicle laws. He sat on the bench opposite Arena's desk and opened the book to chapter 90, section 26, the statute pertaining to leaving the scene of an accident. "Jesus Christ!" he said after a few minutes of study. "Chief, we're in the soup!"

"What're you talking about?" Arena said.

"He left the scene of an accident. You know it better than I do. I haven't tried one of these goddamn automobile cases in fourteen years—that's what I did in my first year in the D.A.'s office in Boston—but it's absolutely clear that he left the scene. There may be some technical defenses, but for Christ's sake we've *got* to get a complaint for that. Now what I want to know is: was the guy stiff or was he not stiff?"

"How the hell do I know?" Arena said.

"Did you ask him?" Steele said, knowing as he spoke that it was a silly question.

"Of course I didn't ask him," Arena said. "He stood here clear-eyed and steady on his feet. He looked fine. How the hell could I ask him a question like that? And he wouldn't have had to answer it anyway. He looked cold sober, and he didn't look hung over, either."

"Yeh, you're right. I got the same impression. Tell you the truth, I never knew the guy to be a big drinking man anyway. Markham looked a little rough to me, but that might have been just tiredness. What the hell was going on over there on Chappy, anyway?"

Arena recited what he knew about the case, and produced Rosemary Keough's pocketbook, and when he had finished reciting the meager list of available facts, Steele jumped up again. "Chief," he said, "I'm sorry, but this doesn't add up at all. Unless they send a couple of knowledgeable lawyers over here and unless they can give a sensible explanation of all this, we're gonna have to get a complaint and get it right away. If they just leave us with this statement and no other explanation, that's the only thing we can do." He leafed through the statute book to the part about medical examiners. "Have you notified the D.A.?" he asked.

"No," Arena said, "only Killen."

"Never mind Killen. Please, call the D.A."

"I'd rather not do that, Walter," Arena said. "It's Saturday, he's off duty, he's probably at home."

"The statute says you have to call him," Steele said, thumping the book down on the chief's desk.

"Okay, okay," Arena said wearily. He looked up the number and dialed it on his wall phone, and very quickly the loud voice of Edmund Dinis came crackling into the little room. Arena outlined the case, told about the dead girl, described Kennedy's role, and informed the district attorney that Kennedy had signed a statement.

Dinis's response was so loud that Arena had to hold the telephone a few inches from his ear. "We're taking over this case right away, Chief! We're in this case right now!" There was a click, and a white-faced Jim Arena hung up the phone and turned to Steele.

"Oh, my God!" Arena said. "What have I done? I've unleashed something. What do we do now?"

Steele stood up and resumed his pacing. "Just stay calm," he said. "Now let's figure it all out. First of all, we've got to keep our left hands high here. Kennedy isn't being very nice to us, leaving us with a statement like that and then taking off. He's practically forcing us to charge him with leaving the scene. Now maybe there's an explanation, but they ought to be over here making it, instead of leaving us in the dark like this." He resumed his seat. "Now what have we got to work with?" he said calmly. "What we've got is an automobile case, pure and simple. And we've got a powerful United States senator on the one hand and you and me representing the people on the other hand. It's a lovely position he's put us in, isn't it?"

The telephone rang again, and Chief Arena began another conversation with Lieutenant Killen. Arena reconstructed the talk later. Inexplicably, Killen seemed to be suggesting that there was no point in the district attorney's office joining in the matter. "Look, Jim!" he said, "this is an automobile case, isn't it?"

"Sure," Arena said. "That's exactly what it is."

"Well, you've handled a lot of 'em. You don't need our help, do you?"

"Not right now, anyway. Kennedy's given me an incriminatory statement."

"Okay. If you need help, let us know. I've talked to the D.A. and he says it's your case."

When Arena had filled Steele in on the conversation, the prosecutor was more puzzled than ever. "Didn't I just hear Dinis say he was taking over the case?" Steele asked.

"Yep."

"And five minutes later his number one investigator calls back and says they're not getting in?"

"Yep."

"And they already said there's no need for an autopsy?"

"Yep."

"I can't figure any of this out," the baffled Steele said. "Here. Let me see the book again." He studied the medical examiners statute and when he was finished, he slammed the book shut and said, "Well, there's *every* reason for an autopsy."

Later, he called Killen and said, "George? This is Walter Steele. Listen, it looks like we should have an autopsy here. You know the old rule: when in doubt, do an autopsy. . . . Yeh, sure, this is a drowning, but it's a drowning where you find a body in a car, and where you have a guy that says, 'Yes, I was operating the car and I went off the bridge.' Not that we think Kennedy's a murderer. We think a few other things at this point, but not that. Anyway, I just read the medical examiners statute for the second time in my life and it seems to me we should think about an autopsy."

To Steele, Killen seemed markedly unenthusiastic about the idea, and the prosecutor impatiently cut the conversation short. "Okay," he snapped into the phone. "Goodbye."

He told Arena, "Okay, we've notified the D.A. as the statute requires, we've talked to his chief investigator, and we've covered all the bases on the autopsy. From now on that decision is up to them. Now the next step won't be so easy."

"What's that?" Arena asked.

"What to do about Kennedy."

By the time he had scrubbed up and returned home and gulped down his lunch, Dr. Donald Mills was fifteen minutes late for his Saturday afternoon office hours, which normally started at 2 P.M. When he stepped from his house into the adjoining office, he noticed that several patients were already waiting. There had been a run of summer colds—sore throats and fever and drip—and by the looks of his waiting room, the run was far from over. He swabbed a few throats and prescribed antibiotics and analgesics and worked his way through about half the waiting patients when the telephone began to ring. The first call was from the Chicago *Tribune*. "Doctor," a reporter asked, "we understand that you treated Senator Kennedy in connection with an accident this morning."

"No, I didn't," Mills said politely. "That's not true. I didn't see Senator Kennedy."

The reporter sounded dubious. "Well, we understood that you saw him *and* treated him this morning," he repeated.

"No, that's just not true. There was an accident, and I functioned on the accident, but I didn't see Senator Kennedy. I've *never* seen him."

By the time the conversation was over, Estey Teller reported that a call was waiting on the other line, and soon the busy physician found himself talking to another reporter long-distance. When he had handled a few more calls and the patients had begun to stir restlessly in his waiting room, he stepped into the house and asked his wife to run to the police station and find out what was going on. A few minutes later she slipped him a note: "Kennedy was the driver of the car and has been flown to Hyannis." Dr. Mills put his hand over the telephone and said, "Well, that's news! Now I'm *really* glad I covered myself on the autopsy."

The afternoon wore on, with the doctor alternately soothing inflamed throats and talking on the telephone. A state policeman came by and picked up a scribbled note authorizing the blood test. Undertaker David Guay and a man who introduced himself as Dun Gifford came to the office with a death certificate that required the medical examiner's signature. "Gee," Mills said, "I don't even know who this girl is."

The man named Gifford said, "I can tell you."

"Well, who are you, Mr. Gifford?" Mills asked. "A reporter?"

"No," the well-spoken young man replied. "I'm representing Senator Kennedy in this matter. I'm on his staff. He called me this morning and asked me to come over from Nantucket and expedite things."

"How are you expediting things?"

"Well, we're taking care of the body. We're authorized by the parents, the Kopechnes, to do that for them. The body will be flown out this afternoon."

Again, Mills felt relieved. He signed the formal death certificate and ushered the two men out, and as he returned to his office to continue seeing patients, he said to himself, "Well, that's the end of *that* case."

But there were calls waiting on both lines. "Do you want us to try to help you handle the calls?" his wife said.

"No," Dr. Mills said. "I think I should take them all myself. We'll get through the afternoon and then it'll quiet down." He picked up a phone and talked to another reporter, finished that call and talked to another, and by the time the second caller had rung off, the first telephone was ringing again.

"Doctor," Estey Teller was saying, "why don't you put the phones on the recorder and not take any more calls today?"

"No, I don't think so, Estey," Mills said. "People know that I'm on duty on Saturday afternoon and they expect me to answer the phone." He was beginning to feel pressed, but he continued to tell himself that he could handle the situation. He succeeded in seeing several more patients, but by midafternoon it was plain that both lines were going to remain busy for the rest of the afternoon. Dr. Mills looked into his ashtray and discovered that he had been chain-smoking, and he told himself that he should cut down. But the telephoners gave him no relief. It was not only that there were constant callers, but that some of them were engaging in verbal harassment. For every reporter who spoke respectfully and called him "sir" and "Dr. Mills," there was another who treated him like a liar and cross-examined him sharply. The gentle country doctor was never at his best in such situations; he tried to explain himself reasonably and honestly, but some of the reporters flatly refused to believe him. There were even a few who suggested that he was covering up for Ted Kennedy, which made the doctor become more flustered than ever.

By late in the afternoon, Dr. Mills had gone through a pack of Pall Malls and his mind was whirling and he was wondering if his trial by telephone was ever going to end. He picked up a ringing phone half-dazedly and began answering the same set of questions all over again. "Tell me, Doctor, how was the girl dressed?" the voice was asking. Dr. Mills tried to remember the scene at the bridge, but all that came to him in his confusion and befuddlement was that the girl had been undressed, of course, as he examined her. He blurted out, "Well, she was nude."

"Oh, Doctor!" the reporter said. "This is terrible! This is more than that poor family should have to bear."

"Yes, it is," Mills said.

"Nothing on at all?"

"All she had on was a blue bra."

A short time later he was sitting at his desk letting the telephones go unanswered, and in this brief moment of silence he realized what he had said. "My God!" he said aloud. "I'll have to call that newspaper back and give them a correction!" He tried to remember the name of the paper, but he had taken so many calls that they blended together. Something told him that the call had come from Boston, but he was anything but certain. "What the hell newspaper was that?" he said to his wife. "I've got to kill that story!"

He telephoned Bob Hyde, a local correspondent for the New

Bedford *Standard-Times.* "Bob," he said, "this is Don Mills. Tell me, what newspapers are there in Boston besides the *Globe?*"

"There's the *Herald-Traveler,*" Hyde said, "the *Record-American . . .*"

"That's it!" Mills said. "Thanks a lot!"

He called the *Record-American,* identified himself, and asked if he could speak to the reporter who had interviewed him earlier. At last he recognized the same voice, and he told the reporter, "Listen, I want to correct a misstatement I made. I was so confused and tired when you called that I made a mistake. I said that the Kopechne girl was naked, and that was untrue. Please retract it."

"I'm glad you got me," the reporter said. "We'll take it out of the story. We just have time."

"Thank God for that," Mills said reverently. He hung up the telephone and switched it to the recorder.

By midafternoon, Police Chief Jim Arena was beginning to feel heavy pressure from the reporters. Now that Senator Kennedy had been sneaked through the back door, there was no longer any reason to keep them waiting outside the town office building, but Arena did not want reporters sitting in Carmen Salvador's office trying to hear his conversations with Walter Steele, either. He compromised by allowing them to wait in the hall, where he could hear them grumbling among themselves. When an hour had gone by and Arena had continued in his closemouthedness, several of the reporters pushed into the outer police office and demanded to know how much longer the silence would last. He told them he was waiting for a telephone call, and then he would give them details. "A telephone call from whom?" one of the reporters said.

"I can't tell you that," Arena said, and went back inside his office.

By midafternoon, the reporters were in a rage, and one of them asked for an audience. Arena recognized James (Scotty) Reston, vice-president of the *New York Times* and owner of the *Vineyard Gazette.* "My God," the chief said to himself, "first I've got to handle Ted Kennedy and now Jim Reston!" The short, world-renowned newsman appeared to be in an uncharacteristically foul mood. He reminded Arena that the press had been kept waiting for hours on a matter that was plainly of public interest, that the press had certain rights in the matter, and that the chief's behavior was beginning to verge on arrogance. Friendly Jim Arena, the most popular cop on Martha's Vineyard, was unnerved. He was torn between cooperating with the angry Reston and his promise to the senator. He compromised by releasing a few details—the girl's name, the fact that Kennedy had been driving, the apparent damage to the car, a few other items. "But we understand you have a signed statement from the senator," the persistent Reston went on. "Will you tell us what it says, please?"

"Just a minute," Arena said. He ducked back into his private office, where Walter Steele sat on the bench studying the statutes.

"They want the statement," Arena said. "Kennedy hasn't called me back, and I'm gonna release it."

"Jim, you'll be making a mistake," Steele said. "That's an incriminatory statement, and if you release it to the press, you'll be giving Kennedy a constitutional defense. He can say that he can't get a fair trial because of adverse publicity, and *you* helped to create it."

Arena considered the matter. He admired and respected Walter Steele, and he knew that the prosecutor was probably right, but there were other considerations. Until a formal complaint was brought, he was in charge, not Walter Steele, and he did not intend to go to war with a dozen angry reporters over the constitutional aspects of a motor vehicle case. Murder or kidnapping, yes, but who ever brought up constitutional defenses in a traffic matter? "I know what you mean, Walter," the chief said, "but Kennedy expects me to release the statement and those reporters are climbing all over me, especially Jim Reston. I'm gonna let it go."

"It's your show," Steele said.

Arena stepped into the corridor, held up his hand for silence, and said, "Gentlemen, Senator Kennedy has given me the following statement." He began to read.

"Louder!" somebody shouted, and someone else said, "Slower!" When Arena finished a second run-through, he began answering questions.

"Chief, Chief," Walter Steele whispered in his ear, "don't do any more talking!"

"Who the hell are you?" a reporter shouted at Steele.

Arena answered a few more questions and stepped back inside with the prosecutor. The telephone rang and a man identified himself as Paul Markham. As Arena remembered later, Markham sounded friendly. "Listen, Chief," he said, "we haven't been able to get hold of Burke Marshall. Could you hold onto the statement a little longer?"

"Gee," Arena said, "I've already given it out." He expected Markham to be angry, but the voice of the former United States attorney remained conciliatory and warm.

"Oh, you gave it out?" Markham said. "Well, that's okay. Goodbye, Chief."

Once again Arena closeted himself with Walter Steele and once again the two men went over the case and what they would have to do about it. "No matter how you slice it," Steele said, "it's leaving the scene of an accident. Unless they come back here with a pretty fancy explanation, I don't see what else you can do except ask for a complaint on that. Let me see the statement again."

As Arena watched, Steele read the typewritten words, and to the chief's surprise the prosecutor's face broke into a smile. "What the hell are you smiling about?" the chief said.

"It's funny how this whole thing came out," Steele said in his Humphrey Bogart lisp. "You know, Chief, you did a good job."

"Thanks, but how do you mean?"

"I mean this: by treating Kennedy with kid gloves, you got a signed confession out of him. And if you didn't have this signed confession, you wouldn't have anything. Under Massachusetts law, there's no presumption whatever that you're the *driver* of a car just because you happen to be the *owner* of the car. If Kennedy had come in here and said, gee, he was sorry about the accident, but he didn't know anything about it and he didn't even know how the girl got into the car, *that would have been the end of it!*"

Arena said he was not so sure, and Steele jumped up and said, "Well, I'm sure! How the hell are you gonna prove that Kennedy is driving that car if he doesn't admit it himself?"

"Huck Look saw him."

"Huck Look saw *shadows*. Huck saw dim figures in the car. He couldn't testify that he saw *Kennedy*."

"Yeh," Arena said, remembering his brief conversation with the deputy sheriff at the Dike Bridge. "I guess you're right."

"Chief," Steele said, smacking the big man on the shoulder with his hand, "I congratulate you! If you had gotten rough with Kennedy, he could have squeezed out of this a dozen ways. Suppose he comes in here and he says, 'The girl was driving. I was a passenger.' Tell me how you prove otherwise."

"I couldn't," Arena said. "Far as I can tell, there's not a single outside witness."

"That's right," Steele said. "The only witness is dead. And if Kennedy says that he was a passenger in the car, he's home free. I've practically memorized these statutes, and there's no legal requirement for a passenger in a wrecked car to report an accident to *anybody*. The law applies only to the driver. So you made your case in the only way it could be made: by a confession from the person involved."

A little later a man of about thirty appeared at the outer office and said that he had come to recover Rosemary Keough's purse. "It's okay, Carmen," Arena said to the policewoman. "I talked to Rosemary earlier. Give the gentleman the pocketbook." Without identifying himself, the tall young man left with the purse. Arena, with Steele's advice, busied himself writing up a citation charging Senator Edward M. Kennedy with leaving the scene of an accident.

When Foster Silva learned that the Lawrence cottage was somehow connected with the incident at Dike Bridge, he let himself into the place with his watchman's key and took a look around. The beds were so neatly made that they looked as though they had not been slept in. The big front room that served as living room, dining room and kitchen was in perfect order, exactly the opposite of what Silva had expected. Usually summer visitors were sloppy, their minds on swimming and sailing and fishing, and they flung clothes and other items all over the place. "Something's funny," he said to himself, "for this cottage to be so empty and orderly on Saturday afternoon." He knew that the clean-up crew had not arrived, and therefore the occupants of the place must have cleaned it themselves.

Not long afterward, Silva's uncle Tony Bettencourt was back on his job as "captain of the dump," the entrance to which was just down the road from the Lawrence cottage. After he raked the new trash and junk into the pit and ignited it in a large ring, his eye was attracted to a cardboard box that contained some bottles. The old man peered across the flaming boundary of the dump and saw that someone had thrown away three unopened bottles of gin.

The first news reports on Saturday afternoon told of the death of "Mary Jo Copachini." Early editions of the nearby New Bedford *Standard-Times* carried a headline: WOMAN KILLED; BELIEVED TO BE KENNEDY AIDE, and a short bulletin: "The body of a woman believed to be a secretary for Senator Edward M. Kennedy (D.-Mass.) between twenty and twenty-five was recovered today in waters at Chappaquiddick Island following an automobile accident. It was not immediately determined if the woman was alone in the car."

The members of the Edgartown Regatta, minus the boats *Victura* and *Resolute* and the skippers Edward M. Kennedy and Joseph P. Kennedy III, tried their best to get to the starting line for the second day of racing, but the wind had dropped to a whisper, and a translucent haze had settled down over the bay. The few yachts that were able to make it to the starting line failed to finish within the allotted period, and the first heats were declared null and void. Old Joe Chase Allen said that he had covered forty-five Edgartown regattas, and this was the poorest of them all. Late in the afternoon, the drizzle resumed, the wind quit altogether, and the races were called off.

Every ferry that arrived at Vineyard Haven from the mainland carried more reporters, and by Saturday evening a group was camped inside the little police station. Jim Arena still had not been home, had not eaten since breakfast, and had not been able to concentrate on anything but the Kennedy case. A summer person named Othmar Cheeseborough came into the station at 5:50 P.M. to report the disappearance of his German shepherd puppy, but Arena had to give the gentleman very short shrift. "It's black and brown and about fifteen weeks old," Cheeseborough said. "It answers to the name of Simba." Arena made a quick note in the log and told the disturbed visitor that he would be on the lookout. At six o'clock a resident called to report that the Francis children were throwing rocks at his boat. "Go take a look, will you?" Arena said to one of his summertime specials, and turned again to the matter at hand, which was a discussion of his notes on the Kennedy-Kopechne case.

By 11:30 P.M., only one or two reporters remained. Arena had written out the citation for leaving the scene of an accident. He answered a few more telephone calls—his seventy-second and seventy-third of the day, including several from overseas—and wearily announced that he was going to walk home.

There were no stars, and a light mist fell as he walked under the old elms and sycamores and maples. He thought back on his thirteen years on the state police, and how the troopers used to sit around and talk about their "top twenty cases." The reminiscences had always embarrassed him, because his own top twenty cases were relatively unglamorous. As an aide on the attorney general's staff, he had been brushed lightly by the Boston Strangler case and the Brink's robberies, but other troopers had been much more highly involved. He could not in honesty list them as cases on which he had worked. The truth was that he had been cursed by robust good looks and a pleasing personality, and as a result he had spent most of his career on "public relations" duty, at airports and office buildings and courthouses and other places where it was important to have a tall, good-looking, knowledgeable trooper on duty. It seemed to him that he had been dealing with celebrities all his life, smiling on them, beaming on them, directing them through crowds, answering their questions. And now—Edward M. Kennedy. For a moment, he wished he were back with his old comrades, playing the game of top twenty cases. This was his own top twenty rolled into one. He walked in the front door and embraced his wife, Yvonne, who had been waiting up.

"Tired?" she said.

"No," Arena answered, but he could hardly keep his eyes open.

An on-duty policeman made the last entry in the Edgartown police log for Saturday, July 19, 1969: "If you want the chief for any emergency, you will have to knock on his door. He has taken his phone off the hook as of twelve midnight." A short time later, around the corner from the station, a young man knocked down an elderly woman, breaking her ankle, and stole her purse. It was the town's first mugging in five years. The night shift patrolmen handled the case themselves. No one could bear to awaken the chief.

IV

The Wheels of Justice

O N Sunday morning, events of varying significance piled one atop the other. Police Chief Dominick "Jim" Arena slept later than usual, then went to St. Andrew's Episcopal Church with his wife and children to sing in the choir. A telegram from Senate Majority Leader Mike Mansfield was sent to the Kennedy compound in Hyannis Port: DEEPLY SHOCKED AND DISTURBED OVER TRAGEDY WHICH OCCURRED OVER WEEKEND. WHAT HAPPENED TO YOU COULD HAVE HAPPENED TO ANY ONE OF US. YOU HAVE OUR FULL CONFIDENCE AND IF IN ANY WAY I CAN BE OF ASSISTANCE PLEASE LET ME KNOW. . . . The district attorney of Barnstable, Bristol, Nantucket and Dukes counties, Edmund Dinis, telephoned from his home in New Bedford to the home of his chief investigator, Lieutenant George Killen, and was told that the body of Mary Jo Kopechne had already been flown from Martha's Vineyard. The Sidney Lawrences of Scarsdale, New York, owners of the Lawrence cottage, had arrived on Chappaquiddick and were borrowing vacuum-cleaner bags from neighbors to do the floors. Newscasts had begun to carry skimpy reports about the tragedy, and Sunday newspapers were on the stands with headlines like those in the local New Bedford *Standard-Times:* ISLAND PLUNGE KILLS GIRL; TED WAS DRIVER. When the *On Time* backed out for its first round trip of the day, a line of cars was waiting. Usually, at this hour on a Sunday morning, there were none. The skies were darkly purple, and it was threatening rain.

Shortly after noon, Jim Arena strolled into the police station to check the log, and a few minutes later he looked up from his desk to shake hands with a young man who introduced himself as Senator Kennedy's aide, Dun Gifford. In the chief's backroom office, the two men talked over the accident. Gifford said he was going to meet undertaker Gene Frieh at Martha's Vineyard Airport at about 12:30, and the body would be put on an airplane and flown to Wilkes-Barre, Pennsylvania, the nearest airport to Plymouth, Pennsylvania, where the Kopechnes wanted their daughter to be buried. The body had been ready for the flight since the evening before, but the weather forecasts had been unfavorable for flying. Gifford inquired politely about the chief's plans. "I don't have much choice," Arena said apologetically. "The senator admitted leaving the scene of an accident. First thing in the morning I'll have to go to the clerk of the district court and ask for a complaint. Of course, there'll be a hearing on that, and the senator is entitled to be represented."

Momentarily, Arena thought of giving Gifford the citation slip to take to Kennedy, but he thought better of the idea. The usual procedure was to send the citation by mail, and in important cases, by registered mail. When one was dealing with the most popular political figure in the state, one went strictly by the book. He chatted briefly with Gifford and kept hoping that the handsome young aide would offer an explanation for what happened on Friday night, but none was forthcoming. "Well, thanks for your help," Arena said, and Gifford left for his appointment with Gene Frieh and the body of Mary Jo Kopechne.

Early Sunday morning, the telephones resumed jangling at the home of Dr. Donald Mills on Summer Street. There were two incoming lines: 627–8262 in his office, ringing into the recording device, and 627–4423, ringing in the residence itself and being answered by the doctor and his wife. The calls were like Saturday's: the telephoners ranged from soft-spoken, courteous interrogators to loud, bombastic inquisitors. Another public figure would have slammed the telephone down on some of them, but the kindly Dr. Mills did not have such abrupt behavior in him. Mrs. Mills, on the other hand, gave as good as she got, and suggested to several reporters that they should return to college and major in manners.

By afternoon, Dr. Mills had taken up permanent station next to the telephone, with his wife occasionally spelling him. He wanted to handle as many of the calls as possible; somehow it seemed to him that insofar as he had functioned as a public medical examiner, he had an obligation to answer the questions of the public press, however annoying and aggravating they might sometimes be. In the middle of a long succession of calls, he picked up the phone and heard a man identify himself as a technician at the Public Safety Department's laboratory in Boston. "Doc," the caller said, "we thought you'd like this information quickly. The alcohol content in the Kopechne girl's blood was .09 percent."

"What does that amount to?" Mills asked.

"Oh, she wasn't really drunk," the technician said. "It sounds like a little social drinking, maybe two or three cocktails and maybe a highball, that's all."

"What else did your tests show?"

"Negative on barbiturates, no organic bases detected, less than five percent carbon monoxide."

Mills jotted the figures down. "Thanks," he said. "You'll be sending a report?"

"Right away," the technician answered. Dr. Mills thanked him again and took another look at the figures on his notepad. They seemed interesting but irrelevant. The girl had been a passenger in the car, and legally or medically it made little difference whether she had been under the influence or not.

The ringing of the telephone shook him back to the immediate problem. He handled another long skein of calls, and then asked his wife to sit in for a few minutes. When he came back, a female reporter from Washington, D.C., was demanding to speak to the doctor personally. "Doctor!" the woman said in a voice that stretched his eardrum. "I understand you have a copy of the blood test on Mary Jo Kopechne."

"I do," Dr. Mills said softly.

"Would you mind reading it to me?" she asked.

Mills hesitated. He had been involved in few police cases, but it seemed to him that such information as the victim's intake of alcohol was highly personal. He would not have minded transmitting the figures to a proper law enforcement authority or to a member of the girl's family, but he could see no reason to give it out to a voice on the telephone. "I'm sorry," he said at last, "but I can't do that."

"Why not?" the woman said. "It's public information."

"I'm not sure whether it's public information or not, miss," Mills said, trying to keep his voice sounding courteous and friendly. "It seems to me that there are ethics involved here, and I wouldn't want to do an injustice to that poor dead child."

"Dr. Mills!" the strident voice said. "The public *demands* this kind of information. The public has every *right* to this. Some things are bigger than your code of ethics!"

"I'm sorry, miss," Mills said. "I can't give the information out." He held on patiently while the reporter castigated him thoroughly. When the lecture on morals and medical responsibility and freedom of the press and the nature of Dr. Donald Mills's ancestry was over, the physician put down the telephone and wiped his brow. "Whew!" he said to his wife. "I'm not sure how much more of this I can take."

"Why don't you call Lieutenant Killen and ask for some help with the press?" Esther Mills suggested.

"Oh, I'd hate to bother him on Sunday," Mills said.

"Well, they're bothering *you* on Sunday," his wife said emphatically. "Killen has experience handling the press. We don't."

"Maybe you're right," the physician said. Leaving Mrs. Mills to answer the residence phone, he put a call through to the mainland. A few minutes later he returned to the living room dejectedly.

"What'd he say?" Mrs. Mills asked.

"He was very sympathetic," the doctor replied. "He's a nice guy. He told me to tell 'em nothing except that it was an accidental drowning and that's all. He said the press was dangerous, whatever you say they'll twist it around, and they'll turn on you in a second. I asked him if he could send somebody to help out with all the calls, but that didn't seem to register. He just said if they keep on calling, slam down the receiver."

"Could you do that?" Esther Mills asked.

"No," Dr. Mills said, and picked up the phone to answer another call.

Shortly after the Dukes County courthouse opened on Monday morning, Jim Arena walked across the street from the police station to bring his charge against Ted Kennedy. Under Massachusetts law, at the outset of a misdemeanor case the court clerk sits as a sort of substitute judge, deciding whether the matter should go any further. This procedure gives the defendant an early opportunity to fight the case. He can demand a hearing about the issuance of the complaint, and if there is no compelling evidence that the law has been violated, the court clerk is empowered to throw the case out. Arena knew that the senator had twenty-four hours in which to take any opposing action, but he was surprised to find that a Kennedy lawyer was already on the scene. It was agreed that a hearing about the complaint would be held before the court clerk on Monday, July 28, seven days later.

"So they asked for a hearing?" Prosecutor Walter Steele said when Arena returned to his office. "Okay, that means we have to protect ourselves in the clinches. We have to know exactly what we're doing at all times."

"I keep hoping we'll hear from Kennedy or his lawyers," Arena said. "Surely they're not gonna let us hang like this?"

"We'll hear from them," Steele said. "Didn't Kennedy say he'd get back to you?"

"Sure. So did Markham."

"Well, they'll probably send somebody over today and help us clear this thing up, give us some kind of explanation that makes sense, like maybe Kennedy was unconscious half the night, or something like that. There's got to be an explanation. Things just don't happen like this. I mean, the guy's a former assistant D.A. himself. He knows the law about reporting an accident. Of course, he could have been dead drunk and spending the night sobering up, but looking at him, I can't believe it."

"Neither can I," Arena said. "You can't be drunk at midnight and look as clear-eyed as he looked in the morning."

The two men finally agreed that no matter what the prospects for an *entente,* they would have to proceed on the assumption that they were going to trial. "We'll also have to see what evidence there is for endangering, drunk driving and even manslaughter," Steele said. "We've simply got to check out everything. Did Killen offer to help?"

"He said he'd help us any way he can," Arena said.

"Good. Let's call him and ask him to get statements from the other people with Kennedy. I don't expect them to be inculpatory, but for Christ's sake let's get *something.* While you're doing that, I'll line up Huck Look and the guys from the registry and we'll go over to Chappy and see what we can find out."

After a day of measuring distances at the Dike Bridge and walking through the scene at the intersection with Huck Look and going over the available information with a representative of the Massachusetts Registry of Motor Vehicles, Steele examined his notes. His rough computations indicated that the car had been traveling at twenty to thirty-five miles per hour when it went off the bridge; the speed might have been considered excessive for the conditions, but there were no speed limit signs or warnings on the approach to the bridge, and Steele knew how a good defense lawyer would handle *that.* There was a charge under Massachusetts law informally called "driving to endanger," roughly equivalent to reckless driving in other states, but a wrecked car and the body of a woman were not sufficient evidence to make an endangering case. A person who drove "to endanger the lives of others" had to be *seen* doing it, and so far not a single witness had come forth. The same drawbacks applied to a possible drunk driving charge. There had to be witnesses either to the driving or to the drinking or both, and there were none. Huck Look's story was impressive, and both Steele and Arena believed every word of it; but even Look had had to admit that his view of the driver had been dim and that he had seen no evidence of driving under the influence of alcohol.

"So it adds up to this," Steele said when they returned to Arena's office. "We can't begin to prove endangering, and if we can't begin to prove endangering, we haven't got a prayer to prove manslaughter. We haven't got the first elements of a drunk driving case, but goddamn it, we can sure as hell prove leaving the scene! And that's as stiff a charge as endangering *or* drunken driving. We've got his own statement, and unless we get some kind of explanation in the meantime, we'll proceed along those lines."

By late Monday afternoon, several dozen reporters had infiltrated the island, and their investigations had begun to turn up the essential facts of the party on Chappaquiddick. A particularly persistent reporter from a television network called on Arena and demanded to know what he was going to do about "the wild party."

"What am I going to do about it?" Arena said incredulously. "What *can* I do about it? It's not against the law to have a party, even if you're a senator."

"Yes," the reporter said, "but there's morality involved."

"The morality involved is none of my damn business," Arena snapped. "I'm dealing with a motor vehicle violation here, not a morals case."

When the reporter left, Arena found himself thinking about the conversation. He had been a law enforcement officer long enough to know that what people did behind their own closed doors was their own business so long as they did not disturb the peace or commit mayhem or violate any of the other laws of the commonwealth. From what he had heard during the day, there had been some sort of affair at the Lawrence cottage the night of the accident, and Kennedy had been present along with ten or twelve others. He wished he knew more about the party, and he wished he had asked Kennedy about it, but so far as he could determine now by making a few telephone calls, every last member of the Kennedy group had fled from Martha's Vineyard on Saturday afternoon. He got out a notebook and began jotting down the names of those who might have attended the party. Certainly Kennedy had been there, and his driver, Jack Crimmins. Paul Markham and Joe Gargan had been in town, and it was a sure bet that they had attended the affair if Kennedy had. The young man who had come to the police station to pick up Rosemary Keough's purse had probably been there, as had the short, courteous man whom Huck Look had seen promenading with the two girls on School Road. That made six men. Arena figured that the most likely one of the six to volunteer information about the party would be friendly Joe Gargan, and he telephoned Lieutenant George Killen in Barnstable and asked him to drive the few miles to the Kennedy compound and interview the pleasant lawyer-banker who had been brought up with Ted Kennedy. Killen gave Arena the impression that he would be glad to help out.

The wrecked Oldsmobile 88 had been towed to the Depot Corner Service Station, a few blocks from the center of Edgartown, and the workers at the station had spent the weekend chasing vandals. By late Monday afternoon an inspection showed what had been stolen: the gas cap, the chrome stripping, the Oldsmobile medallion, door locks and handles, armrests, dashboard knobs, windshield wipers, heater cowling, gas pedal pad, and the windshield visor. There was a four-inch-wide gash in the windshield where souvenir hunters had nicked away at the glass. Jon Ahlbum surveyed the damage and ordered a tarpaulin put over the car. He lettered a sign:

> TO PREVENT ANY FURTHER VANDALISM
> TO THIS CAR WE DECIDED TO COVER IT.
> WARNING—
> ANY FURTHER VANDALISM WILL RESULT
> IN COURT ACTION.

Similar bizarre activity was beginning at the Dike Bridge. The scar on the caplog, where the Oldsmobile's differential had hit, had been greatly enlarged. The sightseers who were rushing to the scene were removing a sliver at a time for souvenirs, and a few of them were doing a more thorough job with hammers and chisels. Someone carved a large heart bearing the words

TED & MARY, and someone else painted on the side of the bridge: TED'S CAR WASH. The macabre season had begun.

Late Monday night, Walter Steele smoked a cigarette and sipped a beer and gazed out the front window of his fishing chalet overlooking Sengekontacket Pond and Nantucket Sound. His wife and children were asleep in various crannies of the little cabin, and each time he lighted another cigarette the flash illuminated a huge headshot of Humphrey Bogart, tacked on the wall by his teen-age daughter to twit him about his lisp and his blunt manner. At the moment, Steele was mulling over the case of the People of Massachusetts versus the Honorable Edward Moore Kennedy. "Of all the things to get messed up in!" he said to himself woefully. "I should have stayed in Boston and minded my own business."

The practical problem was that Walter Edward Steele could not win in the long run. There could be no profit, financial or political or personal, in impaling a member of Massachusetts' royal family on the point of a legal technicality, whether the case could be won or not. And the prosecutor was not even convinced, despite his pep talk to Arena earlier, that the case *could* be won anyway. He had researched the commonwealth's "leaving the scene" statute all the way back to its origins, and it was very plain that the legislature had not contemplated a man's driving off a bridge in the middle of the night when it had specified up to two years in jail for the offense. Massachusetts was a compulsory insurance state, and the intent of the legislation had been to force a driver involved in a two-car collision to make himself known to the other driver and to the police, so that matters of identification and insurance could be worked out. It would be simple for a defense attorney to argue that the law was inappropriate to one-car accidents, and that Senator Kennedy, in his befuddled postaccident state, had not realized that he was legally required to contact the police forthwith. Steele was not even convinced that perfect preparation could win the case for him. He envisaged Ted Kennedy taking the witness stand, his face a mask of tragedy, his blue eyes gazing toward the female jurors, testifying about heroic efforts to save the girl and the agonizing pain in his weakened back and the strange blackout and amnesia that had come over him for nine hours as a result of the shock and the trauma. After such a performance by the only surviving Kennedy brother, the jury would have no problem finding a reasonable doubt.

Steele switched on a small lamp and perused, for about the hundredth time, the statement Kennedy and Markham had composed in the police station. On the face of it, the words still made no sense. The mountain had labored in the back room of the town office building and produced a mouse: a report that raised more questions than it answered. *I was unfamiliar with the road and turned onto Dike Road instead of bearing left on Main Street.* Steele knew that Kennedy had been back and forth on the Dike Road several times during the day; the route from the Lawrence cottage to the ferry was a simple matter of following the blacktop, and it was ludicrous for Kennedy to claim that he accidentally had turned off the asphalt and onto a dirt road and proceeded in precisely the wrong direction. . . . *I descended a hill and came upon a narrow bridge.* There was no hill, only a slight bump in the road about seven hundred feet from the bridge, and one did not "descend" that bump and come upon the bridge; one passed *beyond* the bump and proceeded along an almost flat stretch for a long distance before reaching the bridge, and meanwhile one's headlights would shine squarely on the old humpbacked structure. *I attempted to open the door and window of the car but have no recollection of how I got out of the car.* Steele reckoned that this was possible, but unlikely. Kennedy had given a good description of how the car had gone off the bridge, *turned over and sank into the water and landed with the roof resting on the bottom.* If he knew those details, surely he would have some memory of how he had escaped death himself. *I came to the surface and then repeatedly dove down to the car in an attempt to see if the passenger was still in the car.* Jim Arena, a strong swimmer, had not been able to dive to the car in broad daylight. Would Kennedy, with his fragile spine, have been able to reach the car in

the black of night? Once again Steele had to say to himself that
it was possible, but unlikely. He read the part about the return
to *where my friends were eating . . . I then asked for someone
to bring me back to Edgartown.* But there was no mention of how
this seemingly difficult task had been accomplished. The bald
statement might ring true in Keokuk or Seattle, but it made no
sense here in Edgartown, where everybody knew that the ferry
quit running shortly after midnight and there was a boiling, tide-
ripped channel of water between Chappaquiddick and Edgartown. Others had commented on this part of the statement, and
a reporter from London had advanced the facetious suggestion
that Kennedy had walked across. Steele wished he could see the
humor. The sad truth seemed to be that Kennedy realized he
could say almost anything and make it stick, and if this was true
about a simple handwritten statement, it would be all the more
true in a court of law, where justice was traditionally and properly biased in favor of the defendant and his rights.

Steele flicked out the light, sat down under the print of Bogart, and pondered the situation. The cold reality was that there
could be only one uncomplicated way out of the sticky mess
that the young senator had created. Somewhere under the
mountain of conflicting, confusing reports, there *had* to be a
simple explanation of what had happened, and somebody
should be making that explanation soon. Kennedy and Markham had both promised to get back in touch, and Steele still
clung to the notion that a battery of lawyers would arrive any
minute, ask for a meeting with the prosecutor, and explain everything to his complete satisfaction. Steele could see himself at
the meeting. "Gentlemen," he would say, "Chief Arena and I
are perfectly willing to accept your explanation, but we would
like you to grant us certain courtesies so that we can close this
case in good conscience. We want to talk to every person who
was at the party so that we can satisfy ourselves as to the possibility of drunken driving. We would like the senator to explain
all the discrepancies in his statement and tell us exactly how he
lost control of the car and went into the water. We would like a
better explanation of why it took him nine hours to report to

the police. When that has been done, gentlemen, and we have proved to our satisfaction that nothing of an illegal nature occurred, we will be more than happy to close the case."

But of course such a pleasant conclusion could not be reached unless Kennedy's lawyers made an approach, and now more than two full days had passed without a semblance of an overture. Steele found himself growing more and more annoyed at the young senator and his legal counselors, whoever they were. "Goddamn it," he said to himself, "Jim Arena was more than decent to him, and Kennedy has no right to treat him this way. Kennedy's whole goddamned reputation is on the line, and he ought to be breaking his ass to get over here and answer questions and clean this thing up. Even if his reputation weren't at stake, that's the least he could do as a gentleman." He told himself that the law enforcement authorities of Edgartown, Massachusetts, would have to remain steady on course, as unpleasant as the course might be. Lieutenant George Killen had been requested to interview the girls at the party and call on people at the compound. Maybe he would come up with the explanation that so far had been conspicuously lacking. Steele hoped so. He had no particular fondness for Edward Moore Kennedy, his former co-worker in the Boston district attorney's office, but he was not looking forward to prosecuting him, either. In Massachusetts, there were easier ways to earn an extra five thousand a year.

For three days, Ted Kennedy remained out of sight at the family compound in Hyannis Port, seeing no one except close advisors, and refusing to answer telephone calls from even his most intimate contacts in the press. During those three days, the press and the public tore his "incriminatory" statement to tatters, and right-wing publications seized on the obvious flaws and discrepancies to demand Kennedy's resignation from public life. There was no answer from the compound. Kennedy's relatives made excuses for him: he was torn with grief, he was in physical pain from his ordeal, and he would not be able to speak or answer questions. Meanwhile, high-level advisors began to burst into the place as though another Cuban missile crisis were under discussion, and every house in the compound (except that of Jackie Onassis, who was abroad) soon filled with old Kennedy hands, among them Theodore C. Sorensen, Richard Goodwin, Robert McNamara, Burke Marshall, Kenneth O'Donnell, Lemoyne Billings, U.S. Representatives John Tunney and John Culver, Stephen Smith, David Burke and David Hackett. Illness prevented John Kenneth Galbraith, the Harvard economist and former ambassador to India, from journeying to the compound, but he kept in touch from his summer home in Vermont. Arthur C. Schlesinger, Jr., historian and key advisor to President John F. Kennedy, was attending a conference in Rumania, but he was said to be rushing to the compound by air.

Reporters stood at the limits of the lushly emerald lawns and gawked as the steady procession of luminaries passed in without comment. Now and then one would come out again, and reporters would all but knock him down in their eagerness for information. But the only news was that every visitor to the compound, whether a former cabinet member or an insignificant stenographer, had apparently been sworn to secrecy the instant of his arrival.

On a glum and humid Tuesday morning, eighty hours after the accident, a mute Ted Kennedy made his first public appearance since leaving Martha's Vineyard. Surrounded by a phalanx of aides, including Joseph Gargan, and flanked by his wife Joan and his sister-in-law Ethel, he went to the nearby Barnstable Airport and boarded a private DC–3 for the funeral of Mary Jo Kopechne. Reporters who followed the party noticed that Kennedy wore a surgical collar and appeared uncomfortable. Climbing the metal steps to the airplane, he seemed to lose his balance, and eager hands reached out to help him aboard. The plane, bearing the imprint of the Great Lakes Carbon Company and belonging to Ethel Kennedy's family, lumbered down the runway and disappeared toward the west.

At 8:50 A.M., the twin-engined aircraft landed at the Wilkes-Barre Airport, and another caravan of reporters watched as the funeral party climbed into a white car for the drive to nearby Plymouth, a mined-out anthracite town of some ten thousand people. Plymouth was a few miles down the road from the village of Forty Fort, where May Jo Kopechne had been born twenty-eight years before. The Kopechnes had moved away when the child was a year old, and on this bleak and sunless day in July, they were returning her in a casket to a community that once had hummed and buzzed with mining activity and now lay purposeless and numbed: an empty husk, suitable for funerals and burials. The Kennedy party drove straight to the rectory of St. Vincent's Roman Catholic Church, a block from Plymouth's downtown, and disappeared inside the door to commiserate with Mr. and Mrs. Kopechne. The shades were drawn; the spectators were unable to witness the first meeting between the bereaved parents and the hapless senator. The church was packed to its capacity of five hundred, and hundreds more stood in the back and around the edges. There were few tears in the crowd; Mary Jo Kopechne had no close friends in the community she had left as an infant. A small group of short-skirted young women, looking sophisticated and suntanned and well-to-do, stood slightly apart from the others; occasionally one of them would weep into a handkerchief. A knowing reporter said that these were the girls who had worked in a Kennedy "boiler room" operation together and that some of them had attended the Friday night party at Chappaquiddick. The young women answered no questions. They moved in a group to the back of the church, waiting for the service to begin, and stood near other Kennedy aides, equally tanned and urbanesque, contrasting sharply with the plainly dressed, paler hometowners. There were Kennedy's cousin, Joe Gargan; Representative David Harrison of Gloucester, Massachusetts, a close friend of the senator and chairman of the Massachusetts Democratic Committee; David Burke, Kennedy's administrative assistant; Frank Mankiewicz, who had been Robert Kennedy's press aide; New York lawyer William Van den Heuvel, a family friend who was reputed to be Ethel Kennedy's suitor, and lesser members of the senatorial staff.

A murmur filled the high-ceilinged church when a side door
opened and the funeral party entered from the rectory. Joseph
Kopechne, an insurance salesman with a dignified demeanor,
supported his tiny wife, Gwen Jennings Kopechne, who was
wearing an undersized pair of dark glasses and seemed on the
verge of collapse. The couple walked straight to a pew at the
right front and sat alone, looking neither to right nor left. The
Kennedy party, Joan and Ethel Kennedy, Lemoyne Billings and
the senator, walked slowly to the front pew on the left, and as
they did, another low wave of sound swept through the crowd
outside the church, and someone standing near the main door
let out a stage whisper: "Teddy's inside! He's in!" Kennedy's
eyes did not leave the floor as he walked the short distance to
the pew. He was wearing a dark blue suit, and his dark tie had
been loosened in a wide loop to allow it to fit around the thick
surgical collar. His wife was dressed in white; a black bow accented her blonde curls. Ethel Kennedy wore black, with a
short lace mantilla covering her brown hair. As the party knelt,
Kennedy seemed to have trouble assuming the position, but before anyone could reach out to support him, he had genuflected
and crossed himself. His eyes remained downcast, and reporters
made notes that the Kennedys and the Kopechnes, separated by
the aisle of the church, did not look sideways at each other.
The church was warm and muggy, and as the pallbearers—six
Kopechne cousins and Kennedy aides David Hackett and Dun
Gifford—struggled to carry the heavy bronze casket through
the door, a woman who had fainted was being carried out.

Followed by their acolytes, Monsignor William E. Burchill
and his assistant, the Reverend Charles Smith, began to move
down the center aisle to meet the coffin, and as they walked
with slow dignity the monsignor began reciting the moving
words of *De Profundis:* "Out of the depths I cry to you, O
Lord. . . . My soul waits for the Lord." The coffin was placed
between the Kennedy and Kopechne families, and the priest intoned the Requiem Mass. Joseph Kopechne put his arm tightly
around his sobbing wife's waist and helped her to her feet for
the responses. Once when she was in a sitting position and her

shoulders were shaking, Kopechne clasped her against his side and leaned his head lightly against hers. Edward Kennedy, a few feet away but separated from them by the aisle, turned fleetingly toward the coffin and then averted his eyes. The priest called out, "Do not hand her over to the powers of the enemy and do not forget her, but command that this soul be taken up by the holy angels and brought home to paradise." At the words, Gwen Kopechne buried her face in her hands. Once again Ted Kennedy seemed to be momentarily off balance as he knelt at the rail for communion, and more whispers went through the audience. Then the sister of the mayor of Plymouth sang, "Mother at Your Feet Is Kneeling," and the service was over.

The burial was to be at nearby Larksville Cemetery, at the top of a hill overlooking the cold slag heaps and the neon outskirts of Plymouth, and the black cars of the procession waited in front of the church to recover the body and carry the mourners away. The Kennedys walked down the aisle of the church abreast, looking straight ahead; only Joan nodded her head two or three times to acknowledge friendly greetings. When the party reached the door, there was a loud response from the crowd that had waited patiently outside. Men in coveralls and plain dark suits raised cheap cameras over their heads and shot pictures. Women in housedresses emitted "oohs" and "ahhs," and teen-agers screamed "I see him! I see him!" In the middle of the crowd, someone held aloft a hand-painted sign: KENNEDY FOR PRESIDENT IN '72!

Like a giant amoeba, the throng pressed in on the funeral party, and as Ted Kennedy stood bewilderedly at the front of the church steps, a young woman darted to his side and squeezed his hand. Kennedy seemed not to notice. He glanced toward Mayor Walter Burns, who was standing to one side shouting, "Okay, you spectators. Move back! MOVE BACK!" The funeral party, led by a locked-arm advance guard consisting of Gargan, Gifford and Harrison, struggled for ten minutes to reach the cars parked at the curb, and Kennedy appeared to be on the verge of nausea. "He looks *awful!*" a woman in the crowd said, and another said, "Poor thing. He makes me want to cry." The church bell tolled its mournful cadence over the scene, and at last the funeral cars moved off, driving past the wooden frame houses of the dying town, past little knots of people, descendants of Eastern European immigrants who had worked the mines, and out of town toward the steep road to the Larksville Cemetery. Dozens of unofficial cars fell in behind, and a woman called out as she watched the long procession wend its way through town: "This funeral has put Plymouth on the map!" The mayor and his policemen struggled to clear the traffic jam. "All right, folks," a burly cop said, "the show's over. Let's move on."

At the open grave, several rows of chairs had been protected by a canvas, and the Kennedys and the Kopechnes and the other members of the funeral party took their places under glowering skies. To some of the observers, the senator appeared to be struggling to maintain a calm exterior, staring abstractedly into space, biting his lips, and deliberately looking at no one. After the priest had said a short prayer commending the soul of Mary Jo Kopechne to God, Kennedy continued to stare at the earth beneath him for long seconds, and when he finally raised his eyes, they were filled with tears.

At last the body was laid to rest in its gold-colored casket and the onlookers drifted away. The Kennedys met briefly with the bereaved parents, and then drove the twelve miles back to the airport. Shortly after 1 P.M., the silver airplane landed at Barnstable Airport, and the Kennedy party walked into a swarm of newsmen and photographers. Kennedy had not said a word to the press since the accident; the reporters hoped that now he felt at liberty to speak. "How about a statement?" a reporter shouted.

"I will make one at an appropriate time," Kennedy said tensely, "and I don't think this is an appropriate time."

The newsmen ran alongside as Kennedy and the others hurried toward a waiting car. Kennedy seemed to be making an effort to keep his temper, but when an especially persistent newswoman from one of the television networks climbed almost on his shoetops, he stopped suddenly and said in a voice shaking with anger: "I have just come from the funeral of a very lovely girl, and this is not the appropriate time!" Then he stalked to his car and returned to the protective seclusion of the compound.

On the day of the funeral, *Pravda* carried its first article on the affair. The headline read: UNFORTUNATE ACCIDENT WITH SENATOR E. KENNEDY. The article was datelined "New York," and it reported:

On the night of July 18–19 an automobile with Senator Edward Kennedy at the wheel unexpectedly crashed from a bridge into the Poge Creek, state of Massachusetts. The senator succeeded in getting out of the machine, which ended up on the bottom of the creek with its wheels up. From the written statement of E. Kennedy and the account of the police chief of the town of Edgartown, the following picture of the accident emerged: Senator Kennedy was present that day at the opening of a traditional sailing competition. Returning by night to a hotel, the Senator, not knowing the locality, lost his way and plunged from a narrow wooden bridge unguarded by rails. The machine veered and fell into the water.

In Washington, political circles buzzed with discussions about the effect of the accident on Kennedy, the Democratic party and the country. Privately, top administration officials were gleeful. They were well aware that Richard Nixon had squeaked into office as the result of a series of bizarre incidents that included the assassinations of two Kennedys; now the strongest Democratic candidate, the last one to bear the magic name, seemed to have assassinated himself politically, opening the gate for a second term by the accidental President. A high-ranking White House aide quietly telephoned Massachusetts Republicans and told them to keep after the press to pursue the matter.

Soon the hate mail was running heavy. An Edgartown man received a message: "Mary Jo Kopechne was four months' pregnant. Kennedy dollars persuaded Mills not to perform autopsy. Attorney General Flynn and District Attorney Dinis each got a bundle. The money was paid in hard cash. No checks. The body will not be exhumed. Men in high places can be bought and Kennedy is paying through the nose." Police Chief Jim Arena received postcards addressed to "Whitewash Arena," "Dago Police Chief," and "Chief Wop." One of them bore no message except a large dollar sign in green ink. Another said, "When were you down between Teddy's legs the last time?" A writer addressed Arena as "Dago Creep," and suggested that no red-blooded American would allow himself to go through life with a name like Dominick. Then there were other messages that were not so angry as they were incomprehensible. A long letter suggested that the Kennedy-Kopechne case was part of a giant conspiracy involving the Edgartown Regatta and a University of Southern California football "fix." A communicant from San Francisco advised Arena that the Kennedys were holding a woman captive in a hotel room; she had witnessed the accident at Chappaquiddick, and if he would dispatch officers to slash her bonds and undo her gag, she would tell all. A man telephoned from Alabama and screamed at Arena, "You're gonna take care of Kennedy like you take care of all the other guys in Massachusetts! What kind of justice is that?" An irked Arena said, "You've got a hell of a lot of nerve talking about justice, coming from Alabama!" and slammed down the phone.

"Jesus," Arena said to Walter Steele when they convened for a Tuesday afternoon strategy session, "I don't know how much more of this I can take."

"You can take plenty," Steele said, walloping his friend on the shoulder. "You've got the skin of an elephant and it's a good thing you do, because I've got some bad news for you."

"What's that?" Arena asked.

"You know our friend George Killen, the one who was gonna go over to the compound and interview Gargan and get statements from the girls at the party and give us all kinds of help? Well, one of the Boston reporters told me today that Killen's keeping a strict hands-off policy, that he's leaving the case entirely to you and me."

Arena thumped a heavy fist on the desk. "I understood that he'd give us any help we wanted and that he'd talk to Gargan and the girls for us," Arena said.

"My advice to you is forget about George Killen. This isn't his case, it's ours. We've got to keep on with our own investigation until the case is closed. And I'll tell you something else: we're wasting our time waiting for Ted Kennedy to send his lawyers over here and get this thing straight. The reporters told me that everybody except Madame Pandit has been going to the compound. They've got so many minds working on this little traffic case—you'd think they were defending Sacco and Vanzetti."

"Gee," Arena said. "What can *we* do?"

"Who knows?" Steele said. "Maybe call out the National Guard."

Arena shook his head. "I don't know," he said, his face clouded with disappointment. "You try to be a decent guy. You try to treat a man courteously, give him the benefit of the doubt, and then he clobbers you."

"Jim," Steel said, "if it's any consolation, I agree with you all the way. Kennedy has treated you miserably. There's absolutely no justification for it. Leaving us in the dark for days like this—why, that's an outrageous discourtesy. But it's done. Now there's nothing for us to do but go out and hit all the bases, talk to everybody we can. I'll get Jack Crimmins in Boston and I'll see what he knows. You send your men around to interview everybody you can find."

"But my men are already overworked," Arena said. "That's where Killen was supposed to be so helpful."

"Well, Killen's out of it," Steele said. "You'll have to let the town take care of itself for a while and send some of your guys out with notebooks. You've got a couple of schoolteachers working as summer specials, don't you? They ought to be good on something like this."

Arena summoned a few of the day-shift members of his miniature police department and told them that they were going to be working almost around the clock for the next several days. "Talk to *everybody!*" he said. "We're going to go to court with Senator Kennedy and it's us against the world. Find out when he got here, where he stayed, where the girls stayed, what happened at the party, *everything*. And don't come back till you get it."

When Arena got home that night, he found that a "Judge Clark" had called from the mainland and left word that he wanted to talk about the Kennedy case. "Judge Clark?" Arena said to his wife. "I don't place him, but it looks like the pressure is gonna begin now. They're gonna start telling me to go easy on Ted." Clark had left a Bridgewater, Massachusetts, number, and Arena returned the call. To his surprise, Clark identified himself as counsel for Ted Kennedy and asked for an appointment the next day.

"If it's all the same to you," Arena said, "would it be okay if our prosecutor came along?"

"Fine with us," Clark answered. "Where shall we meet?"

The chief remembered that a small army of reporters was beating the bushes of Edgartown. No place was private, least of all the offices in the building that housed the police station. He knew that it was perfectly proper, indeed advisable, for him and Steele to meet with Kennedy's lawyers and see what they had to say, but he also knew how certain members of the press would handle such a meeting. "We'd better go where we won't be seen," Arena said. A rendezvous was arranged for the next evening at the fishing chalet of Walter Steele, five miles out in the woods.

By Wednesday morning, the earsplitting silence from the Kennedy compound and the lack of hard news developments on Martha's Vineyard had produced a collection of grim-faced, edgy reporters. Their editors, accustomed to a normal flow of news and unaccustomed to Edgartown's high summer rates, were complaining about expense accounts and accusing their correspondents of enjoying paid vacations while failing to do their jobs. "You get in there and *make* Kennedy talk!" a frustrated editor shouted into the telephone, but he had no answer to his reporter's simple question: "How?" A correspondent for a wire service bemoaned the fact that nothing new had turned up since his original story, headlined TED SAFE; BLONDE DIES. All he could write now, he lamented, was BLONDE STILL DEAD.

Walter Steele and Jim Arena had had to take the brunt of the newsmen's hypertensive assaults, and for a few days the two officials walked around heavy-lidded from lack of sleep. Both men were listed in the public telephone book for Martha's Vineyard, and both had found their phones ringing long into the night, sometimes with calls from places like Australia and Germany and Japan. For a day or so, there had been a certain satisfaction in being in touch with the world by telephone, but the thrill quickly wore off in the press of business. Almost every reporter who stepped off the ferry at Vineyard Haven, ten miles away, made a beeline for the police station and requested a complete briefing by the prosecutor or the chief. More than once, Arena's telephone rang and an incoming reporter requested that someone drive over to Vineyard Haven to give him a lift. At first, Arena and Steele were appalled by such audacity, but as time went on they realized that they were watching one of the last bastions of rock-crushing competitiveness, as the gentlemen of the press, radio and television swarmed over the island trying to outdo one another. By the time Wednesday had come around and four full days had passed since the accident, both Steele and Arena had gained a certain respect, commingled with wonderment, for the reporters. There was one television interviewer who, as Steele put it, would have shoved a microphone into the face of Jesus Christ on the cross, and there was another who went from functionary to functionary planting false reports in the hope that someone would slip. An English correspondent spent most of his time at the Harborside Bar boasting of past successes going back to the Zulu wars, and a magazine writer persisted in getting drunk and driving up and down the Dike Road late at night, as though by this process to gain an insight into the happening through the seat of his pants.

Early in the week Steele and Arena had decided that there was no way to cope with the hundreds of news personnel individually, and they had instituted a twice-daily press conference in the basement of the Methodist Church, just across Church Street from the courthouse. There they would stand in the glare of the television lights and give the same answers to the same questions over and over. Sometimes Arena, in his characteristically helpful manner, would start to reveal too much, and Steele would clear his throat loudly or reach under the table to yank on Arena's cuffs. The skinny prosecutor with the hard-boiled manner soon became known as the "heavy" of the "Walter and Dominick" shows. But Steele did not want the case to be tried in the newspapers and later reversed, and he did not mind playing the role of the villain if it would assure the integrity of the case.

On Wednesday morning, the reporters and cameramen were particularly tense and snappy at the press conference, and they refused to take no for an answer to the repeated question: "Have you heard from Kennedy yet?" When Arena denied for about the fourth time that contact had been made, an abrasive reporter from New York City jumped up and said derisively, "Aw, go on, Chief!"

Arena felt his blood pressure rising. "What do you mean, 'Aw, go on'?" he said loudly. "What's the matter with you guys today, anyway? Look, we've been more than cooperative. We've been neglecting our own work, keeping people waiting. There's a kid that's been drinking, and his mother wanted me to talk to him, and I've had to stall her off. Stuff like that's important to me. But we put it off to come in here and try to help you guys, and then you act as though we're a couple of liars. We've held these damned press conferences and we've tried to be helpful, but you guys are never satisfied!"

When the meeting broke up, Arena hurried back to his office. Three or four reporters were standing outside his door and one of them said, "Chief, the Registry of Motor Vehicles announced they're gonna suspend Kennedy's license for negligent driving. Do you have any comment?"

"No," Arena said. The registry was almost a law unto itself, and the suspension was routine and expected, but Arena told himself that soon he would be hearing from the press about the difference between his pace and the registry's. "No comment," he said. "I'll see you this afternoon." He went into his office and slammed the door and buried his head in his hands. He was one of the least hysterical of men, but he felt like bawling. He was also one of the least paranoid of men, but somehow it seemed that the whole world was conspiring against him. First Kennedy had double-crossed him by accepting his courtesy and offering none in return, and then George Killen had cast him adrift to investigate the case alone, and now the press was beginning to doubt his word. "Jesus, what's happening to me?" Arena said to himself. In five days he had barely slept, and his last solid meal had been on the previous Saturday morning. He rubbed his knuckles across his eyes, put on his hat, and strode down the street to the drugstore. "Doc," he said, "what've you got for tension?" The druggist gave him a tranquilizer, and the big ex-Marine swallowed it down and returned to face the day.

Late in the afternoon, when they had completed the matinee performance of the "Walter and Dominick Show," the prosecutor and the police chief met in Arena's office to go over the early results of their investigation. As a side benefit of their relations with the press, they had picked up a few key pieces of information, and a picture was beginning to emerge, albeit an annoyingly incomplete one. "Something I *can* see," Steele said, as he leafed through the handwritten reports from the Edgartown policemen. "While Kennedy was sweet-talking us, everybody was getting off the island as quick as they could. I'm beginning to wonder if he *ever* intended getting back in touch with you."

"I'd hate to believe that," the benign policeman said. "Maybe we'll find out different tonight."

"Maybe we will," Steele said, "but we'd better keep right on investigating and preparing for the worst."

"What do you make of the reports?" Arena asked.

"What I make of the reports," Steele said, waving a few

sheets of paper aloft, "is that Kennedy was registered at the Shiretown Inn and partying at the Lawrence cottage with six girls, and the girls were registered at a place two miles out of town but didn't even sleep there. So you have to begin to wonder. But—" Steele paused.

"But what?"

"But that's none of our business. That's *other* people's business. The whole thing could have been totally innocent. Maybe Teddy was just trying to avoid normal channels because he didn't want the public bugging him. He *is* a senator, you know. And he *is* a Kennedy, and people like that have to do things in strange ways if they want to have any privacy at all."

Steele passed the papers back to the chief, and Arena ran through them quickly. There were interviews with the Malms and the Reverend Smith's family, attesting to the fact that night-lights burned in both places on the Dike Road on the night of July 18–19. There was an interview with Russell E. Peachey, co-owner of the Shiretown Inn, describing how Joseph Gargan had booked three large rooms for a regatta party that was to consist of Senator Kennedy, Gargan, Charles Tretter, Raymond S. LaRosa, John P. Driscoll, Harry Carr and Ross Richards. By now Arena and Steele knew that Carr, Richards and Driscoll had not attended the Chappaquiddick affair, and they knew that the others had. Police Sergeant George Searle had interviewed Peachey, and there was this exchange:

Q: Did you see Senator Kennedy either on the seventeenth, eighteenth or nineteenth [Thursday, Friday or Saturday]?
A: Yes, I saw him early Friday evening at the inn.
Q: How about Saturday?
A: No, but I believe Mrs. Stewart did . . . about 8:30 A.M.

Others had interviewed the realtor who had rented out the Lawrence cottage. The realtor said that Gargan had called early in July and booked the isolated place for the week of July 12–19 on behalf of himself, his wife and another couple. But a few days later Gargan called back to report that his mother-in-law had been taken to the hospital and the party could not get to the Vineyard by the twelfth. Their plans were uncertain, Gargan said, but in any case they wanted the cottage for the weekend of the regatta. On Thursday, July 17, John Crimmins came to the real estate office and picked up the keys. Nothing further was heard from the renting party until Saturday afternoon, July 19, when Gargan called the realtor and reported that the place was vacant.

If the arrangements at the Shiretown and the Lawrence cottage were somewhat unusual, the arrangements at the Katama Shores Motor Inn were downright baffling to Arena and the prosecutor. A policeman had interviewed the motel staff and learned that the reservation had been made by John B. Crimmins several weeks earlier. Crimmins had sent a fifty-dollar check to secure "three twin bedrooms for the weekend of the seventeenth, eighteenth, and nineteenth of July." On plain, white paper, Crimmins had written that he planned to "register on Thursday afternoon the seventeenth," and he had shown up promptly as promised, in the company of four young women. Two of them—Esther Newberg and Rosemary Keough—had signed the register; two others, Susan Tannenbaum and Mary Jo Kopechne, had not. On Thursday night, Rosemary Keough and Mary Jo Kopechne had slept in room 55, Esther Newberg and Susan Tannenbaum in room 56, and Crimmins in room 57. On the following night, the night of the accident, none of the rooms had been slept in, and on Saturday afternoon, a man "about thirty-five or forty and five-nine or five-ten" had checked everyone out, saying that Crimmins would take care of any extra charges. Apparently the final bits of business had been handled by the men of the party, and sometime after 4:30 on Saturday afternoon, a rented white Valiant sedan had been returned to the Hertz offices on West Tisbury Road. The exact time of the return could not be pinpointed; the place had been closed overnight. The car had been driven 105 miles, more than average for a two-day rental on cramped Martha's Vineyard, and the bill was $40.70.

"That's the whole mess," Arena said, passing the papers

back to Steele. "So in a few hours we meet with Kennedy's lawyers and what have we got?"

"Nothing from these reports," Steele said. "They're all beside the point. But here's what we *do* have. One, we have his statement. Two, we can prove that he walked past at least two places that had night-lights on when he was leaving the scene, and his first report was made to you not less than nine hours after the accident. Third, there's no evidence of excessive speed or drunkenness. No *evidence* of speed or drunkenness. A lot of people are making a lot of wild-ass allegations, but I'm talking about *evidence*. Fourth, there's a medical examiner who says it's a classic case of death by drowning. And fifth, there's an unblemished body, and no trace of injury either by human hand or by banging against the car."

"So we've got a case of leaving the scene, period."

"That's it."

"What about all those experts that keep talking about manslaughter?"

"Those experts aren't experts," Steele said. "The law varies from state to state, but in Massachusetts manslaughter is tough to prove even when you *have* the evidence. In Massachusetts, there's no such thing as negligent manslaughter. I mean, you can't convict a man of manslaughter if he just screwed up and somebody died as a result. The act has to be willful, wanton and reckless, which means something more than negligence and something less than murder. There's no way to stretch this case to manslaughter, and we'd be laughed out of court if we tried."

"So we're right back to where we started," Arena said.

"Right," Steele said. "The second that Kennedy walked past the first house on Dike Road, he was guilty of leaving the scene. It sticks out like a sore thumb, and his statement confirms it. That doesn't mean he can't beat the case, but it does mean that leaving the scene is the only criminal charge we can bring, no matter what some of the newspapers are saying. They've got a lot of animosity toward the Kennedys, but goddamned little knowledge of the law."

Just before dark, Arena and Steele met at the chalet to await the arrival of the Kennedy lawyers. Steele was acting noticeably irritated and short-tempered, and Arena asked him what was wrong. "I'm just thinking of the nerve of these horse's asses," Steele said, "letting us sit here for three days without a word, letting *us* handle the whole goddamned press while they pull up the drawbridge over the moat and don't say a word. In all my years in the D.A.'s office, I never had such crummy treatment. And from people that are supposed to have some class!"

"Well, calm down and try to act nice," Arena said. "The lawyers will be here any second."

"Why the hell should I act nice?" Steele snapped. "I don't feel nice, and I haven't been treated nice. I hope to Christ they don't think they're coming here to get him off on a lesser plea, because if they are, I'm gonna tell them to go back and tell Kennedy to shove it. We'll see *him* in court, and we'll see how his story sounds under oath."

"Okay, okay," Arena said. "Just try to calm down."

Soon a car pulled up, and two men, an elderly one and a younger one, wended their way through the fishing rods and squids and battered plugs and boots and entered the front room of the chalet. Steele recognized the older man as former District Judge Robert G. Clark Jr. of Brockton, Massachusetts, and the younger as his son, Robert Clark III. Together, the Clarks were considered to be the best lawyers in the state on accident cases.

As Steele remembered the conversation later, Clark said, "Gentlemen, let's get to the point. Chief, you've asked for a complaint charging Senator Kennedy with leaving the scene of an accident. Now I'm sure I don't have to tell you two gentlemen that there are technical defenses to this charge." Steele jumped up and began pacing. "There are technical defenses," Judge Clark repeated, "but there are also considerations that transcend the usual criminal case and we've got to be guided by those considerations."

"Judge," Walter Steele said in his flat, loud tones, "what do you mean, technical defenses? Why, you couldn't win this case with a winning machine! Judge, please let's not fence around."

Robert Clark III started to speak, but the older man said, "Walter, I'm a country lawyer—"

Steele interrupted, "Judge, you're no country lawyer and I'm no country prosecutor. Now let's get to the point."

"All right," Clark said. "I suggest that my client admit to a finding."

Steele was pleased and displeased. "Admitting to a finding" was almost equivalent to pleading *nolo contendere,* or no defense. It did not require the defendant to stand up and say the ugly word "guilty," but it was a tacit admission that he did not dispute the accuracy of the charge. As for sentencing, there was little difference between a loud plea of guilty and a mute agreement to a finding. Either way, the judge would ask for a summation of the facts in the case, and pronounce sentence accordingly. Steele was pleased that the other side was willing to start off the plea bargaining at such a level, but he was displeased because he knew that tough District Judge James A. Boyle of Martha's Vineyard would never agree to such a plea. He could see the bald-headed judge sitting up there in his red bow tie and black robes pronouncing imperiously, "I want a plea of guilty or not guilty! Now which is it?" Also, an agreement to a finding presupposed an amicable arrangement between the defense and the prosecution, and in this case Walter Steele did not want to make such an arrangement. "No, Mr. Clark," he said slowly. "No dice. This judge wouldn't go for it, and I won't go for it either."

"Well, it's perfectly reasonable in this case, isn't it?" Clark went on.

"I don't think so," Steele said. "Now Judge, please cut it out, will you? The public is clamoring for his ass. It seems to me you either have to plead guilty or not guilty."

"Wait a minute, Walter," Clark said, his own voice rising for the first time. "I'm not kidding now. I think there *are* defenses to this charge."

"Judge, I'm not unaware of that," Steele said, "but technical defenses or no technical defenses, you know we've got enough to hook him, at least in this court. So let's get down to cases.

I'm tired." Even as he spoke sternly, Steele found his respect for old Judge Clark growing. He told himself that Clark was the kind of plainspoken lawyer he admired; the Kennedys could not have chosen better.

"Well, there are other considerations in this case," Clark said. "I have to keep them in mind. Now look: I'm not trying to con you, Walter. I'm not a close friend of the Kennedys, even though I have a place near theirs. Why they've chosen me, I don't know."

"I know why they've chosen you," Steele said. "For once, they're showing intelligence. You're a criminal lawyer and a good one. You don't represent the Mafia or anybody like that, and you're thoroughly identified with Cape Cod. You're a damned good choice."

"I'm not one of those people that are invited over to the compound for cookouts and parties," the judge went on. "I'm not a social friend of the Kennedys. When I go over to the compound on this case, I'm not a free agent. As you know, there's another attorney in charge. At the compound, the ones who seem to have the most to say about the case are Stephen Smith and Ted Sorensen. We have conferences, but Smith and Sorensen seem to be calling the shots. The senator walks in and out, but he really doesn't participate."

"I understand all that," Steele said, "but I think they should rely on you, because you know this game a little better than they do."

"Maybe you're right," Clark said, rising to his feet, "but I've got to clear everything first. Now suppose we start talking out loud about pleading guilty. What would you recommend to the judge?"

"A suspended sentence," Steele said. "Anything else would be preposterous. I'd recommend a suspended sentence for *anybody* on a first offense leaving the scene."

"What about this judge?" Clark said. "Do you think he'd go along?"

"I think so."

"Can you be sure?"

"You can't be sure of anything with Judge Boyle," Steele said, "but he's the judge we've got. If he was a whore, it'd be different. If he was like some judges, we could get on the phone and say, 'Judge, they want to plead guilty and we'll recommend a suspended sentence, how do you feel?' and he'd say, 'Fine, okay.' But if I ever called Judge Boyle up, he'd throw me in jail. I'll tell you this: if you're ever gonna get a fair shot, you'll get it before this guy. He won't be influenced by the press, he won't be influenced by you or Kennedy, and he won't be influenced by me or Arena. He goes strictly by the facts."

Clark turned toward the massive Arena, standing in the shadows against the wall. "How do you feel about it, Chief?" he asked.

"Well, gee, Judge," Arena said hesitantly, "I go along with Walter. I think the judge'll suspend. I think the judge *should* suspend."

"I'm glad to see you're not out to hang the senator," the elder Clark said, smiling.

"No," Steele said. "We're not. A suspended sentence in a case like this would be fair to everybody."

"Okay," Clark said, as he arose to shake hands with the two men. "As I told you, I'm not a free agent. I've got to go to the compound and see what they say about this. We'll fly back and talk tomorrow."

At first, a few of the survivors of the party at Chappaquid-dick had been willing to talk to the press, but only on their own terms and at their own length. By Thursday, it had become possible to take these snippets of information and piece together a rough outline of what had happened: a sort of inside version of the tragedy, minus the testimony of the most important witness of all, Senator Edward M. Kennedy, who was staying in his shell at the compound and reportedly refusing to confide even in some of his oldest friends. The story, as it emerged, contained contradictions and discrepancies, but at least it appeared to be more complete and more reasonable than the statement worked up by Kennedy and Markham at the police station. It went approximately as follows:

The girls were old friends, sharing a common denominator of dedication to the Kennedys. Each had worked in Robert Kennedy's "boiler room" in Washington, where a running count of convention delegates was maintained, and after Kennedy had been assassinated and the girls had gone their separate ways, they had stayed in touch and held occasional reunions. In fact, they had had one a few weeks before Chappaquiddick, but Senator Ted Kennedy had not been able to attend. There was nothing new about the girls getting together with Kennedy, his aides, and/or their wives; they had even partied at the various Kennedy mansions. The reunion at Chappaquiddick had been in the works for at least a month.

On Thursday afternoon, four of the girls had arrived on Martha's Vineyard and were driven to the Katama Shores Motor Inn by Jack Crimmins. The girls were:

Mary Jo Kopechne, twenty-eight, a self-described "novena Catholic" with a flair for "mod" clothes, dancing, and off-beat music like the score from *Hair*. She shared a Georgetown house with other Washington career girls, drove a blue Volkswagen, drank moderately but never smoked, disdained vulgar language, and traveled with a crowd of urbane Washingtonians. She seldom dated, although she was mildly attractive, with shoulder-length blond hair, a slender five-foot-two figure, and handsome legs. She was variously nicknamed Salome, for her dancing talents, and Twiggy, for her figure, but old friends called her M.J. She was totally devoted to politics and to the Kennedys; her adoration of Robert Kennedy had been so intense that she had trailed him down the corridors of the Senate Office Building and kept a picture of him on her desk in the office of Senator George Smathers of Florida. Inevitably, she had joined Kennedy's staff and translated her feelings into hard work. Ethel Kennedy said of her: "She was the kind who stayed up all night and typed Bobby's Vietnam speech, and she retyped it at 6 A.M. She was content to remain in the background and do the drudgery."

When Robert Kennedy was assassinated, she had worked for two months in the silent office, tearfully packing files and closing down the operation; then she had drifted into a series of political jobs, and now was working for Matt Reese, a campaign consultant in Washington.

Esther Newberg, twenty-six, an intelligent and attractive woman, politically astute and possessed of a dignified maturity that made her seem older than her years. She had worked for Senator Abraham Ribicoff of Connecticut before moving to Robert Kennedy's staff in 1968. She was noted for her efficiency ("she follows through," a superior said), but she lacked the head-in-the-clouds attitude of some of the other Kennedy staffers. "She gave the impression of having something else in her life besides working for Robert Kennedy," a friend said. She was extremely poised, dated often, and was employed as special assistant to the vice-president of the Urban Institute in Washington.

Rosemary Keough, twenty-three, a graduate of Manhattanville College, the exclusive Catholic girl's school that was the alma mater of various female Kennedys including Ted's wife Joan and Robert's wife Ethel. Barely five feet tall, "Crickett" Keough was the only "boiler room" girl shorter than Mary Jo Kopechne, but she was noted among the Kennedy workers for her stamina. "She never stopped working or talking," a co-worker said. The daughter of a wealthy Philadelphia businessman, she had worked as a JFK volunteer while in high school, helped answer his post-assassination mail while still a freshman at Manhattanville, and went straight into Robert Kennedy's office on her graduation in 1967. Slightly stocky, freckle-faced and red-haired, she was popular with men, but during a long period of melancholy after RFK's assassination she had dated seldom. She wore her favorite pin, shaped like a PT boat, almost constantly, and worked in Washington for the Children's Foundation, a Kennedy project.

Susan Tannenbaum, twenty-four, daughter of a Greensboro, North Carolina, dentist, graduate of Centenary College in Hackettstown, New Jersey, and Miami University in Oxford,

Ohio. She had worked for Robert Kennedy starting in 1967, mostly in the mail room, although she served her stint with the other girls in the "boiler room." She was intelligent, sensitive and highly competent, and slightly more oriented to liberal causes than some of the other workers, who seemed more mesmerized by the Kennedy charm. After Robert Kennedy's death, she moved smoothly to the staff of Representative Allard Lowenstein of New York, one of the rallying leaders of "the new politics" and a key mover in the 1968 campaign to dump Lyndon Johnson.

The four young women spent a relatively quiet Thursday night, walking around the colorful streets of Edgartown, enjoying a seafood dinner, and returning to the Katama Shores Motor Inn at an early hour. The next morning they were joined by two more "boiler room" girls:

Maryellen Lyons, twenty-seven, who had gone straight into politics after graduation from Regis College in Weston, Massachusetts, in 1963. "John Kennedy said that it was the only way to make things better, and that the whole world needed us," she had said, explaining her postgraduation decision to cancel her application for courses at Boston University. Later Ted Kennedy recruited her to work in RFK's presidential campaign— "a wild and wonderful day," she recalled. "I thought it was just for the weekend, but they wanted me to stay, and of course I did." After the assassination, she went to work for Massachusetts State Senator Beryl Cohen, a Ted Kennedy protégé, and soon became Cohen's administrative assistant. On the wall above her desk was a portrait of Robert Kennedy and a placard: HAPPINESS IS TED KENNEDY IN 1972.

Nance Lyons, twenty-six, Maryellen's sister, a Kennedy volunteer in 1962 and 1964, and the only one of the six girls who worked directly for Senator Ted Kennedy. As a legislative aide she performed such tasks as drafting legislation and writing speeches on the Boston Harbor Islands Bill, the Plymouth Rock National Monument Bill, and the Saugus Ironworks Bill. Robert Kennedy had borrowed her from his brother to work in his 1968 "boiler room," and later she had gone on detached service to help set up Hubert Humphrey's boiler room. After the presidential campaign of 1968, she had helped to run fund-raising dinners to pay off the RFK campaign deficit, and then returned to routine duties in Ted Kennedy's Senate office. Like her sister Maryellen, she was described by intimates as a "straight arrow": bright, hardworking, passionately devoted to politics and the Kennedys.

The six old friends exchanged greetings and brought one another up to date on the news as of that Friday morning, July 18. Then they changed into swimsuits and piled into a black Oldsmobile driven by Ted Kennedy's chauffeur, Jack Crimmins, for the trip to Chappaquiddick, where there was an Atlantic beach at the end of the road that led across the Dike Bridge.

Early in the afternoon, Crimmins left the young women at the beach and drove to Martha's Vineyard Airport to pick up the arriving senator. Kennedy had a reservation at the Shiretown Inn, but instead of registering, he asked Crimmins to take him straight to the rented cottage on Chappaquiddick. There he changed into swimming trunks and went with Crimmins to the beach to greet the girls and enjoy a quick dip before the first heat of the regatta. An hour or so after Kennedy had left to board the *Victura,* the girls had changed clothes and journeyed to the Edgartown Yacht Club dock to watch the races from the *Bonnie Lisa.* After the heat, they returned to the Katama Shores to get ready for the party that evening. At about 8 P.M. a group of twelve converged on the cottage. In addition to the six girls, Crimmins and Kennedy, the group included:

Paul Markham, thirty-nine, debonair, bespectacled former U.S. attorney for Massachusetts (appointed by Lyndon Johnson on the recommendation of Edward M. Kennedy) and a personal friend of the Kennedys. During his three years as U.S. attorney he had been praised for sending Mafia boss Raymond Patriarca to the penitentiary and damned for losing the Plymouth mail robbery case, but when he left the job he was generally credited with having performed in a workmanlike manner. He was not popular with young males; once he had led a contingent of law enforcement officers into the Arlington Street Church in Boston to arrest young men of draft age who had taken sanctuary. His relationship with Ted Kennedy was close; both men shared qualities of charm, gregariousness and wise-cracking affability. He sailed often with Kennedy, played in the family's touch football games, and once distinguished himself in the Kennedy legend by dislocating a shoulder in a game against a group of British students visiting the compound at Hyannis. Married and the father of seven children, he had recently gone into private law practice in Boston.

Joseph F. Gargan, thirty-nine, variously described as "almost a Kennedy," "a flunky," "a very underrated individual," and "a damned good lawyer before he became a damned good banker." Gargan's parents had died when he was a child, and the Kennedys had helped to bring him up. After graduation from Notre Dame he had chosen to submerge himself in the political fortunes of his cousins, and he had worked quietly and effectively for the Kennedy brothers, serving as national campaign manager for Robert in 1968. As children, he and the youngest Kennedy had played together, and the two men were like brothers. They had toured Massachusetts in Ted's 1962 campaign, and Gargan had climbed out on the tailgate of the truck on many a night to proclaim: "I can see that Ted Kennedy needs no introduction here tonight, but I want to introduce to you a man who has traveled this state from the hills of the Berkshires to Post Office Square in Boston, from Lowell in the north to New Bedford in the south, a man of leadership and dedication, from a family long dedicated to this state and to this nation, whose only desire is to carry out this tradition of service. . . ." The two young politicians learned their trade together, and when they were not on the campaign trail they were skiing or sailing or socializing, bosom companions through the years. For his labors, Gargan seemed content with little. He served two brief terms as assistant U.S. attorney in Boston, worked diligently as a courtroom lawyer specializing in liability cases, and finally accepted the position of vice-president of a small bank in Hyannis. He was married, and the father of two children.

Raymond S. LaRosa, forty-one, a short, dark-haired professional fireman now working as a Massachusetts Civil Defense officer. LaRosa had met Ted Kennedy through Edward Moss, the aide who had been killed instantly in the 1964 plane crash, and everyone presumed that LaRosa's advancement from Andover fire lieutenant to Massachusetts Civil Defense field officer had been through his friendship with Kennedy. Long regarded as Ted Kennedy's man in Andover, LaRosa was remembered by some of his former fire department colleagues as a modest person who did not throw his influence around. "Ray never made a big thing about the Kennedys," a firefighter recalled, "but if they wanted something done in Andover they'd do it through him." Married and the father of four children, he sometimes sailed with Ted Kennedy, but he was not regarded as one of the compound intimates.

Charles C. Tretter, thirty, a dean's list graduate of Boston College who had worked from 1963 to 1966 on Ted Kennedy's staff, looking after such constituency matters as missing social security checks and complaints against federal agencies. Tanned and athletic-looking, with a thatch of hair that gave him a superficial resemblance to the Kennedys, Tretter had held various positions in and out of politics after leaving Kennedy's staff in 1966, and now was working as counsel to the New England Regional Commission in Boston. He was married, with three children, and lived in Dedham, Massachusetts.

According to the snatches of information given out in the first week after the incident, the party had started slowly. Gargan busily prepared hors d'oeuvres: miniature shrimp rolls with sherry, chicken liver rolls with burgundy, lobster rolls, ravioli, all purchased frozen from Mercier's market in Edgartown. One of the men had brought a small outdoor barbecue, and it sputtered and smoked on the front lawn of the cottage. After a while, the first frozen two-inch steaks were placed atop the coals, but the capacity of the grill was so small that the partygoers had to eat in shifts, and chef Gargan was ribbed loudly by the hungry group. Early in the evening, Rosemary Keough asked one of the men to drive her to Edgartown, where she picked up a portable radio to enliven the party, and in her eagerness to return her prize to the cottage, she inadvertently left her purse in the black car. It contained the keys to the motel where she and Mary Jo Kopechne would be sleeping, and she knew it would be safe.

By 10:30, the last steak had been eaten and the partygoers began singing, telling jokes, and listening to outrageously funny stories about Boston politics. Because so much time had been spent eating, there had been little drinking; most of the party-goers had confined themselves to one or two drinks, and no one had had more than four or five over the evening. Sometime after 11 P.M. (estimates varied from 11:15 to "after midnight") Ted Kennedy and Mary Jo Kopechne disappeared. No one was worried; Kennedy had been saying that he was tired and wanted to rest up for Saturday's racing, and Mary Jo had been saying that the day had worn her out. It was presumed that the senator was giving her a lift back to the motel. Only Jack Crimmins had any specific memories of the departure. He said that Kennedy had come to him at about 11:15 and said, "Give me the keys, Jack. I've got to sail tomorrow, and I want to get some sleep." To Crimmins, Kennedy did not appear to be under the influence of alcohol. "I've been with the senator on many occasions when there was drinking," Crimmins told an interviewer, "and there was nothing unusual about his appear-ance or behavior on this occasion. I said a few words to him, gave him the keys and walked across the lawn with him toward the car. I didn't see who was with him. He drove off toward the ferry." With his boss gone, the sixty-three-year-old bachelor went into one of the tiny bedrooms in the cottage and dropped off to sleep.

Shortly after midnight, the remaining partygoers realized that they had missed the last ferry to the mainland, and they slept wherever they could find a soft spot—on the remaining bed, on a couch that could be made into a bed, and on mattresses and blankets thrown on the floor. Most of them did not learn about the accident until the next morning, when they all left the cot-tage for Edgartown and the sad trip back to their homes. Esther Newberg, who provided much of the early information about the affair, summed up: "It was a steak cookout, not a Roman orgy." Asked if Kennedy or his lawyers had advised anyone to refuse to discuss the case, she said, "Absolutely not."

But shortly after the various interviews and attempted interviews had begun to find their way into print, reporters noticed a sharp change in the attitude of Esther Newberg and the others. Suddenly doors began to slam in newsmen's faces; telephone numbers were changed, and various of the "boiler room" girls disappeared from their normal haunts. Reporters who had been old acquaintances of the partygoers were told to halt their periodic attempts to make the girls talk, if they valued the friendships. A newspaper reporter spent an entire night at Rosemary Keough's front door, receiving nothing but silence for his vigilance; photographers who staked out for the girls were threatened with invasion of privacy suits. The change in the air was sudden and marked, and a Washington correspondent reported that the girls had been advised to keep quiet. Only loyal Kennedy workers had attended the party; it would not have been necessary to warn them twice. A tabloid weekly newspaper offered the girls twenty thousand dollars each for the "true" story of Chappaquiddick, and a monthly magazine offered five thousand dollars more. There were no takers. A reporter for a syndicate of British and Australian newspapers wangled a date with one of the "boiler room" girls and offered her fifty thousand dollars for her story. The girl continued to sip her scotch and did not so much as dignify the proposal with an answer. As for the men who attended the party, they had not said a word about the case since the accident. They seemed to be taking their cue from Paul Markham, who told a reporter that he could see no reason to discuss the matter, "now or ever"—and from Kennedy, who remained incommunicado at the compound.

At first, the peculiar pattern of silence was puzzling to the top reporters. The story of the party, even though it had come out in tortuous bits and pieces, did not appear to be strongly damaging to anyone's reputation, except insofar as some people would always cast a dubious eye on mixed groups sleeping under the same roof. Certainly nothing that happened in the cottage seemed to be prejudicial to Kennedy's defense on the traffic charge. Correspondents for the world's most influential newspapers and radio and television stations sat in the bars and spas of Edgartown late into the night, theorizing and guessing and pondering the abrupt embargo on news. Comparing notes, they came across some pieces that did not seem to fit into the rest of the puzzle, and they wondered if there were clues to the mysterious night embedded in some of the seemingly inconsistent remarks that had been made earlier. For example, one of the girls had said that Kennedy returned to the cottage after midnight with a story that his car had run off the road and Mary Jo was sitting in it. Another "boiler room" girl had said that Markham and Gargan, looking "normal," came back to the cottage at 2:15 A.M. and said nothing about an automobile accident. And a third girl was quoted as saying that Joe Gargan told her shortly after dawn Saturday, "We can't find Mary Jo." How were the newsmen to make sense out of statements like these that did not fit into any portion of the story that was slowly coming out? They shook their heads and continued seeking clarification, but by now their sources, from the beginning never overly cooperative, had dried up entirely. The best reporters in the world cajoled and implored and entreated and begged, offered tens of thousands of dollars, and received nothing but stony silence and threats.

Rumors and innuendos soon began to fill the vacuum thus created. The most popular was that Joe Kennedy III had somehow been connected with the incident, either that he had been behind the wheel of the Oldsmobile when it went off the bridge (and his uncle was covering up for him) or that he had played a major part in "borrowing" a boat and ferrying his uncle and others back and forth from Chappaquiddick that night. The "proof" was said to be that young Kennedy, disoriented and drenched, had been seen at 3 A.M. Saturday on an Edgartown street, and that he had beaten his way back to Hyannis Port the next day without taking further part in the regatta. Other early theorists spread the word that Kennedy had taken Rosemary Keough and Mary Jo Kopechne out for a midnight ride, and when Kennedy had parked the car and gone for a walk with

Miss Keough, an angry Mary Jo had driven off and crashed into the water. There was a third theory, equally implausible, to the effect that Mary Jo had gone out to the black Oldsmobile for a brief nap, and that Kennedy and Rosemary Keough had accidentally driven the car into the water without knowing that a third person was inside. None of the theories made much sense (and none turned out to be true), but neither gossipy Edgartown nor a panting nation was going to let the matter rest. There had been a tragic accident; a United States Senator had issued a statement full of holes, and certain postaccident comments had confused matters even more. Now there was only silence, and for a while fantasy would have to suffice. There was a single certainty: the blond was still dead.

By Thursday, six days after the accident, Dr. Donald Mills had had several conversations with the district attorney's office in New Bedford. He had insisted to Assistant District Attorney Armand Fernandes that he was being snowed under by telephone calls and needed assistance, but each time Fernandes had gentled him down and told him that he was doing fine. The harassed doctor suggested that the D.A.'s office issue a release about the case covering the important facts, so that he would not have to spend long hours on the telephone repeating them. Fernandes said he would consider it. Once Mills broached similar ideas to District Attorney Dinis himself, but the colorful prosecutor made it plain that he wanted to stay out of the case. "He said he was gonna let Jim Arena handle it," Mills told his wife. "He said, 'I'm gonna keep my office out of it. I don't want another Lee Harvey Oswald affair, and if I get in it's gonna stir up a big Roman holiday in Edgartown.' He said, 'We don't want that, so we'll let Jim handle it.' "

On Thursday afternoon, Mills picked up the ringing phone and recognized the voice of the district attorney again. The two men exchanged small talk about the foul weather that had hung over eastern Massachusetts ever since the accident, and then Dinis said, "Dr. Mills, you're sure of your diagnosis, aren't you?"

Mills was slightly taken aback. This was the first time that

Dinis had mentioned the diagnosis to him; he had thought the matter more or less closed. "Certainly," he said. "I certainly am."

"I don't think there's any particular need for an autopsy then, do you?" Dinis said.

"No, I don't," Mills said. "Of course I don't."

On that same Thursday the grieving Kopechnes were interviewed briefly. They said that the Kennedys had offered to take care of all the funeral arrangements but that they had met the expenses themselves, including the ones on Martha's Vineyard. Mrs. Kopechne said that Ethel Kennedy had called twice and Joan Kennedy once, and that both had been comforting, although no one at the compound was volunteering any inside information about their daughter's death. One of the "boiler room" girls had come to the Kopechne home in Berkeley Heights, New Jersey, to spend a few days with the bereaved couple, and she had told them confidentially that the Chappaquiddick affair had been totally innocent; Kennedy dropped by the party just to say hello, announced that he was fatigued from racing, and agreed to chauffeur an equally tired Mary Jo to the ferry. To the Kopechnes, knowing their daughter's high moral standards, the story sounded perfectly plausible.

"I hate to sneak around like this," Walter Steele was telling Jim Arena as the two men waited in an empty office at the Martha's Vineyard Airport, "but you know how it is. You can be trying a case and whacking away at your opponent and gouging out his eyeballs, but if your client sees you having lunch with the other guy's lawyer, right away he says, 'Oh, those bastards are selling me out.' So you can imagine what five hundred reporters would say if they knew we were having secret meetings with the enemy!"

"Right now I don't give much of a damn," Arena said. "My conscience is clear. I just wish we could get this damn thing over with. I'm not sleeping, I'm not eating, and my wife says I'm not acting myself."

"What makes you think you've got a monopoly?" Steele said. "I'm losing a pound a day. Look at me! I wasn't fat to begin with. I think it's coming out of the bone marrow."

Earlier that morning, Robert Clark Jr. had called Arena and announced that he was bringing Kennedy's decision over on the first available plane, and a meeting had been arranged in an empty office in the airport building. At last the two Clarks walked into the room accompanied by Richard J. McCarron, the Edgartown lawyer who had been hired to fight the issuance of a complaint, and the trio of Kennedy lawyers appeared to be all business. "We want to move with dispatch," the elder Clark said. "There are some very serious security problems to be considered, but first let's decide what we're going to do in court."

"That's fine with us, Judge," Steele said. "What *are* you going to do?"

"Well, I've been studying the statute, and it's peculiar in that it doesn't provide for a fine. All it says is two months' to two years' imprisonment. So we were wondering how you'd feel about our pleading guilty and asking for probation."

"Copping a plea is fine with me," Steele said, "but I don't think probation makes sense where a United States Senator is involved. Can you imagine a senator checking in regularly with his probation officer? Can you imagine a senator asking permission to leave the state, things like that? I think it would be absurd, Judge."

"Maybe you're right," Clark said. The group discussed the idea for a few minutes, with Steele refusing to alter his position and the Clarks and McCarron gradually admitting that he was right.

"Okay, then," Judge Clark said, "here's what we'll do. We'll take a plea and a suspended sentence. Dick McCarron will get up and make a brief statement about the plea. He'll say that we're pleading guilty even though we have some technical defenses—"

"Don't do that!" Steele advised the older man. "You'll get in all kinds of trouble with Judge Boyle. I've seen it happen eighty-five times in his court. The judge'll say, 'Either you plead guilty or not guilty. If that man's not guilty, then I don't want a plea of guilty. If he pleads guilty, I don't want an explanation of how he's really technically not guilty.' And he'd be right. He'd stop you from making a statement like that if you plead."

"Well," Clark said, "what's more important now is the timing. The security people are scared to death that there's a nut lurking around someplace. This case has inflamed a lot of people, and we'll have to go to extraordinary lengths to protect the senator. I think you'll agree, Walter. It's only common sense. You don't want to get the man killed."

"Of course not," Steele said. "What do you suggest?"

Clark said that the best security was to quietly alter the publicly announced timetable of the case. The hearing on issuance of the complaint against Kennedy was scheduled for Monday morning, four days away, and if there were any psychopaths around, they would be likely to show up on that date. "What we propose is to go to court the first thing tomorrow morning and get the whole thing over with," Clark said. "We'll waive our right to a hearing on the complaint, we'll plead guilty, and we'll get the hell out of here before any psychos can find out what's happening."

"Does that make sense to you, Jim?" Steele said to Arena.

"It makes a lot of sense," Arena said, "provided I can get the state police ready and my own men ready and really tighten down on the security. What about the Secret Service, and transportation for the senator?"

"All that can be handled at the compound," Clark said. "They'll have a plane standing by to bring him over first thing in the morning, and if the weather's bad he had come by private boat. Where would he dock?"

"Oak Bluffs wharf would be simplest," Arena said. "Nobody'd be looking for him to land there, and it's only five miles away. We could have the state police pick him up and give him an escort to the courthouse."

With the outline of the plan in hand, the group started to split up, the Clarks to fly back to the compound and make last-minute arrangements, and Steele and Arena to return to the police station and get to work on security. A final pretrial meeting was scheduled for seven o'clock that night. The press had discovered Steele's fishing chalet, but he also owned an equally remote rental cabin nearby, and the group would meet there to coordinate their arrangements for the next day's hearing.

Through the early afternoon, Steele and Arena worked busily on their telephones, making sure that the courtroom and the round-trip routes would be secure. Swearing everyone to secrecy, they lined up a crew of deputy sheriffs, all ten officers of the Edgartown Police Department plus the two policewomen, extra bailiffs and courtroom assistants, and a contingent of state policemen. When every security arrangement had been nailed down, they called in patrolman Robert Bruguiere and told him that the 4 P.M. edition of the "Walter and Dominick Show" would have to be scrapped for the day and he would have to stand up before the reporters and announce the cancellation. "My God!" Bruguiere said. "They'll tear me limb from limb!"

"Well, I'm sorry, Bob," Arena said, "but Walter and I have too many things to do. Just tell them we'll make it up to them in the morning." Bruguiere went off, talking to himself, and Steele and Arena sat back to exchange congratulations on their efficiency. Suddenly Steele blanched and stood up, and before Arena could ask him what was the matter he had grabbed the telephone with trembling hands and begun to dial a number. "The judge!" Steele was mumbling. "We forgot to tell the judge!"

"Oh, my God!" Arena said.

Steele got Court Clerk Thomas Teller on the telephone. "Tommy!" he said. "Where's the judge?"

"Off-island, visiting relatives," Teller said. "Why?"

"Will he be here in the morning?"

"Not that I know of. There's nothing docketed."

"Oh, my God," Steele said. "Listen, Tommy, we've put the Kennedy case down for tomorrow morning, first thing."

"And you haven't cleared it with the judge?"

"No, but we've had to move fast for security reasons. We don't want to serve notice that Kennedy's gonna come down here and then have somebody hit him with a shotgun."

"Sure, Walter," Teller said. "That's fine reasoning, but you know Judge Boyle. He wouldn't change his calendar around for the Pope."

"Tommy, see what you can do, will you?" Steele begged. "We're meeting with the Clarks tonight, and they're over at Hyannis right now making all the arrangements with the Secret Service and everybody. Call the judge up and see what you can do, will you?"

"I'll do my best, but I can't promise anything. You better get over here right away in case I need you."

A few minutes later Steele arrived at Teller's house to find the court clerk putting down the telephone and rubbing a reddened ear. "Whew!" Teller said. "Did he chew me out!"

"What'd he say?" Steele asked. "Is it okay for tomorrow?"

"Don't know yet," Teller said. "He said he'd be back tonight at seven and he'd talk to me at his place in Vineyard Haven."

"How'd he sound?"

"Awful. Like he was gonna throw *me* in jail! You know how he is. He doesn't see any difference between Ted Kennedy and any other defendant. They all have to be handled the same. First thing he said was, 'This is highly unusual.' I was expecting *that*. Then he says, 'Why should we put this case down for any date *they* ask?' I said something to the effect that you thought there was a security problem, and he said, 'What security?' so I said, 'Well, Mr. Steele's been talking about the possibility of an assassination.' He says real loud, 'Well, Steele's an alarmist.' Finally he says, 'Now you just get this straight, you and Steele can't change my schedule. I won't talk about it now.' So I asked him when he *would* talk about it, and he said at seven o'clock at his place and hung up."

"Jesus Christ," Steele said. "You know him better than I do, Tommy. Do you think he'll come around?"

Teller shrugged his shoulders. "We won't know till tonight," he said.

Just before dark, Steele and Arena met the incoming delegation of Kennedy lawyers at the prosecutor's rental cabin in Ocean Beach, five miles from the center of Edgartown. "Everything's worked out at our end," Robert Clark Jr. announced. "How about yours?"

"Well, everything's worked out here," Steele said, gulping hard, "except the judge."

"Except the judge?" Clark said.

"Yeh, we lined up everybody else, but we don't know if the judge'll be sitting in the morning."

"Good God," Clark said. "When *will* you know? We've moved heaven and earth to get everything arranged."

"So have we," Steele said, "but this judge doesn't move easy. We're going over to see him in Vineyard Haven right now. We'll know soon."

Judge Clark looked more upset than Steele could remember. "Get back here right away and let us know, will you?" he said. "Because if we're *not* going to court in the morning, we've got an awful lot of plans to change."

"So do we," Steele said. He drove his sputtering red Land Rover downtown, picked up Teller, and headed across the beach road toward Vineyard Haven. "Now for Christ's sake *you* stay out of this," Teller said. "Let me handle the judge. I don't even want him to *see* you. The way he is, he'd throw the whole case out if he even saw you and me in the same car together."

Steele parked a half-block from Judge Boyle's house and waited. Five minutes passed, then ten, then fifteen, then twenty. Steele chain-smoked and looked at his watch, and soon the half-hour mark had gone by. He wondered what was happening inside the judge's house, and what the others were doing back in the cabin. He had left the two Clarks and McCarron with Chief Arena and instructed all of them to stay away from the windows and remain quiet if anyone knocked on the door. If a single smart reporter were to see the Kennedy lawyers closeted with the chief of police in a cottage belonging to the prosecutor, the security would be seriously compromised.

It was just turning dark when Steele looked through a cloud of bluish cigarette smoke and saw the usually placid Thomas Teller hurrying toward the car. Teller looked both ways, opened the door and climbed in.

"Well?" Steele said, his fingers trembling.

"You lucked out," Teller said. "He'll hear the case tomorrow."

"Beautiful!" Steele threw the Land Rover into gear. "Now we've got to get back and tell the other guys before they panic. The whole thing will be over tomorrow. I can't believe it. I'm so goddamned sick of it I'm taking the first boat back to Boston."

"What do you think's happening at the cabin?" Teller asked.

"I think Arena and the lawyers are wondering what's gone wrong, and I think they may be getting ready to alert everybody that we blew it."

"Is this the fastest this thing'll do?"

"No," Steele said. "I think I can get it up a little." He tromped on the gas pedal and watched the needle climb, and the red Land Rover careened into the limits of Oak Bluffs. Then the engine died.

"What's the matter?" Teller said.

"I think we're out of gas."

"Well, Jesus Christ, don't you ever look at the gas gauge?"

"The gas gauge hasn't worked in five years," Steele said. "It was the first thing that went."

"Come on," Teller said, climbing out of the car. "We're not far from the state police barracks. I know a shortcut."

The two men stumbled through a field of weeds and ran up to the front door of the barracks puffing and grunting. They knocked, and there was no answer. They pounded on the door, but no lights were showing and it was plain that the place was empty.

"Now what?" Teller said.

"There's a phone booth over there," Steele said, "but with my luck I won't have a dime." He fished in his pockets as he ran toward the single telephone booth, came up with a coin, and then discovered that the booth was occupied. Steele took up a position a few inches from the glass exterior and tapped his foot loudly. Minutes passed, and the conversation showed no signs of abating. Steele tapped on the glass and the young man inside ignored him. Steele flung open the door and said, "Please, get out! I've got to make an important call."

"What?" the young man said, gripping the phone more tightly than ever.

"Look," Steele said loudly, "I'm a cop. Now get out of here before I have you arrested!"

The young man hung up the telephone and ran off, looking back over his shoulder as he disappeared. Steele dialed the number at his cabin, and relaxed when the voice of Jim Arena came on the line with a low "Hello?"

"Jim," Steele said, "we're on our way. We ran out of gas. We'll be there in ten minutes."

Arena responded in a strange whispered croak, and Steele had to ask him to repeat. "I said there's a four-hundred-pound albino trying to get in the door!" Arena said. "What do I do now?"

"Oh, my God!" Steele said. "Keep him out. We'll be right over!"

Back at the cabin, no one had been cracking wise or telling jokes as the long waiting period passed. There were no curtains in the place, and Arena had advised the Kennedy lawyers to remain as far back in the shadows as possible. Few cars passed on the dirt road that ran outside the windows, but there was no point in unnecessary risks. Arena had brought along the first draft of his summary of the case; the wording would help to determine the judge's attitude toward punishment, and the Clarks asked if they could check the statement for accuracy. "I don't see why not," Arena said. "You're going to plead guilty anyway." Someone had started to turn on a light, but Arena cautioned them against it. "There's just enough light left in the sky," he said. "Come on, we'll go into the bedroom and hold it up to the window."

Robert Clark Jr. perused the typewritten statement and handed it to his son and then to McCarron. "Do you mind a little editing?" old Judge Clark said.

"Not if it doesn't change the facts," the chief said.

"Well, here where you've written: 'There were opportunities for the defendant to have made himself known to the proper authorities after the accident.' Don't you think that should say, *'immediately* after the accident'?"

"Good idea," Arena said, and penciled in the correction. The Clarks suggested a few more innocuous changes and Arena made the alterations. Just as Judge Clark was holding the paper up to the failing light for a final look, a voice boomed from outside: "Walter!"

"Jesus Christ!" Arena said. "Who's that?"

"Walter!" the voice shouted. "Hey, Walter!"

Arena beckoned the three lawyers into the farthest corner of the tiny bedroom and tiptoed into the living room. Outside, he could discern the figure of a huge man with the unmistakable coloring of an albino. The man tipped back his cowboy hat and shouted, "Hey, Walter, it's me!" and just then the phone rang.

When the chief had finished talking to Steele, he took another look outside and saw that the big man was laying a pair of boards up the steps of the house. He dashed into the bedroom and told the lawyers to stay put, and then he returned to his vantage point. As he watched, the albino backed a small truck around to the doorway and began unloading a refrigerator. "Jesus!" Arena said to himself. "What's he gonna think when he sees me in here? What a goddamn stupid time for this to happen!"

The doorknob began to rattle, and Arena swallowed hard and opened it. "Hi, there!" he said to the big man. "How are you tonight?"

"Fine," the man said. "I brought Walter's refrigerator."

"Well, you just go right ahead," Arena said. "Don't let me bother you." He stepped into the bedroom and signaled the lawyers not to move, and continued to make small talk with the delivery man. At last the refrigerator was installed and Steele drove up in the Land Rover.

"Everything's okay," Steele said, after a few words with the refrigerator man. "We go to court in the morning."

"How about *him?*" Arena asked, beckoning toward the delivery truck disappearing down the road. "Can we trust him?"

"My refrigerator man? He's the most trustworthy guy on the island," Steele said. "I doubt if he'll even tell his wife he saw anything. But he did say something to me before he left."

"What was that?"

"He said there were some suspicious-looking guys hiding in my bedroom."

Friday dawned gloomy, wet and heavy, like Thursday and Wednesday and every day since the accident. No red ball of sun climbed over the ocean in the east; instead, a dull, leaden glow signaled the approach of day, and raindrops spattered the pavements intermittently. Cameramen on the courthouse steps covered their equipment and themselves with plastic sheets, and cursed softly as they worked, like a company of infantry ready to move out. The night before, they had been relaxed and calm; nothing had been scheduled until Monday, when Kennedy's lawyers would appear to resist the issuance of a complaint, and most of the gentlemen of the press, radio and television had been engaged in informal conference in the various spas of the little town. Then messengers had begun arriving and shaking up the groups. "There's going to be a press conference at the church, right away!" they had said, and everyone had rushed into the night to hear a distinguished-looking man in a charcoal-gray suit identify himself as Judge Robert G. Clark Jr., Senator Kennedy's attorney, and report that the senator would appear for arraignment in the morning. That had ended the brief respite. Many of the TV technicians had worked without sleep, and some of the cameramen and reporters had been up since long before daybreak. Few were feeling sympathetic to the cause of the senior senator from Massachusetts.

Shortly after 8 A.M. the *Marlin* docked at the Oak Bluffs wharf, and three persons disembarked: Senator and Mrs. Ted Kennedy and his brother-in-law Stephen E. Smith. The threesome climbed into an unmarked gray Chevrolet that was driven by a state policeman and protected, fore and aft, by more cars full of troopers. At exactly 8:35 the caravan pulled up in front of the red brick "County of Dukes County Courthouse," and the party stepped into a swarm of newsmen. Kennedy wore a dark blue suit, white shirt and dark tie, and he had discarded the surgical collar that had brought sneers and snickers from cynics at the funeral three days before. He wore neither outer coat nor hat against the rain, and his wife was modestly stylish in a black-and-white plaid coatdress and matching hairband. Old Kennedy hands barely recognized Smith; his hair had been trimmed close, and the last time anyone had seen him in public his hair had been modishly long. The three walked briskly up the steps of the old courthouse, ignoring the questions that peppered them, and were ushered into the tiny probation office, where Kennedy filled out an identity card. The courtroom was one flight up, and as the little party waited in the closed jury room for 9 A.M. and the appearance of Judge Boyle, the door opened and a big, smiling man entered. "Good morning, Chief," Kennedy said, and his wife echoed, "Good morning, Chief."

"Good morning," Arena said. "Here's your summons." He handed over a white piece of paper and disappeared into the courtroom.

Walter Steele had overslept in his fishing chalet overlooking Nantucket Sound, and he rushed about shaving and dressing and repeating his courtroom arguments to the picture of Humphrey Bogart on the wall. Like the newsmen, he was suffering from lack of sleep. The courtroom would not accommodate all the reporters who wanted to get in, and Steele had sat up till 3 A.M. working out the "pooling" arrangements. Then he had pitched and tossed and suffered nightmares.

As Steele shaved erratically in front of the mirror in the closet-sized bathroom of the cabin, he clung to a single consoling thought. The case was almost over. The reporters and cameramen who had been pestering him for six days would hop on the ferry and go home. He would be able to return to Boston himself and see if his law partners still recognized him. He would be able to eat solid food again. All he had to do was recite his lines in the final short scene of the last act of the tragedy.

Steele parked the red Land Rover with the defective gas gauge a block from the courthouse and headed for the steps. "No, fellows!" he said as the reporters pressed around him. "I can't say anything. *No,* fellows! No comment right now." As he started to enter the building, he felt a tug on his sleeve and turned to see a game warden who had a reputation for strict enforcement of the law. The man was in uniform, and he seemed to have something extremely urgent on his mind. For an instant Steele wondered what could be more urgent than the case about to be heard upstairs, but he stopped as the warden whispered something inaudible. "What is it?" Steele asked.

"Walter," the man said, "I've been watching that fellow and I've got to speak to you."

Steele felt a chill up and down his backbone. From the very beginning, it had struck him as odd that no one had seen Kennedy driving up and down the roads of Chappaquiddick, no one had seen the black car careening toward the Dike Bridge, and no one had seen him make the long walk from the bridge back to the Lawrence cottage. Now here was the game warden showing up at the last second, a man who prowled around the waterside at all hours of the day and night, a man who lurked in shadows to catch poachers. "Oh, God," Steele said to himself. "We're about to go on trial and this guy was at the dike that night and he saw something and *now* he tells me!" He beckoned the game warden aside. "Yes, what is it?" he whispered.

"I got a whole bushel," the warden said.

Steele was mystified. "A bushel of what?"

"Come over here," the warden said, pulling Steele away from the flow of traffic. He looked to both sides, cupped his hands together and said into the prosecutor's ear, "Seed clams!"

"Seed clams," Steele said. *"Seed clams?"* Suddenly he realized that the man was talking about a poaching case. "For Christ's sake," he shouted, "stick 'em up your ass!" He hurried up the winding staircase and into the courtroom.

Reporters leaned forward for a better look as Ted Kennedy walked through a back door of the courtroom behind his short, ruddy-complexioned local lawyer, Richard J. McCarron, and took a place alone in a row of chairs just behind the bar. He clasped and unclasped his hands, looked at the floor, and occasionally rested his head on his knuckles as though deep in meditation. Fifty feet away, Joan Kennedy and Stephen Smith watched like medical attendants ready to spring to the patient's aid. Jim Arena sat a few feet away from Smith and Mrs. Kennedy, and the various lawyers, including McCarron and the Clarks and Steele, took up positions at counsel's tables just under the high wall of the bench. The courtroom was silent, except for mumbled conversations among the reporters. From the peach-colored walls, portraits of judges dead and gone gazed upon the scene, and uniformed policemen stood at the top of the stairwell in the back and shushed those who were chattering below. There was a silence when the church bells across the street chimed nine times, and then the voice of the bailiff, John O'Neil, a lean, spare man who looked as though he had just stepped off a whaling ship, boomed across the courtroom: "The District Court of Dukes County is now in session. God save the Commonwealth of Massachusetts!"

Judge James A. Boyle, white-moustached and balding and wearing his trademarked red bow tie, adjusted his robes around him; he looked a little like a juridical Andy Gump, and all eyes focused on him as he nodded to the clerk of the court, Thomas Teller. Everyone resumed his seat as the clerk began reading: "Commonwealth versus Edward M. Kennedy. This complaint charges that Edward M. Kennedy of Boston, Massachusetts, on the 19th day of July, 1969, at Edgartown, did operate a certain motor vehicle upon a public way in said Edgartown and did go away after knowingly causing injury to Mary Jo Kopechne without stopping and making known his name, residence, and the number of his motor vehicle. How do you plead, guilty or not guilty?"

Kennedy stood up. His wife glanced at him and touched her face nervously, but she retained her composure. Kennedy said, "Guilty," in a voice that barely carried to the first row of the courtroom, and quickly repeated loudly: "Guilty!"

Teller motioned him to take his seat, and the judge leaned forward and said, "As is my custom, I'd like to hear a summary of the evidence."

"May I call the officer, your honor?" Walter Steele said, blinking behind his brown-rimmed glasses.

"You may."

Jim Arena walked across the front of the courtroom, raised his hand to take the oath, identified himself as "the officer in charge of this matter," and began reading from his notes. "Your honor, while on duty at Edgartown on the morning of July 19, 1969, at approximately 8:20 A.M., I was advised of a call made to the Communications Center by a person who lived on Chappaquiddick that two boys had reported to her that there was a car submerged in the water near the Dike Bridge." The notes fell from his hands, and Arena stooped over embarrassedly to retrieve them. "I went immediately to the scene," he continued, "and was later joined by a member of the Edgartown Fire Department scuba team, and through his efforts learned there was a young woman in the vehicle. She was brought to the surface and taken up to the shore, where she was placed in the Edgartown police cruiser to await the arrival of the Edgartown medical examiner."

As Arena read, Kennedy appeared sometimes to hang on every word and sometimes to be lost in thoughts of his own, his eyes directed downward. Reporters whispered to one another that he looked ill, and they noticed that throughout the proceedings Joan Kennedy and Stephen Smith continued to watch the young senator almost to the exclusion of the other activities in the courtroom. Raindrops beat against the closed windows, and the crowded courtroom was sultry and warm; several of the spectators found themselves hoping that the hearing would end quickly so that they could go outside for fresh air.

"The medical examiner, Dr. Donald R. Mills of Edgartown, pronounced the victim dead by reason of drowning," Arena went on. "During this investigation, it was learned that the car belonged to Edward M. Kennedy of Boston, and an attempt was made to locate him. In a call made by me to the Edgartown police station in this regard, I learned that Mr. Kennedy was at the station. I returned to the station and was advised by Mr. Kennedy that he had been the operator of the vehicle involved. Mr. Kennedy advised that he believed that the accident had happened sometime after 11:15 P.M. on July 18, 1969." Arena paused and cleared his throat. To this point, he had alleged no violation of the law, and when he began speaking again, in a slightly firmer voice, the judge rested his arms on the oaken bench and paid close attention. "This accident was reported by Mr. Kennedy at some time after 9 A.M. on the morning of July 19, 1969," Arena read. "Investigation of the accident and accident scene produced no evidence of negligence on the part of the defendant. However, there appears that there were opportunities for the defendant to have made himself known to the proper authorities immediately after the accident. Therefore, a complaint was sought against him for leaving the scene of an accident involving personal injury without immediately making himself known." Arena closed his notes and looked at the judge.

Steele stood up. "May I ask the defense counsel, Mr. Clark, if he has questions from this officer?" he said.

The Robert Clarks remained seated, but Richard J. McCarron, who had argued many cases before Judge Boyle, took to his feet and said, "No questions of the officer."

Arena started to leave the witness stand, but Judge Boyle said, "I have a question. Were you in charge of the investigation?"

"Yes, sir," Arena answered.

"I would be most interested in determining from the defendant or the Commonwealth if there was a deliberate effort to conceal the identity of the defendant."

"Identity of the defendant?" Arena repeated, slightly flustered. "Not to my knowledge, your honor."

There was a momentary silence, and Steele said, "Thank you, Chief."

As Arena was walking back to his seat in the audience, the young McCarron began to address the bench. "Your honor—"

"I should be glad to hear you gentlemen on disposition," the judge said.

"Your honor," McCarron went on, "the attorneys representing Edward M. Kennedy have advised him that there are legal defenses that could be presented in this case. However—"

The judge's face clouded over, and he pointed an admonishing finger at McCarron and said, "Mr. McCarron, just a moment. I don't think that is a proper statement to make. Do you now desire to say you want to plead not guilty?"

The lawyer reddened. "No, your honor," he said.

"I am concerned now with the question of disposition, mitigating circumstances, aggravated circumstances," the judge said, making it plain that the subject of "technical defenses" was not to be pursued.

McCarron paused, looked at his co-counsels the Clarks and said, "The defendant is adamant in this matter, your honor, that he wishes to plead guilty to the offense of operating a motor vehicle and going away after causing personal injury—it is his direction that this plea enter—and leave the disposition to this court. I believe your honor has had experience in disposition on motor vehicle accidents of this nature. It is the contention of the defendant, your honor, and the defendant's attorneys, that confinement to the House of Correction to this defendant would not be the proper course. I believe his character is well known to the world. We would therefore ask that any sentence that the court may impose be suspended."

When McCarron had finished, Steele stood up and said, "May it please your honor, the Commonwealth suggests for your honor's consideration that this defendant be incarcerated in the House of Correction for a period of two months and that the execution of this sentence be suspended. It would seem that having in mind the character of the defendant, his age, his reputation, that the ends of justice would best be served were he given a suspended sentence."

The judge turned to the probation officer. "There is no record, Mrs. Tyra?" he asked. Mrs. Helen Tyra said there was none. Boyle looked down at the attorney's table and said, "Considering the unblemished record of the defendant, and the Commonwealth represents this is not a case where he was really trying to conceal his identity—"

"No, sir," Steele interjected.

"—Where, it is my understanding, he has already been and will continue to be punished far beyond anything this court can impose, the ends of justice would be satisfied by the imposition of the minimum jail sentence and the suspension of that sentence, assuming the defendant accepts the suspension."

"The defendant will accept the suspension, your honor," McCarron said quickly.

The judge beckoned to Teller, and the court clerk said loudly, "Edward M. Kennedy." The senator stood up. "On the complaint," Teller announced, "the court has found you guilty and has sentenced you to serve two months in the House of Correction at Barnstable; sentence is suspended."

As bailiff O'Neil shouted for order, reporters exploded out the doors of the courtroom to find telephones. A twenty-year-old defendant shuffled toward the front of the courtroom to stand trial on a charge of driving without a license, and at the same time the Kennedy party was escorted out the back door of the courtroom and down a flight of steps to the first floor. At the head of the main entrance staircase, Kennedy motioned the packed group of cameramen and reporters for quiet, but there was so much racket coming from spectators who spilled out into the street and onto the lawns on the other side that hardly anyone heard his words. "I have asked the television networks for time this evening to make my statement to the people of

Massachusetts and the nation," he said; then he followed a V-wedge of state troopers down the stairs and into a car.

As the vehicle pulled slowly away, shoving its own path through the hundreds of spectators, a reporter shouted, "Chief, Chief!" at the tall man walking across the street toward the town offices. "Chief," the reporter asked, "what's next?"

"What's *next?*" Jim Arena said, smiling broadly and looking fully relaxed for the first time all week. "Nothing's next. The case is closed."

By that afternoon, enough news had leaked out of the compound at Hyannis Port to convince reporters that something very strange had been going on inside. There had been little enough action for the eyes of the newsmen who had ringed the grounds night and day for a week. Once Joan Kennedy had gone out to buy a candy bar. Another time Ted and Joan were seen strolling in the rain that had hardly stopped falling since the accident. Rose Kennedy, head held high as always, periodically walked among the flowers, and each morning a priest came in to say Mass. Ethel, looking more distraught than she had since the death of her husband, struggled through several sets of tennis, and somehow managed to make room in her already overcrowded house for old friends like Robert McNamara, the former defense secretary, who showed up to help. ("Well, Bob," another Kennedy advisor had said when McNamara appeared, "you handled the Bay of Pigs and Vietnam. Now let's see what you can do with this one.")

At first, the reporters standing watch had come to the conclusion that the dignitaries inside the compound were engaged in round table discussions over the accident and the senator's future, with everyone speaking up and everyone's counsel being considered. But despite the vows of secrecy administered to each trusted visitor, the press soon discerned a pattern that did not indicate such an atmosphere of free and open discussion and mutual respect. In the early hours, not even Ethel and Rose Kennedy had been let in on the true picture. The senator, remorseful and wracked by back pain, apparently had not confided in them, and they were unaware of the damning time lag between the accident and its reporting. On Saturday afternoon and evening, after Kennedy returned home, the atmosphere around the compound had been one of sadness over the death of Mary Jo Kopechne and relief that the last of the four brothers had not been killed. Until newspapers began arriving, the true dimensions of the tragedy were largely unknown.

Then the avalanche of voluntary assistants began to descend on the neat white mansions in the compound. There were former JFK advisors like McNamara, Theodore Sorensen and Kenneth O'Donnell, former RFK advisors like David Hackett and Burke Marshall, and Ted Kennedy's own confidants, men like David Burke and John Tunney and John Culver, as well as Joseph Gargan and Paul Markham and a dozen or so others, invited and uninvited. At first, some of the visitors were puzzled by Kennedy's absence from most of the early councils. He was hardly seen by anyone, and when he did show up he seemed distant, distracted, and vague. A few days went by before some of his old friends concluded that the senator was in a kind of delayed shock, that he was barely able to discuss what had happened. He was said to be spending long hours alone in his nearby Squaw Island home, mourning by himself. On Monday, three days after the incident at the Dike Bridge, he had placed his second telephone call to the Kopechne family, but after managing to get out a few words he had broken down completely, and Joseph Kopechne had barely been able to understand him.

By Wednesday, after the ordeal of the funeral, Kennedy had pulled himself together enough to speak about the incident, but to the surprise of certain of the compound visitors, he gave the distinct impression that he was not telling everything. There appeared to be councils within councils, and varying levels of trust. Some of the most reliable of the Kennedy family advisors began to feel left out. One early arrival, a member of the innermost circle of Kennedy politics, left the compound in dismay when it appeared that his suggestions for full and immediate disclosure of the accident details were somehow repugnant to the others and that he was not being told the truth about the incident. Even Robert McNamara, after insisting that the silence was jeopardizing Kennedy's standing with the public, reportedly felt that major pieces of the puzzle had been kept from him. Other old members of the Kennedy political family were finding out, mostly by indirection, that their assistance was not wanted. A man who had been one of RFK's closest confidants was unable to reach Ted Kennedy on the phone; he was shunted to one of the senator's advisors, who listened to his suggestion that a detailed statement of facts be released as quickly as possible, thanked him, and hung up. There was no further contact between the RFK advisor and the compound. Another famous political figure, a crony of John F. Kennedy, called the compound, leaving his name and number. The call was not returned.

By midweek the picture that emerged from behind the perimeter was one of barely controlled chaos. Sorensen, who seemed to have taken over direction of the affair, was said to have bawled out Markham and Gargan for failing to report the accident promptly, as though theirs had been the primary responsibility. Kennedy was said to have broken down twice in front of the others, once after someone had upset his dying father by trying to explain the accident to him. The idea that the senator should appear on television was bitterly argued; some felt that the ordeal would be too trying, others that television was the wrong medium. When it was decided that Kennedy should plead guilty on Friday and appear on television on Monday, Robert McNamara reportedly said in disgust: "He'll have no credibility at all by then." After fierce arguments that went on until early each morning, it was agreed that Kennedy must speak at the first opportunity, but since the case was pending in the courts, he should not comment publicly until its disposition. The networks were called and asked to clear time on Friday night.

But what should be said? Kennedy could not seem to make up his mind, and on those rare occasions when he sat down with his advisors and discussed strategy, it was clear that his thinking processes were still muddled by the events of the week and his own physical misery. Finally he was advised flatly that only a few courses were open to him on television, and that he would have to choose one. He could discuss the accident but not relate it in any way to his Senate career or his future. He could discuss the accident and announce that he intended to complete his Senate term. He could announce his resignation from the Senate. Or he could leave the whole matter up to his constituents. The last course seemed to appeal to the troubled politician; it gave him time, and he needed time to decide on his own course of action. When the theme of the TV message had been worked out, Sorensen enlisted the aid of David Burke, Kennedy's administrative assistant, and Milton Gwirtzman, a former Kennedy staffer, and began to hammer out the wording. Burke Marshall, who had been a Justice Department aide to Robert Kennedy, stood by to review the lines, and the final changes in the text were not made until a few hours before air time on Friday night, July 25, one week after the accident.

The address was scheduled to originate from the home of Joseph P. Kennedy Sr., but even that minor detail had been the subject of discussion. Wiring problems eliminated the senator's Squaw Island residence from consideration, but a few thought the speech should be made from Ethel's or Jackie's home. Kennedy vetoed the idea; he felt that it would appear that he was trying to gain sympathy from the previous tragedies, a suggestion that had always been a touchy point with him. Shortly before the scheduled air time of 7:30 P.M., members of the Kennedy clan began to gather in the home of the patriarch, while the old man dozed in his bedroom upstairs, oblivious to what was happening. There were Stephen and Jean Kennedy Smith, Patricia Kennedy Lawford, Eunice Kennedy Shriver, Ethel Kennedy, and Rose Kennedy, at seventy-nine one of the most cheerful in the group. None of the grandchildren were in the room with the big TV cameras, but Joseph III and Robert Jr. and Bobby Shriver were elsewhere in the house. The three children of Ted and Joan Kennedy remained in their Squaw Island home, a few minutes away. When the senator arrived the conversation in the big room was subdued. Family members made small talk and watched him anxiously for signs of mental stress, but he appeared to be in full control, slightly tense and nervous but in command of his emotions. At last he seated himself in front of the lenses, a red light flicked on, and he began to speak:

My fellow citizens:

I have requested this opportunity to talk to the people of Massachusetts about the tragedy which happened last Friday evening. This morning I entered a plea of guilty to the charge of leaving the scene of an accident. Prior to my appearance in court it would have been improper for me to comment on these matters. But tonight I am free to tell you what happened and to say what it means to me.

On the weekend of July 18 I was on Martha's Vineyard Island participating with my nephew Joe Kennedy—as for thirty years my family has participated—in the annual Edgartown sailing regatta. Only reasons of health prevented my wife from accompanying me.

On Chappaquiddick Island, off Martha's Vineyard, I attended on Friday evening, July 18, a cookout I had encouraged and helped sponsor for a devoted group of Kennedy campaign secretaries. When I left the party, around 11:15 P.M., I was accompanied by one of these girls, Miss Mary Jo Kopechne. Mary Jo was one of the most devoted members of the staff of Senator Robert Kennedy. She worked for him for four years and was broken up over his death. For this reason, and because she was such a gentle, kind and idealistic person, all of us tried to help her feel that she still had a home with the Kennedy family.

There is no truth, no truth whatever, to the widely circulated suspicions of immoral conduct that have been leveled at my behavior and hers regarding that evening. There has never been a private relationship between us of any kind. I know of nothing in Mary Jo's conduct on that or any other occasion—the same is true of the other girls at that party—that would lend any substance to such ugly speculation about their character. Nor was I driving under the influence of liquor.

Little over one mile away, the car that I was driving on an unlit road went off a narrow bridge which had no guardrails and was built on a left angle to the road. The car overturned in a deep pond and immediately filled with water. I remember thinking as the cold water rushed in around my head that I was for certain drowning. Then water entered my lungs and I actually felt the sensation of drowning. But somehow I struggled to the surface alive. I made immediate and repeated efforts to save Mary Jo by diving into the strong and murky current but succeeded only in increasing my state of utter exhaustion and alarm.

My conduct and conversations during the next several hours to the extent that I can remember them make no sense to me at all. Although my doctors informed me that I suffered a cerebral concussion as well as shock, I do not seek to escape responsibility for my actions by placing the blame either on the physical, emotional trauma brought on by the accident or on anyone else. I regard as indefensible the fact that I did not report the accident to the police immediately.

Instead of looking directly for a telephone after lying exhausted in the grass for an undetermined time, I walked back to the cottage where the party was being held and requested the help of two friends, my cousin Joseph Gargan and Paul Markham, and directed them to return immediately to the scene with me—this was some time after midnight—in order to undertake a new effort to dive down and locate Miss Kopechne. Their strenuous efforts, undertaken at some risks to their own lives, also proved futile.

All kinds of scrambled thoughts—all of them confused, some of them irrational, many of them which I cannot recall and some of which I would not have seriously entertained under normal circumstances—went through my mind during this period. They were reflected in the various inexplicable, inconsistent and inconclusive things I said and did, including such questions as whether the girl might still be alive somewhere out of that immediate area, whether some awful curse did actually hang over all the Kennedys, whether there was some justifiable reason for me to doubt what had happened and to delay my report, whether somehow the awful weight of this incredible incident might in some way pass from my shoulders. I was overcome, I'm frank to say, by a jumble of emotions—grief, fear, doubt, exhaustion, panic, confusion and shock.

Instructing Gargan and Markham not to alarm Mary Jo's friends that night, I had them take me to the ferry crossing. The ferry having shut down for the night, I suddenly jumped into the water and impulsively swam across, nearly drowning once again in the effort, and returned to my hotel about 2 A.M. and collapsed in my room. I remember going out at one point and saying something to the room clerk.

In the morning, with my mind somewhat more lucid, I made an effort to call a family legal adviser, Burke Marshall, from a public telephone on the Chappaquiddick side of the ferry and belatedly reported the accident to the Martha's Vineyard police.

Today, as I mentioned, I felt morally obligated to plead guilty to the charge of leaving the scene of an accident. No words on my part can possibly express the terrible pain and suffering I feel over this tragic incident. This last week has been an agonizing one for me and the members of my family, and the grief we feel over the loss of a wonderful friend will remain with us the rest of our lives.

These events, the publicity, innuendo and whispers which have surrounded them and my admission of guilt this morning raise the question in my mind of whether my standing among the people of my state has been so impaired that I should resign my seat in the United States Senate. If at any time the citizens of Massachusetts should lack confidence in their senator's character or his ability, with or without justification, he could not in my opinion adequately perform his duty and should not continue in office.

The people of this state, the state which sent John Quincy Adams and Daniel Webster and Charles Sumner and Henry Cabot Lodge and John Kennedy to the United States Senate, are entitled to representation in that body by men who inspire their utmost confidence. For this reason, I would understand full well why some might think it right for me to resign. For me this will be a difficult decision to make.

It has been seven years since my first election to the Senate. You and I share many memories—some of them have been glorious, some have been very sad. The opportunity to work with you and serve Massachusetts has made my life worthwhile.

And so I ask you tonight, people of Massachusetts, to think this through with me. In facing this decision, I seek your advice and opinion. In making it, I seek your prayers. For this is a decision that I will have finally to make on my own.

It has been written a man does what he must in spite of personal consequences, in spite of obstacles and dangers and pressures, and that is the basis of all human morality. Whatever may be the sacrifices he faces, if he follows his conscience—the loss of his friends,

his fortune, his contentment, even the esteem of his fellow man—
each man must decide for himself the course he will follow. The
stories of past courage cannot supply courage itself. For this, each
man must look into his own soul.

I pray that I can have the courage to make the right decision.
Whatever is decided and whatever the future holds for me, I hope
that I shall be able to put this most recent tragedy behind me and
make some further contribution to our state and mankind, whether
it be in public or private life.

Thank you and good night.

When the address was over, Kennedy seemed relieved, and
the family members congratulated him on his delivery. "He said
what he had to say," someone observed, and the group sat down
to a quiet dinner at Ethel's. At 10 P.M. Kennedy excused himself
and went home, and at 10:30, exhausted from a day that had
begun in court in Edgartown, he was in bed.

The reaction to the Kennedy speech came in waves. The first
was an outpouring of almost hysterical sympathy and compassion such as had not been seen in public life since the assassination of Robert Kennedy the year before. Western Union's
Hyannis office received thirty thousand telegrams over the
weekend; they were almost unanimous in their support of the
young prince of American politics. About twenty-five hundred
telegrams arrived in Boston, and another five hundred in Washington. By Monday evening the tiny Hyannis post office was
knee-deep in letters, and the postmaster ordered the mail
trucked to Kennedy's Boston office for sorting.

Small-town Massachusetts newspaper comment was similarly
favorable, though at a somewhat lower pitch. The *Berkshire
Eagle* said that the speech "came as a considerable relief to
those of us who feel he is too valuable a public servant to be
lost to the state and the union." The Springfield *Daily News*
commented that Kennedy had "decided properly that he can
still be of service to the people of Massachusetts and the country." Other newspapers said that Kennedy had explained himself manfully and it was time the case was closed.

At Edgartown, the proprietors of the Shiretown Inn posted a

sign on their bulletin board: "We fully endorse Senator Kennedy, fully appreciate his statement and encourage his remaining in office." A university professor almost got into a fight at a Martha's Vineyard cocktail party over his own pro-Kennedy leanings. He shouted to the scoffing partygoers: "Look, if Senator Kennedy says he swam across to Edgartown, he swam across to Edgartown! If Senator Kennedy says he turned down the Dike Road by mistake, he turned down the Dike Road by mistake! Is that clear?"

But after the early wave of approbation had receded, another wave came curling in. It was made up of extreme distaste, disdain and contempt for the speech and its authors. "Devious and mawkish," wrote John Marquand Jr., longtime resident of Martha's Vineyard and student of Massachusetts politics. David Halberstam wrote in *Harper's:* "The statement itself was of such cheapness and bathos as to be a rejection of everything the Kennedys had stood for in candor and style. It was as if these men had forgotten everything which made the Kennedys distinctive in American politics and simply told the youngest brother that he could get away with whatever he wanted because he was a Kennedy in Massachusetts." Barry Farrell wrote in *Life:* "He was simply hustling heartstrings, using words, cashing in on the family credibility. For the first time ever, I felt embarrassed for a Kennedy." The Washington *Evening Star* took note of the Massachusetts telegrams and letters backing the senator, but added that "letters to the editor of the *Star,* however, have been overwhelmingly critical," and printed a few excerpts: "Instead of its being contrite, Kennedy's statement to his docile serfs in Massachusetts was a cold, heartless, political maneuver." "I'm appalled at what Kennedy and the brains around him believe the intelligence of most Americans to be. Or do they really believe us to be nothing but sheep after all? This is one lamb who says, 'Bah!' " "Kennedy's fireside chat was a masterpiece of careful contrivance. Delivery was superb. The message came through loud and clear. To paraphrase an oft-repeated quotation: 'Ask not what I did at a time of crisis; ask instead how you can help me get out of a bad hole.' "

Nowhere was the criticism of Kennedy and the speech writers more cutting than in the place where the accident had happened. The Shiretown owners stood almost alone in approving their guest's actions. An Edgartown newspaperman took the pulse of the community and reported privately: "Edgartown got sick to its stomach watching him on TV. People here know this area and they know the Dike Bridge, and they can't be conned. They sat in front of their screens and listened to Ted Kennedy tell stories that made him sound like Superman, and they laughed and said, 'Come on, Teddy, you've got to be kidding!' Phones were ringing all over town as soon as he went off the air. Everybody agreed he must be lying, that he must be covering up for something much worse. Now they're wondering what that *something* is."

V
The Trap

THE irony of Chappaquiddick was that certain patterns were visible from the beginning, like an optometrist's mosaic that shows a vivid red symbol through one lens and a jumbled mass of dots through another. One only had to look through the correct lens. Kennedy said that he drove the car off the bridge, and people nodded and said: *How* did it happen? But perhaps they should have said: *Did* it happen? By unquestioningly accepting Kennedy's version of the accident itself, they may have put themselves in the position of the dupe in the classical algebraic puzzle, who fails to recognize that the first equation of a series is nonsense and that therefore everything that follows in the series, no matter how logical and orderly, must also be nonsense.

From the time of the publication of Kennedy's first statement, the one drawn up by him and Markham in the back room of the Edgartown town office building, there were doubters on all sides. There were the automatic doubters of the far right, who would have questioned Kennedy if he had read the 1-to-9 multiplication tables. There were doubters in the middle, neutral or ambivalent in their feelings toward the youngest Kennedy brother but able to reason logically and see inconsistencies in his narration. And there were even doubters on the left, where Kennedy's appeal was reckoned to be strongest. The left traditionally harbors the cerebral types, Spiro Agnew's "effete corps of impudent snobs," and to such mentally active persons the original Kennedy statement was its own refutation.

But what, specifically, were these doubters doubting? First, they were doubting that Ted Kennedy, thirty-seven years old, lifelong sailor and navigator, old hand behind the wheel of an automobile, had managed to make a turn that was exactly 180 degrees off course. They were doubting that his rescue attempts had been quite so heroic as his description. And they were doubting that he had spent a whole night in such befuddlement that he could not report the fatal accident. When the young senator went on television a week later "to tell you what happened and to say what it means to me," he only increased the doubts. He said he had not been driving under the influence of liquor, whereupon the doubters insisted that one supposition or the other had to be correct: either he had been drunk, or his mind had been clear enough to report the accident (or if not *his* mind, then certainly the minds of Paul Markham and Joseph Gargan). People doubted the new version of the postmidnight diving acrobatics, which now had been broadened to include Gargan and Markham, and they doubted the Kennedy explanation of how he returned to Edgartown, "impulsively" swimming across the tidal channel and nearly drowning in the effort.

But in all the thousands of words that were written about the two statements, hardly any dubious comment was made about Kennedy's version of the accident itself. The whole subject of how the black Oldsmobile 88 went out of control on the bridge had been covered by two sentences in his police report (". . . I descended a hill and came upon a narrow bridge. The car went off the side of the bridge") and a single sentence in his lengthy television speech (". . . The car that I was driving on an unlit road went off a narrow bridge which had no guardrails and was built on a left angle to the road"). Apparently that was all that he could remember. He was even less enlightening about his escape from the submerged car. His overall explanation for the skimpy detail was his shock and trauma, a shock and trauma which did not keep him from executing a whole galaxy of postaccident maneuvers and remembering them clearly.

Under close examination, Ted Kennedy's story of losing control and going off the Dike Bridge seemed to make far less sense than any other part of his story. But he could not be

closely questioned about it. He had been shocked and trauma-
tized. His memories were faint. He had "no recollection of how
I got out of the car." But other points were reasonably clear.
He had "actually felt the sensation of drowning." He had dived
down to the car to rescue Mary Jo. He had walked "to where
my friends were eating" and climbed into the back seat of a
parked car. He had enlisted "the help of two friends, my cousin
Joseph Gargan and Paul Markham, and directed them to return
immediately to the scene with me." He had led the men in renewed efforts to save the girl. He had instructed Markham and
Gargan "not to alarm Mary Jo's friends that night." He had
asked them to take him to the ferry landing. He had swum the
120 yards of channel to Edgartown, walked around for a while,
said something to a "room clerk," and gone to bed. All of these
memories were recounted in Kennedy's two reports, but the accident itself seemed to fall into a short period of blackout.

Thus deprived of accident details, the public skipped over
Kennedy's first description of the plunge into Poucha Pond and
lingered long and deliciously on such questions as how he could
possibly have made a wrong turn, how he could possibly have
swum the boiling channel between Chappaquiddick and Edgartown, and what he was doing at a late party with unmarried
women in the first place. The accident details, if they were not
examined too closely, seemed to make a certain amount of
sense. He had been driving on an unlighted, narrow dirt road;
he had come over the top of a hill and suddenly confronted an
off-angle bridge with no guardrails. No wonder he had gone
off. As Mike Mansfield had said in his telegram from Washington, it could have happened to anyone.

But it had *not* happened to anyone before. The Dike Bridge,
ugly and primitive and unrailed and unmarked, twelve feet wide
and some seventy-five feet long, had been in place for twenty
years, and no one had ever driven off it. The bridge lay almost
at the end of a washboard road, a road used by students learning
to drive, by fishermen rushing like lemmings toward the sea, by
lovers preoccupied with the oldest impulses, by wild-eyed young
men full of beer and showing off. The very location dictated a

slackening of inhibitions. Dike Road was at the end of nowhere. Traffic cops did not police it; warning signs did not grace it, and highway engineers left its potholes and ripples till last on their schedules. And yet no one had ever gone off the bridge until Ted Kennedy came along on a moonless night two decades after the bridge's construction. Why did such a dangerous-looking structure have a perfect safety record?

The answer lay in the nature of the road and the nature of the bridge. As Kennedy said on TV, they were unlighted. So is the New York Thruway. Powerful headlamps are built into modern automobiles to help drivers cope with the darkness. But suppose a motorist comes over the top of a hill and suddenly his lights play across a hazard that cannot be avoided? Suppose that "after proceeding for approximately a half mile on Dike Road I descended a hill and came upon a narrow bridge." Then the accident begins to sound plausible, at least to those who have never seen the Dike Road.

The bump which Kennedy called a hill is 670 feet from the Dike Bridge. The drop from the apex of the bump to the lowest point in the road ahead is about one foot per hundred. To call such a gradient an "incline" would be misleading, and to call it a "hill" would be downright exaggeration. The fact is that the approach to the Dike Bridge is almost perfectly flat and perfectly straight, and the driver picks up the bridge squarely in his headlights at distances ranging as far as 300 or 400 feet away. Kennedy's own investigators reportedly found that the bridge was visible at no less than 150 feet, depending on the condition of one's headlights, and a photograph that appeared in *Time* showed the bridge standing out through the photographer's windshield like a wooden monument in the night.

Moreover, Dike Road provides the discerning motorist with ample warnings of other kinds. As one drives down the road, trees and bushes that have crowded the edges suddenly disappear, and one passes a few cottages and comes into an open area, all at a range of some 600 feet from the bridge. Plainly a change is coming. One knows that the sea is somewhere ahead, and that the road cannot go on much farther. Now the road widens into a parking area; the ripples increase in depth, and at 70 feet from the bridge, there is a pronounced hole in the roadway, made by previous drivers applying their brakes. Another such hole jounces the car at 50 feet from the bridge. Even if the driver refuses to believe the sight that has been so clearly visible through his windshield for 300 to 400 feet, he has been warned by the changes in scenery, by the bumpiness of the road, by the parking area, and by the two deep ruts. If after all these natural warnings, he drives up and off the side of the bridge, he has made a driving error so grandiose as to defy the imagination. And if he has been traveling at a speed of only twenty miles an hour, as Ted Kennedy claimed later, *no amount of driving error seems to explain the accident.* It becomes, apparently, unexplainable. It appears that a skilled driver accustomed to high speed (like Ted Kennedy) could hurtle down the Dike Road at eighty miles an hour (if he could retain control on the washboard surface) and have more than enough time and warning to stop at the bridge. How did Kennedy manage to go off at twenty miles an hour? And how did he manage to go off in a straight line, plunging up and over the side of the angled bridge almost as though the car were on a track, as though the steering wheel had been frozen into position? Accident experts who investigated the scene later could not even be positive that the brakes had been jammed on. Light scuff marks showed where the car had continued steady on course and off the right side of the bridge, but the wood had been damp and easily scored. No rubber residue had been left on the planks, and no deep braking gouges were visible in the sandy approach. The accident could not be explained by speed. It could not be explained by poor visibility (the night had been humid but clear); it could not be explained by faulty equipment (the car was examined and found to be in excellent working condition), and it could not be explained by any apparent driver error, at least by any driver error within the normal range of human behavior. And yet it had happened. Manifestly, an Oldsmobile 88 sedan had gone off the Dike Bridge and carried Mary Jo Kopechne to her death, and none of the talk about the bridge's twenty-year safety record, and none of the facts and figures about the road and the bridge and the markings, could alter what happened. There *had* to be an explanation. But where was one to look?

The first and most popular explanation was circulated widely in Edgartown and later around the country: Ted Kennedy had been drunk; he had used the nine hours of silence after the accident to sober up. When word got out that there had been a party at the Lawrence cottage, the proponents of this theory rubbed their hands together and pronounced the puzzle solved, conveniently ignoring the fact that thoroughly incompetent drivers had been passing back and forth over the Dike Bridge since 1949 without incident. There were too many warnings, real and implied, even for those whose minds were elsewhere. Only one type of intoxication could begin to explain the accident, and that was plain, old-fashioned, *blind* drunkenness, in the most literal sense. But if Kennedy had been blind drunk, he would have lost control of the car long before the Dike Bridge, and he would have exhibited pronounced symptoms afterward. One is entitled to doubt various self-serving statements to the effect that drinking at the party was light, but how does one explain that Russell Peachey conversed with Kennedy a short time after the accident and noticed nothing untoward about his speech or his manner? Or that Jim Arena and Walter Steele, expert observers of the effects of intoxication, had come to independent conclusions the next morning that Kennedy was not even slightly "hung over"? Or that Mrs. Frances Stewart had conversed with him twice at 8:30 A.M. and noticed nothing out of the ordinary, except that Kennedy seemed preoccupied? Beyond these human observations, always subject to error, one had the young senator's entire history. His worst enemies did not claim that he was a heavy drinker. Washington correspondents who had followed him around for seven years searched their memories after the accident, and except for rare periods of letdown like the flight home from Alaska, were hard pressed to remember a single example of heavy drinking. Even in his own home, at parties where liquor flowed in generous amounts, Kennedy had remained sober and composed. One correspondent remembered an Irish stag party, like most such affairs almost consecrated to intoxication, where Kennedy had sung a few ballads and gone home, completely steady on his feet. Some of the newsmen's memories stretched back through the histories of three Kennedy brothers, and the expert consensus was that none of them had been a two-fisted drinker. JFK had enjoyed an occasional scotch and water, and RFK had sipped politely at parties, and Ted had had his occasional airborne pillow fight and vaults into the swimming pool, but generally speaking one did not associate alcohol with the Kennedys as one associated it with certain other nationally known politicians. Perhaps the young Kennedys had been influenced by their father, who had neither drunk nor smoked and had promised each of his sons a thousand dollars for abstaining until the age of twenty-one. Whatever the reason, Ted Kennedy was not a heavy drinker, and alcohol was an unlikely explanation for the incident at Dike Bridge. The answer had to be sought elsewhere.

But information was hard to come by. From the very beginning, the only person who knew the precise details was Ted Kennedy, and he was suffering from a sort of pinpoint amnesia. His memory was clear, however, on the time of his departure from the party at the Lawrence cottage. He had left at 11:15 P.M. to drive himself and Mary Jo Kopechne to the Edgartown ferry, which closed down at midnight. Only a wrong turn had kept him from the completion of his innocent journey. In pronounced contradiction to this account stood Huck Look, who swore that he had seen Kennedy's car disappear down the Dike Road at about 12:45 A.M.

In between the senator's statement to Arena and his public statement on television, an apparently plausible explanation for Huck Look's story turned up. According to Kennedy, he had returned to the cottage after the accident, enlisted the help of his friends Gargan and Markham, and returned to the Dike Bridge to dive on the car. It was clear from this that Look could have spotted the three men on their mission of mercy. But the deputy sheriff, beleaguered by the press and besieged by admirers of Kennedy, stood fast. He could not have mistaken the car bearing Kennedy, Markham and Gargan for the car bearing Kennedy and Mary Jo, he explained, because the car he had seen was black and bore a license beginning with L and containing a few 7's. The only other car available to the Kennedy party had been a white Valiant sedan, rented from Hertz. "I can tell black from white," Look said blandly.

No amount of pressure or intimidation could sway him from his story, nor could Kennedy partisans offer a logical explanation of why the deputy sheriff should be lying. He was, after all, a "Kennedy man," one of the few in Edgartown. But more than that, he was an observant officer of the law; he had done what all good law enforcement officers do in remote areas. Unable to remember the full license number and description of every strange automobile they see, they try to remember a salient detail or two: a body style, a fender nick, a letter or number from the license plate. If it develops later that a crime was committed in the neighborhood, they at least have some small fact on which to begin an investigation. Look had been doing this for years. The white lettering on his oil truck was spotted with hastily penciled license numbers and descriptions, placed there against the possibility of crime later divulged. And there was hardly a night when he did not make a mental note of a car or two on Chappaquiddick. On this night it had been a black sedan. He had told himself to remember that the license plate began with an L, and that there were 7's in the number; seven had been his favorite number ever since he had worn it on the local high school basketball team. Even after efforts had been made to gain information that would impeach Look's character and his credibility, the deputy refused to change his story. "I can't help what I saw," he said apologetically. "Investigators for Kennedy are knocking on doors all over Edgartown asking old ladies if I get drunk or run around with women. Well, everybody knows that I don't, but even if I did, it wouldn't change what I saw."

Was there a way to reconcile the contrasting stories? As Walter Steele observed, no one had seen the accident except Kennedy and the late Mary Jo Kopechne; there was not a single independent witness. The Sylvia Malms, mother and daughter, had heard a car pass directly in front of their cottage four hundred fifty feet down the road from the Dike Bridge, but they were inexact about the time and neither professed to have heard the banging of the stricken car's undercarriage on the bridge or the loud splash it would have made on entering the water. The night had been still and windless; earlier visitors to the bridge had heard fish jumping a half-mile down the lagoon; the Malms' windows were wide open. It seemed unlikely that the car they heard late in the evening, while they were still awake, had been the same car that had plunged into the water. Their evidence settled nothing.

A roundabout but revealing approach to the question of time was the study of the tides that spurted into Poucha Pond on mysterious schedules. "Figuring out these tides is no exact science, I can guarantee you that," Foster Silva said later. "You can't go by the charts for Edgartown, because there's a big difference between Edgartown and Poucha Pond. The tides vary at the dike with the moon and the winds and the ocean currents and everything else." Old-timers said that the tides at Poucha ran forty-five minutes to two hours later than the posted times at Edgartown, but the only way to be certain was to go to the pond and look. Low tide at Edgartown had been at 9:54 P.M. on Friday, July 18, and therefore the water must have been low at the Dike Bridge between 10:45 and midnight. Witnesses on Saturday morning watched the tidal flow and counted backward to place the low tide more exactly. They said the pond's low tide had been between 11:00 and 11:30 Friday night. Therefore, by Kennedy's own version of the accident, the car had gone off the Dike Bridge into a dead low tide.

But this information seemed to contradict another portion of Kennedy's statement. On television, he had said, "I made immediate and repeated efforts to save Mary Jo by diving into the strong and murky current. . . ." But if the car went off the bridge just after 11:15 P.M., and if the locals were right about the tides, there could not have been a "strong and murky current"; indeed, there could hardly have been any current at all. Even at a narrow bottleneck like the one under the Dike Bridge, the tide did not change instantly from outgoing to incoming. The change began slowly, and it was not until an hour or so after change of tide that the water began ripping at its accustomed pace of one and a half miles an hour. By specifying that the current had been strong, Kennedy seemed to be contradicting his own estimated time of the accident. As one observer put it later, "He can have it one way or the other, but not both. Either he went off the bridge at 11:15 and dived into a slack tide, or he went off the bridge later and dived into a strong current."

There were other passages in Kennedy's statement that seemed to have far more bearing on the facts than such matters as whether he made the wrong turn accidentally or whether he had swum the Edgartown channel or whether he had been drinking. "The car turned over and sank into the water and landed with the roof resting on the bottom," he said in his statement to Arena. "I attempted to open the door and window of the car but have no recollection of how I got out of the car." In his TV statement, he added a few details: "I remember thinking as the cold water rushed in around my head that I was for certain drowning," he said. "Then water entered my lungs and I actually felt the sensation of drowning. But somehow I struggled to the surface alive."

According to information compiled by the National Safety Council and other concerned groups, there are ways to escape from submerged automobiles, but such escapes are difficult and rare. If the windows are closed, the victim may sit tight and hope that rescue comes before the car fills with water. Under such circumstances, it will be almost impossible to open the doors of the submerged automobile against the tons of water pressure. If the trapped person can summon the coolness and resourcefulness, he can wait until the water had risen to just below his nose, and the pressure inside and out has become almost equalized. Then, in a burst of effort, he can attempt to shove open the door and beat his way to the surface.

But an automobile with three windows out is an almost certain deathtrap. The air burbles out and the water cascades in, and all the weight and pressure are on the side of the inflow. The National Safety Council has no examples in its files of anyone's ever being sucked out of such a car. Assuming that Kennedy was unscathed by the whirling and tumbling action of the car as it gyrated through the air, and that he remained fully oriented and in control of his wits after the car turned over and came to rest in the total blackness of the bottom, the odds against his escape would remain all but insuperable. According to Kennedy, "I attempted to open the door and window of the car but have no recollection of how I got out. . . ." The strongest probabilities are that he did not open the door (it was closed and locked when Farrar reached it the next morning), and that the window on the driver's side was already open (the night had been warm and sultry). Farrar found it rolled down to within an inch of the bottom.

If Kennedy's story of his miraculous escape did not seem to square with the known realities of such situations, his accounts of diving down and trying to rescue his companion also raised doubts. Jim Arena, a strong and healthy swimmer, was forced to give up in daylight after a few dives. Ted Kennedy, like the other members of his family, was also a strong swimmer, but his back was weak. It needed the support of a tight cloth brace, and according to his own accounts he had just undergone a frightful physical ordeal by water. It was difficult to imagine him surface diving down to the submerged sedan in the black of night, while the tide boiled and swirled through the choked passageway. It was equally difficult to imagine him returning later and repeating his dives in the company of his two friends. "Their strenuous efforts, undertaken at some risks to their own lives, also proved futile," Kennedy said on television. But one of the "boiler room" girls was quoted as saying that Gargan and Markham had returned to the cottage at 2:15 in the morning, bone-dry.

There were other statements in Kennedy's narrations that appeared plausible to the general public but drew insiders up short. He said on television: "In the morning, with my mind somewhat more lucid, I made an effort to call a family legal advisor, Burke Marshall, from a public telephone on the Chappaquiddick side of the ferry. . . ." Both the police report and the television address were full of "throwaway" lines like these, uttered flatly and without amplification. But nowhere was there the slightest explanation of what Kennedy was doing on Chappaquiddick at 9:30 in the morning. Presumably he (and the two men with him) had known for some nine hours that Mary Jo Kopechne was lying at the bottom of Poucha Pond. Kennedy had just left the Shiretown Inn, where he appeared to be preparing for a normal day, ordering the *New York Times* and the *Boston Globe,* dropping into the breakfast room, and walking off in the typical attire of a racing yachtsman. He had waved a greeting to sixteen-year-old Steve Ewing on the *On Time,* and disappeared with his friends into the tiny ferry shack on the Chappaquiddick side, where he "made an effort to call a family legal advisor. . . ." Another advisor, Ted Sorensen, attempted to explain the use of the Chappaquiddick telephone later. On a CBS news program with Walter Cronkite, he was asked why Kennedy had not made the call from his hotel. "I'm told that the only telephone in the hotel is one of those that's out in the lobby," Sorensen said. "There's no booth. There's no privacy whatsoever. One does not normally call his lawyer from such a telephone." But in such circumstances, does one take a ferry to search for a private telephone? Edgartown, like most resorts, is littered with telephone booths. Within a one- or two-minute walk of the Shiretown Inn, Kennedy could have taken his choice of twenty-five or thirty, and never boarded the *On Time* at all.

On top of such puzzlements, there were contradictions inherent in the very warp and fiber of the story that Kennedy told and assertions that were totally inconsistent with his own personality, behavior and reputation. For a time it seemed impossible to believe that he had walked past lighted cottages while Mary Jo Kopechne might still have been fighting for her life.

But how could there be any doubt about it when Kennedy himself had admitted making no telephone calls till morning and
when Kennedy himself had called the delay "indefensible"?
What was the point of looking for another explanation when
Kennedy's own *mea culpa* had been so definite and so final?
The public simply had to accept the fact that the youngest of
the Kennedy brothers had blundered in a matter of life and
death. It was not a pleasant thought. One contrasted the picture
of Senator Edward M. Kennedy, arranging for his morning
newspaper delivery, with the picture of Mary Jo Kopechne, her
head pressed up in a footwell filled with salt water. One had to
reconcile an image of Ted Kennedy, climbing aboard the *On
Time* and waving a greeting, with an image of a corpse in a
submerged car. Some were able to make the reconciliation, to
assimilate the unassimilable, to accept the apparent fact that
Ted Kennedy, whether because of shock or trauma or natural
inclination, had been able to function almost normally for long
hours after such an accident. Some said that he was a cold fish,
concerned only with his political image, and that the tragedy of
Chappaquiddick had reached him only as an impediment to his
political ambitions. If such thinking were correct, then Kennedy's extreme depressions in the days after the accident and his
almost hysterical attempt to telephone the Kopechnes and his
tear-filled eyes at the graveside in Pennsylvania had been Academy Award performances, more worthy of a Machiavelli than a
Kennedy. Some simply could not bring themselves to see him in
these terms. They said that they did not care how many confes-
sions of guilt Kennedy made or how conclusive the evidence
was against him. They said that the story did not add up; something *different* had happened at Chappaquiddick.

One can accept a given framework of information and try to
arrange the available facts to fit into it, or one can hypothesize
an entirely different set of conclusions and see if the available
information correlates. In the case of the affair at Chappaquiddick, the tendency was to accept Kennedy's framework and tuck
all the facts inside, even though the story seemed to be no more

logical than Alice's wildest adventures through the looking glass. But what other explanation could there be? What other hypothesis could be made?

One returns to the Dike Bridge, but this time with a new lens. One sets out to *prove* Kennedy's statement that he drove the car off the bridge. But no matter how long one remains at the bridge, measuring and pondering and stepping off distances, the story remains implausible, unprovable. No normal motorist could commit such egregious error. But what if the driver was in a wildly abnormal state or the driving conditions were markedly difficult? Suppose, for example, that the driver was handling a strange car for the first time and that the car was bigger and more powerful than the driver was accustomed to? What if the seat was adjusted for someone much taller? What if visibility was difficult and the driver's feet could barely reach the accelerator or the brake? What if this handicapped driver had also been drinking, and was in a state of nerves? What, in other words, if the driver was Mary Jo Kopechne?

At first glance, a suggestion that Ted Kennedy stepped out of the car on the Dike Road and left Mary Jo Kopechne to drive into the night would seem to raise as many questions as Kennedy's own miscellaneous versions of the incident. The difference is that these questions can be answered more credibly. Certain hypotheses must be accepted along the way, but they are not nearly as difficult to accept as certain hypotheses of Kennedy's, namely, that he drove off a bridge that was almost impossible to drive off, that he failed to take adequate steps to save the girl's life, and that he waited nine hours to report a fatal accident.

Why would Kennedy step out of his car on a lonely road and give it over to the control of a young woman whose name he could not even spell? The answer may lie in his own history and the history of his family. One willingly accepts Kennedy's claim that "there is no truth, no truth whatever, to the widely circulated suspicions of immoral conduct that have been leveled at my behavior and hers regarding that evening." But this did

not change the *appearances*. Kennedy and his helpers had fash-
ioned a private party on a lonely island, using three different
residences to house the partygoers and the party itself, and now
in the twinkling of an eye a nosy policeman was threatening to
undo the security of the whole affair. Kennedy would have had
to consider his reputation and his brothers', and if he knew the
truth fell far short of the legend, he would also know it was the
legend that would be revived if word got out that he had been
partying on Chappaquiddick with five other men and six unmarried women. Now he was on the Dike Road with a few
drinks under his belt, in the company of a young woman with a
few drinks under *her* belt, and probably wondering whether the
man in uniform who had stalked toward his car was planning to
follow. Certainly Kennedy had done nothing illegal; he had
blundered into a private road, backed out, and returned to the
public way. But the cop had kept approaching; now there was
every reason to suspect that he would jump into his station
wagon and speed down the Dike Road to ask them questions.
Rural cops did things like that, and rural cops could be nasty.
Some of them were highly political, and the prospect of netting
a Kennedy in a car with a woman other than his wife would
have titillated many of them.

If thoughts like these did indeed go through Kennedy's head,
his first instinct might have been to flee, as he had fled years
before in Virginia. But he would have realized quickly that he
had no chance to outdistance the law on a dirt road; he was
going to be caught and embarrassed. Probably nothing would
come of it, but much was at stake. It would have been a very
logical step for Kennedy to stop the car between the high walls
of underbrush on either side, jump out, and tell Mary Jo to circle back and pick him up in a few minutes if the policeman did
not give chase. If the cop caught up, she could explain that she
had borrowed the car and was out for a cooling drive. Thus
Kennedy would be completely left out. The plan might well
have appealed to Mary Jo more than the prospect of being interrogated in the car with the senator. She had a sterling repu-

tation to protect and a long history of loyal dedication to the Kennedys; she would have been eager to help him avoid a scandal, especially one based on so little.

It does not take the imagination of a dime novelist to see Mary Jo Kopechne at the wheel of the car, struggling to control two tons of equipment on a strange road while her own adrenalin flowed at high pressure. She might not have taken time to readjust the seat so that her feet could reach the pedals comfortably. At five feet two, she was exactly one foot shorter than Kennedy; her own car was a Volkswagen, about half the size of an Oldsmobile 88, and most of her driving had been done on city streets. As a road racer, she would have been sadly miscast, lurching and bumping down the Dike Road. In less than one minute she would reach the bridge, but she would never see it. Hunched down in the seat, barely able to see, she would continue in a straight line off the bridge.

If this was what happened, Kennedy would have been in a state of confusion and frustration as he waited in the bushes by the side of the road. Quickly he would have realized that the policeman was not going to follow; now all he had to do was fight off the mosquitoes and wait for the girl to return. One can only guess at his possible thought processes as the long minutes went by and the car did not show up. He was waiting halfway down the Dike Road in impenetrable darkness; the moon had set hours earlier, and the situation was entirely out of his control. After a while, he might have wondered if Mary Jo, fortified by a few drinks, was playing a trick on him, playfully making him suffer. Or she might have taken a side road and headed back toward the Lawrence cottage, as a double precaution that she would not be found in the company of the married senator. Finally, he might have guessed that she had managed to get stuck. Off-islanders were prone to that; their wheels went into the sandy shoulders and all their amateurish attempts to extricate their cars only enmired them more deeply. In any case, Kennedy could not have stood by the side of the road slapping mosquitoes all night. If Mary Jo had taken another route and lost her way, or if she was stuck in the sand, he would need a car to help her, and since he was only a short walk from the cottage and the other car, he would turn back instead of walking down the Stygian corridor where the Oldsmobile had disappeared. From his midway point on the Dike Road, he would see no house lights on his way back; there would be none to see. (This hypothesis would explain why Kennedy reportedly told friends later, in obvious confusion, that he could not understand all the allegations about his walking past two lighted houses; he said he had seen nothing. The statement seemed to be as revealing as his comment about the "strong and murky current." If he had walked to the Lawrence cottage from the scene of the accident itself, he could not have missed the Malm house, alongside the road on the left, and the Smith house, alongside the road on the right, both with lights that showed distinctly on this black night.)

If these suppositions are correct, one begins to understand what might have aroused Foster Silva's dogs. Huck Look had seen the roadside dancers at 12:50 just to the north of Silva's house. A few minutes after Look drove on, the two women and the man had passed Silva's house on foot, arousing the animals. After Silva had quieted them, he returned to bed, and a half-hour later, at 1:30 A.M., the dogs resumed their caterwauling. This time they might well have heard Kennedy, making his way back to the Lawrence cottage, and the sounds that Foster Silva heard dimly from the direction of the road might well have been Kennedy telling some of the partygoers what had happened. But if so, exactly what was he saying? *Newsweek* reported that Kennedy had returned to the cottage and given the impression that "his car had merely run off the road somewhere and that Mary Jo was simply sitting in it." Viewed in the light of the possibility that Mary Jo had driven the Oldsmobile, the remark seemed to be illuminating. If Kennedy had indeed been at the wheel and had tried without success to save the girl, why would he return to the cottage and report to close friends that she was sitting in the car by the side of the road? There was reason to conclude that the *Newsweek* version of the story was exactly what Kennedy *did* believe and that at 1:30 in

the morning he did not have the slightest idea that anything serious had happened at the Dike Bridge.

If this is true, one may assume that Kennedy and a few of
his friends piled into the rented white Valiant and began
searching the back roads of Chappaquiddick for the missing car
and driver. But even if they had gone straight to the Dike
Bridge, they might well have missed the evidence of the accident. The scuff marks left by the tires were not conspicuous,
and the dents in the four-inch-high caplog were minor. The
headlights of the Valiant would have illuminated the road and
the bridge, but they would not have shown down into the water
where the car lay concealed by the incoming tide. Sooner or
later, the men in the Valiant might have decided that whatever
had happened, there was no point in involving the senator; it
would be best for him to return to the Shiretown Inn and make
his presence known. Thus he could not be associated with the
incident on Chappaquiddick. Besides, Mary Jo would certainly
be found by morning, and the whole silly matter cleared up. If
she had become stuck in the sand and was trying to find her
way back to the party through the matted vines and bushes, she
might be a long time in returning.

If these assumptions are correct, there must have been trepi-
dation in the Kennedy camp when dawn came and there was no
trace of Mary Jo Kopechne. The *New York Times* reported
later that Joe Gargan showed up at the cottage and told some
of the sleepy-eyed girls: "We can't find Mary Jo." Three men,
including Ted Kennedy, stood in the privacy of the Chappaquiddick ferry shack to talk the problem over. Perhaps they
thought she had become stuck in the sand and had slept in the
car. Perhaps they decided that a daytime hunt would have to be
started. As the three men talked, it seems probable that they
still did not know what had happened, though they must have
begun to realize that something was very wrong. Then a little
old man stepped up and told them that a girl was dead in the
senator's car at the Dike Bridge. A hearse drove by, and a
wrecker, and a few minutes later, when one of the ferrymen repeated the information about the accident, one of the men said,

"Yes, we just heard about it." Kennedy and his two companions took the first available ferry for town, and the senator dashed to the police station. If these hypotheses are valid, Kennedy had not waited long hours to report the accident. Instead, he had not known about it, and now he was rushing to get on record.

But if so, then why did Kennedy sit down and write out an entirely different story at the police station? A number of possible reasons come quickly to mind. His wife, who had had two miscarriages, was lying pregnant a few miles away at Squaw Island. Even if she knew and approved of the party, and even if she knew and approved of the nighttime drive with Mary Jo, no wife could fail to be upset by public insinuations that would be made if full details came out. How would Kennedy explain his motivation for stepping from the car, and how would he explain his being in the car on the Dike Road in the first place? Inevitably, there would be more snickers about the Kennedy men and problems for the marriage.

Moreover, Kennedy had a public image to consider. No intelligent politician would begin a police report by writing, "My brothers and I have a certain reputation. It is not deserved but we have it. And when I realized that I was in a very compromising position and might be interrogated by a police officer, I jumped out of the car." The statement might have rung true and it might have *been* true, but it would have ended his public life. It would have been far simpler for Kennedy to fudge a few minutes on the time and claim that he and Mary Jo had been headed for the ferry, had taken a wrong turn, and had gone over the "hill" and off the bridge.

If these suppositions are correct, Kennedy seems to have made two conspicuous errors. The first was to attend such a gathering. One does not have to take the leering approach to recognize that the party, however innocent in concept, appeared to compromise everyone who attended. Indeed, it was the inevitable *suggestion* of improper behavior that fueled the long and hectic aftermath of the accident. People kept wondering about the men and women assembled in the cottage overnight, as though this had anything to do with what happened at the Dike Bridge. Others spoke pompously of the rights of witnesses and fair trials and other legal subtleties, when in fact they were most concerned about what had gone on (or had *not* gone on) behind the closed doors of the Lawrence cottage. As the plain-spoken Walter Steele put it, "What's keeping this case alive, besides politics, is the public wants to know what the hell is a United States Senator doing on the island of Chappaquiddick, having a few pops and ending up on a lonely road with a blonde. Now that's all very interesting but it's not a criminal matter. The public's gonna keep on kidding itself for months and months, when in fact there's not a single goddamned reason to keep this case open."

As though to confirm Steele's diagnosis, a Los Angeles newspaper printed an apparently straight-faced remark by an unidentified pathologist. Referring to the prospect of an autopsy on the dead woman, he said, "The possibility of sexual intercourse shortly prior to death should also be resolved." But why? Mary Jo Kopechne was buttoned up from the sandals to the neck when her body was removed from Poucha Pond; tests for semen on her clothes were negative. But even if there had been the most blatant indications of sexual intercourse before the accident, the legalities would have remained the same. The traffic case would have remained a traffic case. The West Coast doctor seemed inadvertently to be expressing the unspoken thoughts of the people rather than discussing genuine legal considerations. But there would have been no such morbid curiosity if the party had been of a different nature. The case of Mary Jo Kopechne would have died quickly if, for example, a wife or two had attended the affair, or if all concerned had hopped aboard the midnight ferry and returned discreetly to their quarters. The public must be excused for wondering, and Edward M. Kennedy must remain stigmatized for putting himself into such a position in the first place. There is more to life than reality; one can be ruined by appearances as well, and it would seem that a United States Senator would know that better than most.

Kennedy's other mistake might have been in assuming that a naive public would accept his version of an accident that he had not even seen, let alone participated in. But it was precisely the sketchiness of his report to Arena that caused newsmen to bear down on the case, and it was this pressure that elicited the apparently offhand remarks that helped to provoke the theorizing: the statement that Kennedy returned to the cottage on foot and explained that the car had gone off the road and Mary Jo was sitting in it; the statement that Gargan and Markham had returned at 2:15 in dry clothes, and the statement that Gargan had announced the next morning, "We can't find Mary Jo." These seemingly innocuous adlibs came early in the week after the accident, before the "boiler room" girls fell silent, and there is reason to suppose that it was because of these random comments that the request for silence had been made. There was a secret to be kept, and glib disclosures by the party guests were threatening it. Taken one by one, the remarks seemed merely to reflect the confusion of the evening, but with the inconsistencies in Kennedy's statements and the possibility that Mary Jo had driven herself to her death, the quotes seemed to fit a distinct pattern. After all, if Ted Kennedy came jogging out of the night and reported that Mary Jo was sitting in his car by the roadside, when in fact she was at the bottom of Poucha Pond, he was either frightfully disoriented or telling what he believed to be the truth. An hour or so later, he showed up at the Shiretown Inn, acting fully in control of himself.

In his TV speech, Kennedy attempted to provide explanations. "All kinds of scrambled thoughts . . . went through my mind during this period," he said. "They were reflected in the various inexplicable, inconsistent and inconclusive things I said and did, including such questions as *whether the girl might still be alive somewhere out of that immediate area. . . .*" (italics added). He also noted that "my doctors informed me that I suffered a cerebral concussion as well as shock"; early newspaper reports about his medical examination by a Hyannis physician had listed "possible concussion," a diagnosis that is almost routine in the case of a patient who says he has been struck on the head. The words "cerebral concussion" had an awesome medical sound to them; one could not help but be sympathetic and understanding of a man who was suffering from such a condition.

For five days after his television speech, Senator Ted Kennedy remained in seclusion at Squaw Island, sailing in Nantucket Sound, fishing from the family yacht in the lee of a nearby breakwater, flying kites from the porch with his son Ted Jr., and looking over some of the communications that had swamped the local post office. If he was still totally inaccessible to the press, he was somewhat more available to the old friends he had shunned in his first few days of depression and remorse. Now old friends had long talks on the telephone with him, or they came to the compound and sailed on the *Marlin* and stayed for lunch or dinner. Like Kennedy's political advisors, his friends recommended that he put the incident from his mind and return to the Senate. Some even argued that the accident, unfortunate though it had been, had twanged a sympathetic chord in the hearts of others with troubles of their own. People who had only felt sorry for him when his brothers died were now saying that they could *understand* Ted Kennedy; he was a human being with a human being's frailties, and they loved him all the more for it. If some of the conclusions were strained and exaggerated, there were nevertheless early evidences that Kennedy's actions at Chappaquiddick were being taken largely as tragic happenstance by the man in the street. The first polls showed that a preponderance of the voters, especially in Massachusetts, tended to believe Kennedy's version of the story, despite its inconsistencies. An extreme example of this docile acceptance could be seen in a letter from a Boston woman to a Kennedy detractor: "You say the senator should have reported the accident sooner. The reason he didn't was because the moonshot was on and he didn't want to steal the publicity from the astronauts. That is typical of the modest attitude of this dear person." As John Marquand Jr. observed, Kennedy's television speech had been "a masterly appeal to the silver-haired Irish mother who abides in the core of the Kennedys' home constituency. Her voice is heard in early party council and if anybody can save him, it will be she." Early returns indicated that she was already hard at work on behalf of "this dear person."

There were others, some of them more sophisticated, who also tended to minimize the effect of the incident on the young nobleman's future. "I would never count a Kennedy out of anything," Senator Edmund Muskie announced. "I wish him well in every way. If his political posture has not been weakened, I would be delighted." A Harvard professor praised Kennedy for his "stamina and coherence of character," and went on to explain that Kennedy's political prospects had been improved by the affair, that he had become "less remote" to the public. "They will have gone through that terrible experience with him," the professor said, "and as they think about it they will participate in his personality. There is no remoteness about a man who has shared this kind of experience with an individual. Kennedy is a round and complete person now, not one of those blank figures of the type of politicians and celebrities we see today." One almost came away with the impression that two or three more Mary Jo Kopechne cases would lead Ted Kennedy straight into the White House. The Kopechnes themselves seemed satisfied with the senator's story; they told reporters that their questions had been answered and they hoped that Kennedy would return to his duties.

But the majority of the public did not remain sympathetic. Later polls started showing a sharp diminution in Kennedy's credibility, and soon pollsters were turning up more nonbelievers than believers. As though to solicit public patience, Kennedy and his aides and friends dropped hints that the senator would explain himself after the legalities were cleared up. A friendly article in *Life* quoted him as saying, "It will all come out. The questions . . . all the answers . . . it will all come out, and I think people will understand." Senator Birch Bayh, the gritty Indianan who had saved Kennedy's life five years before, said, "I think the matter has to be cleared up completely. I think he'll do this. I think Ted wants to make available all the information." There were suggestions that Kennedy would appear before a panel of television newsmen to answer any and all questions.

Such a step would entail certain risks. If it were indeed true that Mary Jo Kopechne had driven the car off the bridge, Kennedy, despite his innocence, could face further legal charges by saying so, and also run the risk of involving friends who had stood by him loyally. If he gave a new version of the facts, he could open himself to a charge of making a false report, and Markham (and possibly others in the party group) to a charge of conspiring to make a false report. Such charges, like the one of leaving the scene of an accident, are misdemeanors, petty offenses, but they presumably would be heard by Judge Boyle, and no one could predict the reaction of that straitlaced jurist when the young senator came before him again. With these dire possibilities in mind, some speculated that Kennedy would make a dramatic public appearance later and give the *impression* that he was answering any and all questions, while sticking to the gist of his first reports. He would explain the discrepancies in terms of his "cerebral concussion," amplify some of the less important details, and hope to emerge unscathed from the performance. There were suggestions that Kennedy would have no choice. He had provided two explanations of the occurrence, and both contained implausibilities, but who would believe him now if he came out with a third? And if he did produce a new account before a television panel, and convinced the electorate of his ultimate honesty, how would he handle Jim Arena and Walter Steele? Like Judge Boyle, their attitude toward the young senator might undergo a sharp change the next time around.

For the moment, however, Ted Kennedy kept quiet and took the public criticism. He faced life in the knowledge that he had been labeled an irresponsible child-man who would run away from a drowning woman without bothering to summon help. He let his guilty plea stand undenied, even though it was entirely possible that he had not committed the offense of leaving the scene of an accident, and even though the outbreak of insinuation and innuendo and cheap moralizing that he might have hoped to avoid had descended upon him anyway.

His recourse seemed to lie in good works, in rebuilding his fallen image, in returning to the Senate and immersing himself in the busy round of detail and confusion in his job of whip. Still refusing to discuss the accident with reporters, he arrived at his McLean, Virginia, home on Wednesday night, July 30, twelve days after the accident, just as newscasters were reading the text of a statement released that afternoon by his office: "Senator Edward M. Kennedy is returning to Washington to resume his duties as United States Senator and assistant majority leader. He is grateful to the people of Massachusetts for their expressions of confidence and expects to submit his record to them as a candidate for re-election in 1970. If re-elected, he will serve out his entire six-year term."

Reaction to his return was predictable and somewhat partisan. Majority Leader Mike Mansfield said, "I'm delighted. I've been encouraging him to do so." Russell Long said, "Fine." William Fulbright said, "I'm very glad. He is a young man who I think will overcome his difficulties." Senator Fred Harris, the Democratic national chairman, said that the decision was good for the party and the country, and another Democratic senator, Daniel K. Inouye of Hawaii, said, "If I were up for re-election, I'd be delighted to have him come into my state."

Republicans were understandably less ecstatic about the prodigal's return, but the rules of the Club prevented any sly remarks about the nature of the young senator's predicament. Senator Everett Dirksen, the minority leader, said coolly, "Should I have a reaction? I haven't got one," and Senator George Aiken of Vermont said, "So what else is new? Didn't you expect it? You don't think thirty million Democrats are going to stand by idly and see another Republican senator come here, do you?" The reference was to the fact that the governor of Massachusetts was a member of the GOP, and presumably would have appointed a Republican had Kennedy stepped down.

The Senate press and public galleries were packed the next

day. Everyone wondered how the Club would react to Kennedy's return, and they were not long in finding out. Mike Mansfield said loudly, "Come in, Ted! You're right back where you belong," and accompanied his assistant on the long walk from the back of the Senate to the front row. Senator John Pastore of Rhode Island rushed over and pumped Kennedy's hand vigorously, saying something into the young senator's ear that brought a wan smile. Everett Dirksen beamed warmly and said hello. George McGovern and Edmund Muskie presented friendly greetings, and the spectators could see Kennedy's lips repeating over and over, "Thank you, thank you very much." Mississippi Senator James Eastland passed by and patted Kennedy's shoulder, and Eugene McCarthy of Minnesota shook hands. Russell Long, defeated for the post of whip by Kennedy, slipped into an adjoining seat and began whispering and confiding to his young colleague, as though to show the viewers that the Club members had closed ranks. Kennedy nodded and said an occasional word in return. Then he picked up the *Congressional Record* and started leafing through the pages as a debate opened on the income tax surcharge bill. Upstairs in the galleries, reporters exchanged knowing glances. "I'll bet he's not reading," said one to another. From time to time Kennedy would turn slightly, drop the hand that had been shielding his eyes, and appear to flick a quick glance toward the galleries. To some, he seemed to flinch involuntarily on the three occasions when his name was sounded loudly on roll calls. Once he rubbed the back of his hand across his eyes as though deeply fatigued, and those who watched him realized that he must be immensely uncomfortable. When the session was over at last, and Kennedy walked back into the outer hall, the effects of Chappaquiddick could be seen in his stance and demeanor. He stood in a slouched position, his head hanging down, his eyes expressionless behind his deep suntan. To some, he appeared to be quivering under his blue suit; others were shocked at the weight he had so obviously lost during his ordeal. He looked few in the eye, and his voice was tremulous. "This isn't Senator

Ted Kennedy," an old friend whispered. "This is Ted Kennedy of Chappaquiddick. I wonder if he'll ever get over it."

The recovery was slow, but as the weeks went by the young senator seemed to gain strength from his readmission to the Club and his activities in party councils. Like a person taking a deep breath and plunging into cold water, he began to accept speaking engagements and to make public appearances. On the first such occasion after the accident, he spoke at a dinner of the American Cancer Society in Boston, attacked the administration, and worried the middle button off his jacket with nervousness. But with each succeeding appearance, he seemed to gain in strength and aplomb. If the demand for his appearance at fund-raising banquets and dinners had declined slightly, his voice was still welcome in many quarters. The headlines flowed: TED HOPES TO BEAT NIXON ON DRAFT REFORM . . . TED URGES U.S. ACCEPT REFUGEES . . . TED CHARGES [AGNEW] TALK DIVISIVE . . . KENNEDY TACKLES SENATE WORK WITH VIGOR . . . TED SAYS U.S. FAILS INDIANS . . . TED RENEWS ATTACK ON U.S. WAR POLICY . . . KENNEDY RAPS NIXON . . . Renewed by the therapy of public service, Kennedy regained some of the weight that he had lost during the ordeal, and once again began to take on the appearance of robust health that had always characterized him before.

Those who had tended to write him off completely after Chappaquiddick now began to revise their prognostications. Despite polls that showed a continuing erosion of public belief in his version of the accident, he remained a likely prospect for re-election to the Senate in 1970. To be sure, his chances for the Presidency were dimmed, at least for 1972, but at the age of thirty-seven he could bear this deprivation. He came back to Massachusetts early to begin his 1970 campaign for re-election to the Senate, and he told his aides that the campaign was to be taken seriously; the remarks of Senator Edward Brooke and other Massachusetts Republicans to the effect that Kennedy was a "shoo-in" were to be ignored. More than a year before the scheduled election, Kennedy was politicking on his own behalf all over the Bay State, listening to speechmakers like his friend U.S. Representative Edward Boland introduce him as "a man we all love." "If there is a man in the United States who has more compassion for the people, I've never seen him," Boland said one night. "If there is a man who has more courage, I've never seen him. If there is a man who has more guts, I've never seen him." And while some in the audience nodded agreement, Kennedy stepped up and revealed his own future plans. "We'll be out here again—and again, and again and again," he said. "The greatest wealth of the Kennedy family has always been in the loyalty of its friends."

As his political image slowly improved, Kennedy allowed himself the luxury of an occasional confidential remark about Chappaquiddick. To his closest friends, he continued to make no bones about his "indefensible" conduct, but he wondered aloud how much more abjection was expected of him. He had pleaded guilty in court; he had appeared on television and castigated himself; he had never denied the inadequacy of his behavior on that dark night in July. What else was expected? He ignored long questionnaires from respected newspapers like the *Washington Post* and the *Chicago Daily News* and the *New York Times* on the grounds that he would have to answer all if he answered one. Only rarely was he quoted directly on the subject. Once he told his friend Matthew V. Storin of the *Boston Globe:* "I can live with myself. I feel the tragedy of the girl's death. That's on my mind. That's what I will always have to live with. But what I don't have to live with are the whispers and innuendos and falsehoods, because these have no basis in fact." Later he told reporters: "I would say those who tend to look for things in this case are going to be disappointed."

The rest was anticlimax, but an anticlimax that dragged on for months. Kennedy had told his story, and it seemed unlikely that any number of hearings or inquests or grand jury sessions would change it. His hopes had to rest with the shortness of the public memory, and the capacity of the electorate to forgive.

The *Pilot,* the publication of the Roman Catholic Archdiocese of Boston, had said, "It is time, we think, that this case were closed. It becomes too easily an occasion for rash judgments and self-righteous assertions; it feeds the weakness of those who rejoice in another's misery, who reach for the mote and miss the beam. What had to be said has been said; what answers are available have been given."

Edward Moore Kennedy put his own feelings in the simplest of terms, as he had always tended to do. "This was a summer," he said, "I was anxious to have end."

The summer did end, as summers do, but the ordeal continued in the form of the tedious legal maneuverings. Fall came, and with it the death, at eighty-one, of Senator Kennedy's father, old Joe Kennedy, who had survived all but this last one of his beloved sons. There was yet another mournful gathering of the clan, another eulogy, another burial. Now Ted Kennedy, alone of all the remarkable Kennedy men, remained to face his own justice, and fate, and truth.

Rollinsville, Colorado
December 15, 1969

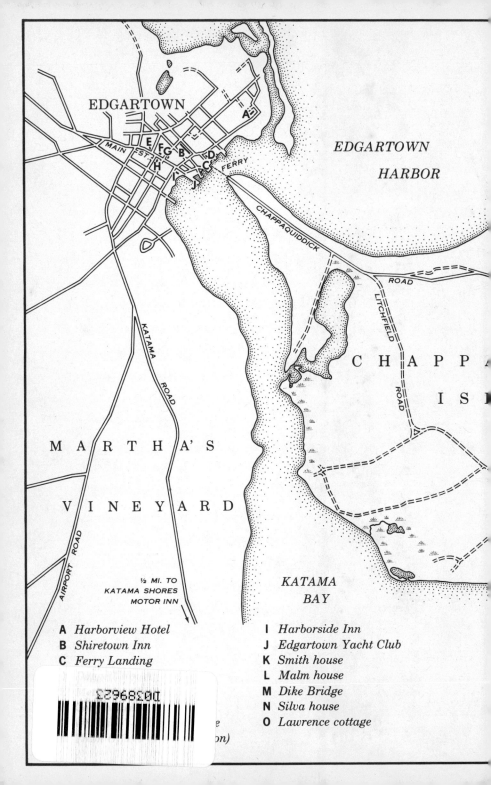

EDGARTOWN

EDGARTOWN
HARBOR

MAIN ST.

E F G B D
H C
J FERRY

CHAPPAQUIDDICK

ROAD

LITCHFIELD ROAD

KATAMA ROAD

C H A P P A
I S I

M A R T H A'S

V I N E Y A R D

AIRPORT ROAD

½ MI. TO
KATAMA SHORES
MOTOR INN

KATAMA
BAY

A *Harborview Hotel*
B *Shiretown Inn*
C *Ferry Landing*

I *Harborside Inn*
J *Edgartown Yacht Club*
K *Smith house*
L *Malm house*
M *Dike Bridge*
N *Silva house*
O *Lawrence cottage*